The ACIM Mentor Articles

Volume 3

Answers for Students of A Course in Miracles *and* 4 Habits for Inner Peace

ISBN: 9781793096289

Other Books by Liz Cronkhite

Non-Fiction

The Plain Language *A Course in Miracles*:

 The Message of A Course in Miracles: *A translation of the Text in Plain Language*

 Practicing A Course in Miracles/The Way of A Course in Miracles: *A translation of the Workbook and Manual for Teachers in Plain Language*

The ACIM Mentor Articles: Answers for Students of *A Course in Miracles*

4 Habits for Inner Peace

Releasing Guilt for Inner Peace: A companion to *4 Habits for Inner Peace*

The ACIM Mentor Articles, Volume 2: Answers for Students of *A Course in Miracles* and *4 Habits for Inner Peace*

Fiction

A Good Woman

You can learn more about these books at www.lizcronkhite.net.

Contents

Preface

Preface

In 2010 I published the first volume of *The ACIM Mentor Articles*, a collection of my newsletters between 2006 and 2009. Last year, in 2018, I published the articles I had written between 2010 and 2014, all but one of which was an answer to questions from readers. It was for students of *A Course in Miracles* as well as a book I published in 2011, *4 Habits for Inner Peace*. This third volume of articles covers 2015 thru 2018 and is a collection of answers to questions from readers of ACIM and my other books, as well as new essays. The answers to questions are prefaced with "Ask".

The articles in this book have not been touched, but for some formatting corrections, and are as they were at the time they were printed in my newsletter. They cover an important period in my spiritual evolution. In 2014 the ego fell away from my mind, leaving behind only its "echo", only I didn't recognize it at the time. However, many of my articles following that occurrence—the articles in this book—reveal I knew something big had happened. Finally, in 2018, I came to realize what had occurred as I experienced a radical shift in the life of the self. In October of that year I traveled to Australia. Just before I left I became aware I am Spirit, an awareness that has not left me. All of this is covered in articles in this book.

You, too, are evolving, and some articles will resonate with you more than others. And there will probably come a time when you put this book aside. Until then, I hope you find it useful.

If you wish to read or make comments on these articles you may do so at my blogsite, www.acimmentor.blogspot.com.

Liz Cronkhite
Elleker, Western Australia, 2019

1. Safety in Defenselessness (January 2, 2015)

"In my defenselessness my safety lies." (W-153)

You have two thought systems in your mind. The ego is the thought system that teaches you that you are a self in a body in a world. Because this isn't true when you identify with the self you experience lack and vulnerability. You spend your time defining and defending the self's identity in an attempt to undo your sense of lack and to feel safe.

The "defenselessness" referred to in this lesson is the other thought system in your mind, what *A Course in Miracles* calls the Holy Spirit. This thought system comes from the part of your mind that is always aware of God, or True Being. In this awareness you feel whole and complete. You feel safe so you have nothing to defend.

So this lesson is not asking you to be defenseless in the ego. This is not possible, since it is inherently insecure. It is asking you to turn away from the ego thought system which teaches you that you lack and are vulnerable. Turn instead to the Truth within you in Which you are eternally Whole and Safe.

Defensiveness shows up as anger. Defenselessness shows up as not taking a situation personally so you are charge-neutral, or without an emotional response. The ego always speaks first and emotionally. This will not change. But as you become aware of your wholeness in God you will learn to let the ego's emotional reactions come up and go by. Then you will be able to choose to come from a rational, detached place rather than an emotional, personal place.

As long as you identify with the ego you will be defensive. Accept this. There isn't any reason to add to your guilt. It is not wrong or bad to be defensive. It comes from a mistaken idea about yourself. You will stop being defensive when God is real enough to you that you will be able to turn to your wholeness in God when you feel vulnerable and get relief. Until then, use conflicts to grow your awareness of God by turning inward and opening to God when you experience them. You will receive an answer that is helpful to you where you are.

2. Ask: What is the best way to deal with idols? (January 9, 2015)

"I now see clearly my attachment to various false idols—the so-called special relationships—those things of the world that appear as sources of peace but which I know intellectually, intuitively, and through endless disappointing experience can never deliver lasting peace. Nevertheless, they feel so real and appealing as I covet and pursue them on a daily basis. As bright as these golden calves seem to be, worshiping them is fraught with fear, and a gnawing sense of lack. Obsessing over them leads me down a distracting, dead end path. How best to deal with these obstacles to peace and ultimately get past them?" – ES

The mind is always looking for relief from lack. You won't let go of idols until you have something to replace them even though you recognize that ultimately they do not work.

Only your awareness of Truth will bring the lasting sense of wholeness that you seek in idols. When you find your mind turning to an idol for relief remind yourself how you've learned it does not work. Remember specific examples of how it does not work. Then turn to Truth instead. Remember your experiences of Truth and remind yourself that only in Truth can you find the wholeness that you seek. Let yourself rest in Truth for a while. As your awareness of

Truth grows you will find yourself longing less and less for the old, futile ways of looking for relief from lack.

3. Acceptance (January 16, 2015)

Acceptance is one of those ideas that I see students resisting, largely because they confuse "acceptance" with "embracing" or "liking" or "condoning". So when I say "Accept that growing your awareness of Truth is a process" or "Accept that your boss is unfair" or "Accept that you have a chronic illness" they think I am suggesting that they try to like or approve of these things. But what I mean by "acceptance" is "acknowledge a situation the way it is without resisting it or judging it". Resisting or judging a situation is the way that you keep it in mind. It is the way that you hold onto it. Acceptance is the way that you let it go.

Resisting and judging close your mind. And a closed mind cannot hear the Holy Spirit (Teacher of Truth) in your mind. So acceptance is the way to open your mind to solutions to problems or to another way of looking at a situation. Judgment and resistance also add to the discomfort or pain of a situation. With acceptance you do not add to the discomfort or pain of an already uncomfortable or painful situation.

So "accepting that growing your awareness of Truth is a process" becomes the way in which you let the process unfold naturally. It keeps you open and willing. "Accepting that your boss is unfair" opens your mind to ways of working with her in the context of what you know about her. And "Accepting that you have a chronic illness" becomes the way in which you open your mind to ideas for taking care of the body.

4. Ask: I had an insight and then seemed to totally lose it. What happened? (January 23, 2015)

"Let's say I'm embroiled in some struggle with another person. They 'appear' as some kind of threat and the usual defend/attack scenario plays out - mostly in my head but sometimes spilling out into acting out behavior. Suddenly, a realization comes to me that the perceived threat is all made up (by me) ie. I had been attaching certain meaning to their behavior while in fact this person that I had demonized now appears as weak, clueless, ignorant or just can't help themselves or simply has another point of view. Now that the drama has been drained from the story, and all the meaning neutralized, I then realize that I need simply state my needs to that person, work out some compromise or move on. Peace at last. But then, a couple of hours later, much to my chagrin, the whole thing starts up all over again, sometimes with an even greater intensity than before! What happened?" – ES

You are simply experiencing the process of accepting a new thought system (Holy Spirit/Teacher of Truth). The new thought system brings blessed relief. But you don't trust it yet. And the old thought system (ego/personal thought system), though painful, is familiar. It seems to give you something that you feel you lose with the new thought system. Going forward you will be in a process of learning that the old thought system does not give you anything of value. And you will learn to trust the new thought system.

These flashes of insight are how accepting the thought system of the Holy Spirit begins. Take comfort in that you have begun the process. You will be back and forth between the two thought systems for a long while, but there is no turning back. You now know there is another way to look at things. And even though you may consciously forget this sometimes your subconscious knows it. The process will now happen of itself.

5. The Problem With "Love" (January 30, 2015)

"Love" is one of those words that I wish was not used in spirituality. We use the word in two ways when discussing human love and only one of them describes the experience of True Love. This leads to confusion as the two ideas become conflated.

As humans when we say "I love you" we mean "I like you a lot", "I enjoy you", "I enjoy being with you", "I like how I feel about myself when I am with you", "I enjoy the role that I play in our relationship", "I am grateful to you for the role that you play in our relationship" and/or "I'm obligated to you through a family connection". In these contexts "I love you" really means "I am attached to you in some way".

We feel attachment-love only when we love others not when others love us. When others attachment-love us what we experience is a safe place to be ourselves. Others' attachment-love for us brings emotional and practical support to our lives in the world. But their experience of attachment-love for us does not leave them and then go into us. If we don't value ourselves their stating, or even demonstrating, their attachment-love for us is meaningless to us.

The experience of attachment-love is valuable for preserving the human race and for preserving and enhancing individual human lives. But the experience does not make you feel whole. And "wholeness" is the other meaning we have for "love".

When we speak of True Love—spiritual "love", or "God's Love"—what we mean is an experience of wholeness. It is an experience of abundance rather than lack. And this is what we really seek in our relationships with others. This is what we hope to find in our love for others or in their love for us. And human attachment-love does not provide this. It is inherently limited.

Human attachment-love is always directed toward someone or something. True Love, as an experience of wholeness, is not directed toward anyone or anything. It is an internal experience that you carry with you. So you can understand the confusion that comes with spiritual directives like, "Love your neighbor as yourself." From a human point of view you think this means you have to *like* everyone! And this is of course not possible so you end up feeling like a failure. But if you understand that "love" in this context means "wholeness" you understand that to love your neighbor as yourself is to come from your awareness of your wholeness in Truth in your relationship with them. And to recognize that no matter how they appear to you or what they seem to think that they too are whole in the Truth in their mind. You hold in your mind that Truth *is all that is true* no matter what is appearing.

In your awareness of True Love you do not direct love only toward certain others. You come from your awareness of your wholeness in your relationships with all, regardless of whether they are close to you or are strangers; whether you *like* them or not. You still feel attachment to those close to you simply out of familiarity. And your personality will enjoy some people more than others. But you do not ask anyone to make you whole. You accept others as they are. And you are willing to let anyone go should it become necessary.

When you find yourself seeking to feel whole then you are not seeking human attachment-love. You are seeking for the True Love (abundant wholeness) that is your True Being. And you can only find this within. You grow your awareness that you already have It within you by choosing to come from this awareness in your relationships with others. This is the practice of "what you give you receive" or "what you teach you learn" that *A Course in Miracles* emphasizes. You can give only to yourself. And you can teach only yourself. You give to and teach yourself that lack is real when you choose to look for wholeness where you will not find it. And you give to and teach yourself that you are whole when you come from your awareness of abundant wholeness (True Love) within you as you interact with the world.

6. I Am Whole and You Are Whole (February 6, 2015)

To follow up on the last article about "Love", when you enter into relationships from the awareness that "I am whole and you are whole" you change the dynamic of personal relationships. Personal relationships usually start from "I lack, please fill me". In an attempt to feel whole you drop the boundaries between you and another. This shows up as you demanding that another meet your needs. If they don't you feel abandoned or attacked. You also may insist that the other change to meet your needs or change because you are uncomfortable with how they show up. Without boundaries you feel that how they show up reflects on you. Or you may be uncomfortable with how they show up and think that they are responsible for your discomfort.

You also experience the other side of this in personal relationships. Others demand that you fill their needs or that you change to make them happy or comfortable. You can see why personal relationships are so contentious! Everyone is pulling against everyone else.

This is not easy to address because often our identities are tied up in the role we play with others. That role may be the helpless one in need of fixing. This is the victim role. You are a victim of your childhood or circumstances or a god or something that makes you lack. You are powerless and dependent on others to make you feel better. And if they do not then you are their victim, too. Everyone plays this role in some, if not all, areas of their life. It is central to the personal thought system (ego).

You may also play the role of the fixer-of-others. You may feel that it this is your purpose in life; maybe even a "God-given" purpose. Eventually you may find relationships to be a burden because you are overwhelmed taking responsibility for others' bad feelings and problems. So you may avoid relationships. Of course you cannot fix others and they often resent you trying. This makes you feel unappreciated in your relationships and becomes another victim role for you. But when you feel that this is your assigned role in life you feel guilty if you do not take responsibility for others.

You can see how coming from True Love, or the recognition that "I am whole and you are whole", changes the dynamic of personal relationships. Not only do you not need others to make you whole. You also do not need to make others whole. You do not need to play a certain role with others to be whole. And since you are already whole you do not have a purpose to fulfill to make you whole. In Wholeness you recognize that you do not have to do anything. You are free! And you are with others because you want to be with them not because you need them or need to play a role.

Some think that coming from True Love means being a doormat. But an awareness of Wholeness shows up as self-respect. Your relationship with others is your relationship with yourself. And in self-respect you expect respect from others. So you set boundaries with others who do not behave respectfully. This honors not just your wholeness but theirs. Their acting out and inappropriate behavior is a sign that they are not aware of their inherent wholeness. When you set boundaries you give them a chance to look at themselves and to grow into an awareness of their wholeness. Whether or not they take this opportunity is up to them.

In self-respect you decide how far out boundaries need to be or how close in they can be based on what you need to take care of yourself. Students will say, "But don't I need to look at myself in this situation?" Yes! But you do that behind healthy boundaries. You don't have to hang around abuse to figure out what you may be projecting or using in the situation to perpetuate your story of victimhood. Eventually you will stop taking personally others' responses to you and you won't feel attacked. But even then you will put up boundaries. Even if you don't feel attacked allowing others to disrespect you only teaches them that their dysfunction is okay. Again, your boundaries are for you as well as for them. It's a way of saying, "I'm whole and so are you. This is your chance to learn this."

7. Assertion is Not Aggression (February 13, 2015)

(To clarify: The boundaries discussed here are about boundaries for the self at the level of form. They are the practical result at the level of form of being aware of your wholeness in Truth. Discussions in spiritual teachings about the dropping away of the boundary of the self refer to an experience that transcends the level of form.)

Sometimes students tell me that they feel that setting boundaries is an attack on others. This is because in the past they didn't set boundaries until they felt so violated that they felt they had to become angry and aggressive to protect themselves. They would blow up at others or cut them out of their life for not respecting boundaries that they never clarified. Their anger seemed to be about others. But really they were angry with themselves for allowing others to abuse or to manipulate them.

When you are confused about your worth you feel uncertain about where to set your boundaries. You feel that you do not have the right to expect respect from others. You feel, unconsciously or consciously, that their abuse is justified. So asking for respect feels as though it requires you to "confront" others. This is a projection of your own inward conflict. Internally you feel so guilty and conflicted about your own worth that you don't feel right simply asking for respect. You feel you have to "steal" it from others and that this makes you even more wrong.

But when you come from self-respect you assert your feelings, boundaries, and desires matter-of-factly. You don't feel guilty so you are not defensive, angry, or aggressive. So if you feel confused about your right to set boundaries or you feel that setting boundaries requires a huge confrontation then look, with the Holy Spirit (the awareness of Truth in your mind), for the guilt and unworthiness in your mind. When you have undone them you will find taking care of yourself around others by setting healthy boundaries comes naturally.

8. Ask: What about PMS making it hard to get past the ego? (February 20, 2015)

"I notice that despite all of my work with the Holy Spirit and using correct perception of my ego's thoughts that PMS time still gives me a difficult time. It seems that a hormone shift just changes my ability to deny the ego its 'voice'. I know Eckhart Tolle addressed this as a manifestation of our collective experience here....I was wondering what your understanding is." – MB

Mood-swings are just part of the experience of female selves. The degree varies from woman to woman and month to month. If you know your cycle you know that negative emotions can be chemically induced or exaggerated when you are pre-menstrual and when you are ovulating. You know not to take them seriously and to ride out the episodes each month. Sometimes, if it's bad enough, it does make it seem like you cannot get past the ego. Irritability, depression, foreboding, and/or sadness are its playground and if you aren't aware of what is going on it can have a field day with you! But if you pay attention to your cycle you can learn to detach from these episodes.

Since I have been in peri-menopause for the past few years, and negative mood-swings are par for the course during this stage, it has become crystal clear to me that peace does not come to the ego or to the self. I have peace, but the ego is still judgmental and the self still goes through the normal life processes. The peace allows me to detach from the ego and the self. But it has not changed them. It has changed my relationship to them. They are not reality.

It has also made it clear to me for how long I made the mistake of judging my progress toward peace by the mere moods of the ego or the self. I was looking in the wrong place! Peace came *despite* the ego and the self. It is wholly apart from them. This has allowed me to let them go—to forgive them. I rest in peace and observe the ego and the self without judging them or judging myself by them.

9. Ask: What comfort can you give a child whose father just died? (February 27, 2015)

"I know this world/body is not real it something I created out of my vane imaging {ego}. I understand that but What comfort can you share with an eight year old child whose father just died. I know the usual 'He's in heaven with God'", etc. Confused on how to counsel My Great Grandaughter from an ACIM VIEW POINT. I GET TEARS EYES THINKING WHAT SHE IS GOING THRU." – JP

It is the same comforting a child as it is comforting an adult. First, get yourself out of the way. Put aside your own need to comfort and ask what *the other* needs. Most people just want to be heard and understood. So listen to your great-granddaughter and validate what you hear. "I see you are missing your Dad. I know it's very painful", etc. And you may want to give a lot of hugs! But make sure she actually wants the hugs and that you are not just satisfying your own urge to "fix" her.

Loss is a part of life in the world. Grief is not bad or wrong. It is the normal response that the body and the human psyche have to loss. It is a process and you may want to educate yourself about the process to help your great-granddaughter understand her physical and emotional feelings. She is going to experience loss in many forms as she goes through life and she needs to understand the experience. You can reassure her that time does make it better.

Don't try to give your great-granddaughter more information than she's asking for. Put aside your own need to inform or to educate. If you try to give her more information than she's seeking then you will only confuse or overload her in her already overwhelmed state. If she does ask about where her father has gone, ask her what she thinks happened to him and let that be your guide. If she has her own ideas, then let them be. If she's truly open and wants to know what you believe then you can share what you believe.

It is difficult as students of *A Course in Miracles* to share what we've learned and experienced with others because even though it is comforting to us it is not comforting to others who are not seeking Truth and are still identified with an ego (personal thought system). So you probably don't want to say, "Your Dad never really existed in the first place so nothing happened when he died." But you can point out that he is still with her in her thoughts. Or you can say something like there is a part of God (or whatever she will understand) in everyone and It is Eternal and That she shares with her dad.

10. All A Mind Needs Is Willingness (March 6, 2015)

For a mind to be aware of Truth and at peace it really is all about willingness *and nothing else*.

Looking back to when peace began for this mind so much time and energy were wasted trying to make peace happen when "my" part was over as soon as Peace came into the awareness of this mind. This awareness could not be sustained so this mind thought "I" had to make it happen again. But in hindsight it is clear that for this mind time has been about undoing the obstacles that stood in the way of this mind keeping Peace in its awareness. All of this was done within this mind as the natural unfolding in time of the awareness of Truth that came to it all those years ago. For this mind this is the meaning of "the script is written". It does not mean that every detail of the self's story in time was pre-ordained. It simply means that the outcome of this mind's experience in time was inevitable once Truth came into its awareness. This awareness changed the trajectory of this mind's story in time. In fact, time was really over for it once Truth came into this mind. And all it's really had to do since then is to accept this.

This mind's mistake over the years was focusing too much on whether it was happy or comfortable in its identification with a self. It looked and worked for the ego (personal thought system) to become peaceful. It expected the self would not go through the usual life processes. But when Peace came into the awareness of this mind it was not to the ego or to the self. The ego is still in this mind, blathering on with its judgments, conflicts, and confusion. The self's story continues on with the usual life processes. But Peace is here in this mind despite the ego and the self. This is how this mind came to see it is not an ego or a self.

When this mind recognized that Peace was not leaving its awareness it wondered why there was still a world in its thoughts. And the Holy Spirit (this mind's awareness of Truth) noted, "What difference does it make? You have peace." Of course! This mind was focused on the wrong thing. Peace is what is real, not the story of a universe of form and the ego's interpretation of it. Whatever this mind attends to grows in its awareness.

Despite this mind thinking what it needed for Peace, Peace came anyway. Not because this mind knew how to make peace happen in its identification with a self and an ego. But because this mind was was *willing* to have It in its awareness. Willingness allowed the awareness of Truth (Holy Spirit/Teacher of Truth) to work in this mind to undo its obstacles to Peace. Any obstacle that it needed to look at and undo, any technique that it needed for centering itself in Truth, came into its awareness because it was willing not because of any effort it made.

What does it mean for a mind to be willing? It means for it to be open, despite obstacles and fear, to letting the Truth work in it. The transformation occurs mostly on an unconscious level. This mind had shifts toward Peace, insights, miracles, and Revelations. And none of these ever came where this mind was "working on" the ego and the self trying to get them to change. These came *despite* this mind's efforts in the ego and the self.

This mind's willingness was demonstrated by its invitation to Truth to come into its awareness with no agenda but to be aware of Truth. It was demonstrated by its inviting the Teacher of Truth (Holy Spirit/awareness of Truth) to be its Constant Companion, Guide, and Teacher. It was demonstrated by its turning to Truth throughout the day simply to remember that It is here.

This mind's willingness was never perfect. But as *A Course in Miracles* says, you only need a little. It does not have to be perfect; it just has to be there. If this mind had accepted this long ago it would've saved itself a lot of effort and pain and guilt. But it couldn't accept it because it found it unbelievable, and somewhat insulting, that "I" did not have to *make peace happen*. It was all wrong about what is real. A mind naturally at peace is real. The rest is just a meaningless story.

11. Ask: Can you go into more detail about "the script is written"? (March 13, 2015)

"I have a question I hope you will consider answering for me and others. In your most recent post; 'All A Mind Needs Is Willingness,' you speak a little about the meaning of 'the script is written,' and mention 'it does not mean that every detail of the self's story in time is pre-ordained.' As I understand this to be true, being that our choices can alter our course in time, I still have so many questions the rotate around this one statement. I was wondering if you could go into more detail about what 'The Script Is Written,' actually means. When I think of this I believe it is saying that everything that seems to come our way we have asked for being that we chose to listen to the ego's voice instead of the Holy Spirit's—which was the detour into fear. And from that choice, we set into motion everything we think is happening. Also, God's Will is done, meaning that the separation never happened, just the desire to listen to another voice which caused us to sleep rather than wake into God's Will. Outside of that, It is at large to me. Would you care to touch on this? It would be most helpful." – BO

Like "I need do nothing", "the script is written" is one of those phrases in *A Course in Miracles* that the ego latches onto, reads totally out of context, and runs wild with. Here's how that phrase is used in ACIM:

*"Time is a trick, a sleight of hand, a vast illusion in which figures come and go as if by magic. Yet there is a plan behind appearances that does not change. **The script is written**. When experience will come to end your doubting has been set. For we but see the journey from the point at which it ended, looking back on it, imagining we make it once again; reviewing mentally what has gone by."* (W-158.4)

Here is this paragraph in my translation of the Workbook into plain-language, *Practicing A Course in Miracles*":

*"Time is a trick, a sleight of hand; a vast illusion in which illusory figures seem to come and go as if by magic. Yet, there is a plan behind these appearances that does not change. **It is as though there is a script with the ending already written**; the Experiences that will end your doubting have been set. There really is no journey, but you imagine that you are taking one, learning what you have really already learned."* (PACIM-158.4)

And here is what I said about this paragraph in my mentor's notes in PACIM:

"Paragraphs 3, and 4 are referring to the fact that the moment that the idea of not-God occurred it was undone, because God is All-encompassing and cannot have an opposite. But the idea of not-God contains the concept of time, and only in time does it seem that you separated

from God in a distant past, and that you will return to God at an indefinite time in the future. Time is the illusion on which all other illusions rest. This is why the Experience of the Holy Instant is so important. In the Holy Instant, you step out of time and into Eternity, and you realize that you have never left God; there is no time, no world, and no journey. And when you return to time from a Holy Instant, it never again has the same hold over you." (PACIM-158.mn)

Time is only an idea that is an expression of that instant of the-idea-of-not-God/the-undoing-of-the-idea-of-not-God. So one's life in the world is an expression of one of these ideas. The idea-of-not-God, which you are born into by default, is expressed by a life that moves away from God. It expresses the concept of "separation from God". But you can become aware of God and at that point your life becomes an expression of the undoing-of-the-idea-of-not God. You "retrace your steps" back to God. In any case, both are meaningless stories (except to you while you still identify with one of them) because not-God is not possible so the undoing-of-not-God is not necessary. So "the script is written" is a figurative phrase that means that once you've chosen God the outcome is inevitable. The "theme" or trajectory of your life has changed and you cannot go back. You cannot unlearn what you have learned.

Keep in mind that the ego thought system gets caught up in the details of what is or is not occurring in the unfolding story. It cannot see beyond what is right in front of it, or its own desires, so it is always in lack. But the thought system of the Holy Spirit (your awareness of God) in your mind sees the larger unfolding story. It sees the whole picture. Where the ego sees minutiae the Holy Spirit sees the larger unfolding theme. The ego sees what is not yet done in time. The Holy Spirit sees that time is over.

So you can relax and trust your unfolding awareness. You don't have to nitpick the details of your every thought and mood and choice every moment of the day. The arc of your life has changed. The outcome is inevitable.

12. How "the world isn't real" Shows Up (March 20, 2015)

I often tell students that much of this path has not unfolded in the way that I expected. I had ideas about how it was going to look and feel. So I often missed shifts in my experience because I was looking elsewhere for a shift. Or I simply didn't recognize them for what they were. Eventually I learned I have no idea how this will unfold! I learned to release expectations, to trust the process, and to keep an open mind.

One of the first examples of this is with the awareness that the world isn't real. It's hard to know how I expected this would show up. I think I expected a wholesale shift in my perception and that the world would disappear. But the shift in awareness began almost immediately after I became a student of *A Course in Miracles* with a shift in my values.

A Course in Miracles tells us that we believe in what we value:

"Remember that where your heart is, there is your treasure also. You believe in what you value." (T-2.II.1)

"And your thinking but reflects your choice of what you want to see. Your values are determiners of this, for what you value you must want to see, believing what you see is really there." (W-130.1)

"I am grateful that this world is not real, and that I need not see it at all unless I choose to value it." (W-53.2 [12])

This used to confound me. I thought it was backwards. Don't I have to believe something is real before I value it? No, ACIM was telling me my giving something value is what makes it real to me. I did not understand this until I experienced it. The way that "this isn't real" first showed up for me was in my no longer according value to certain thing that I once valued. They no longer seemed significant or to have meaning for me. So I did not think about something "this is not real" or "this is an illusion". Instead I just stopped thinking about it. It no longer had meaning for me. It "disappeared" for me in that it was no longer *on* my mind even if in form it was still *in* my mind. What has no meaning to me does not exist for me. Eventually, this generalized to the whole world as I found value and meaning in my awareness of Truth instead of in the world.

This is not a foreign experience. Everyone does this all the time. You do not give your attention to thousands of things that pass before you every day. The whole world does not exist for you all of the time. Your attention automatically goes to what has value for you. And things that once had value for you fall away from your attention when something you value more comes into your awareness.

Another way that "the world is not real" showed up for me was in the acceptance that everything in the universe of form passes. This includes not just painful things but also pleasures. Only the Eternal is real because it always *is*. What passes is not real *because* it passes. Interestingly, this not only mitigated the pain of life in the world for me. But I enjoy pleasures more because I do not cling to them in desperation to "save" me from the pain of the human experience. I accept them for the time that they are present and then let them go. So my enjoyment of them is not diminished by my desperation to hold on to them. All in the world passes but the Eternal is always with me.

Lately another way that the world isn't real shows up for me is in how stories in my mind about the world fall away easily. They can be about the past, present, or future. They can be a story for this self or a person I know or a public figure. As soon as I start to give anything any real thought I become acutely aware that it is *only* a story in my mind and nothing more. Then it seems to turn to dust and fall away and my mind is set free.

I do not go around thinking "this is not real" all of the time because that awareness has quietly become my "new normal". This came about through a slow and steady shift in my mind over time. I become aware of how dramatically my mind has changed only when I hear how much others still believe in the world and are so invested in it. Then I remember that I used to be that way, too, and I feel the contrast. I can remember that I used to be that way but I cannot recall the actual experience. It seems alien to me now and it doesn't make sense.

13. In the Flow of the Universe (March 27, 2015)

Many years ago I met a woman who told me that as soon as she wanted something for the self it manifested for her. This had never been my experience. In fact, I was confused about the whole manifesting thing. (This has since become popularly known as the "Law of Attraction" because of the book that brought together long held ideas behind manifesting what you want). I was left wondering if she truly did manifest what she wanted or if the desire for something grew in her just before it showed up. Maybe she was just in tune with the universe of form.

I first learned about manifesting when I was a new student of *A Course in Miracles*. The theory, as I understood it anyway, was that what did or did not show up in the self's life was determined by my own thoughts. If I didn't have what I wanted for the self it must be because of obstacles within me. For example, maybe I felt unworthy of or afraid of what I wanted. I was supposed to dig around in my mind for those obstacles and, if I removed them, lo and behold what I wanted would show up. My initial discomfort with the idea of manifesting, or attracting, what I wanted was the recognition that I would only be concerned with what did or did not show up for the self if I thought that this was the cause of my peace or conflict. Wasn't I learning that being aware of God (True Being) was the only lasting source of peace and happiness? I wasn't there yet, but I felt early on that concerning my mind with manifesting was a distraction from being aware of God (True Being).

My other problem with the concept of manifesting was that I had always intuited the flow of the universe of form, whether I wanted to or not. Sometimes I wanted something for this self but would feel that it was not going to happen. Sometimes the feeling was "not yet". Other times I would know that what I wanted was coming soon. Also, desires for the self would shift. They would show up or fall away. Yes, I was sometimes aware of unworthiness or fear when it came to something I wanted. But more significant to me was the sense that I was trying to force something to happen if what I wanted didn't jive with my intuition about the flow of the universe. And how was I supposed to know what was best for this self, anyway? It doesn't live in a vacuum. Anything that shows up for this self affects others selves, too, especially those close to it. Wasn't this self's life part of a larger picture? It always felt that way to me.

I learned to look for the "flow" rather than to try to force what I wanted to happen. I was not happy with this, because I wanted what I wanted. But I always eventually concluded that it was easier to ride the flow than to swim against it. Especially since swimming against it wasn't going to make happen what I wanted to happen anyway!

Eventually I gave more and more of the self's life to the Holy Spirit (Teacher of Truth in my mind). It has become clear to me recently that some of what I thought was guidance from the Holy Spirit over the years was really my tuning into the flow of the universe. Where the Holy Spirit came into it was in my willingness to be rational, open, and without judgment. This opened my mind to the flow of the universe of form. So the Holy Spirit was not so much my guide as my mind-set. But even though I sought the flow, rather than to manifest what I wanted, I still lived through the self. I sought through it for happiness and peace. But when I undid guilt I let go of a need for a story – for a self. I let the self go into the flow of the universe – where it always was, anyway. It was always just a character in a story, though I selfishly thought it was there for me to live through! Now I simply watch it, without judgment. Since I don't identify with it I am not concerned with controlling its life. It is only part of a meaningless story that has nothing to do with Truth.

14. One Story (April 3, 2015)

I have come to a higher vision where I see the universe of form as a tapestry; a unitary, unified story where once I saw it as a collective (macro story) of independent stories (micro stories) all playing on each other. The choices for this self have not been independent choices influenced by and influencing the larger macro story as I thought they were. The choices for this self have all been *part of one whole unfolding story*. I experienced those choices, and still experience the choices for this self now, as though they were made by a singular independent split-mind among many independent split-minds. But now I know they are simply the singular unfolding of one larger story. Every choice is the effect of only one split mind. And none of the choices have any real effects. The Truth goes on untouched by any of it. It is *just a story*.

I knew back when I studied *A Course in Miracles* that the "you" it was speaking to was not what I experienced as the individual "me". For example, where it speaks to the choice to be separate from God I knew it was not referring to a choice that I made as an individual. This individual, like all individuals, is an expression of the choice of one split-mind (what ACIM calls the "Son of God") to be separate from God. But only now do I *see* this. And of course this choice, again, is not a real choice. Nothing real is occurring. It is just the playing out of the idea of the opposite-of-God.

I went from being almost wholly ego-identified and feeling that the self was reality. I thought this self was one among many. Then I shifted to being aware of a mind split between ego (personal thought system) and the Holy Spirit (the thought system that comes from an awareness of Truth). I thought this split mind was one among many. Eventually I saw that there is really only one split mind that takes many forms. The content of all of these minds is the same though their forms are different. So I came to understand that these minds were a projection in the likeness of one split mind. But I still thought of them as independent of that one split mind. And now I *see* that they are not.

Does this change anything for the self? No. Whatever its choices they are part of the one story. They cannot be anything else. But I say this vision is "higher" because, apart from the self, I can see the whole story, as though I am above it, rather than in the midst of it seeing only what is in front of me.

15. The Sanest One in the Room (April 10, 2015)

I used to intellectually understand that the ego was insane. Now I experience it as such. I get what I call the "falling down the rabbit hole" sensation of disorientation when I try to understand an ego (personal thought system). This includes the one in my mind. What I experience is the chaos of a multitude of possible interpretations and responses without any criteria to establish which is the best to choose. The mere fact that there is choice indicates that there is no absolute correct interpretation or response except to acknowledge it is insane and not engage with it. Not engaging with the ego is easy now that I experience it as insane. While I still thought it made some sense I couldn't let it go.

"Whoever is saner at the time the threat is perceived should remember how deep is his indebtedness to the other and how much gratitude is due him, and be glad that he can pay his debt by bringing happiness to both. Let him remember this, and say:

I desire this holy instant for myself, that I may share it with my brother, whom I love.
It is not possible that I can have it without him, or he without me.
Yet it is wholly possible for us to share it now.
And so I choose this instant as the one to offer to the Holy Spirit, that His blessing may descend on us, and keep us both in peace." (T-18.V.7)

The above quote was the suggestion made to Helen and Bill in *A Course in Miracles* for those times when they were in conflict. Of course they were in a unique teaching-learning relationship where what one experienced the other did as well. But what about the rest of us who do not have a partner in this practice? The "saner" one at any given moment is the one who is able to put aside the ego (personal thought system) and access the Truth in their minds. Since the vast majority of people you come across are not aware of the Truth in their minds this most often means you. If you want harmony in your relationships with others you are going to have to be the one to find that harmony for yourself in your awareness of Truth. The Holy Spirit (your awareness of Truth) in your mind will help you find another way of looking at the other or the relationship or help you to find ways of approaching the other so that you do not increase fear in either of you.

When dealing with others it helps to remember that just as you view things through the filters of your mind they view things from the filters in their mind, too. This can help you to not take their responses personally and escalate a conflict. What they feel and how they respond is never about you. If you can take a deep breath and focus on what they need in the moment rather than on your personal response of fear you will drop your defenses. And when you drop your defenses you will often find that they drop theirs, too. Then you can get on with a rational discussion to deal with the conflict between you.

As you grow closer to Truth and sanity and away from the insanity of the ego there will be fewer people to whom you can relate. You will feel increasingly different from others and apart from the world. The ego will tell you that you should feel lonely. But you will feel whole in your awareness of Truth so you will not feel lack or "loneliness". True Oneness is not the joining of egos but an inward experience of Wholeness. And because the mind always sees itself you will see the same Wholeness in others even when they are manifestly not aware of It themselves. Wholeness will feel more present to you and the superficial, passing ego drama will be insignificant to you.

16. Death, Reincarnation, and Guilt (April 17, 2015)

"In the ultimate sense, reincarnation is impossible. There is no past or future, and the idea of birth into a body has no meaning either once or many times. Reincarnation cannot, then, be true in any real sense. Our only question should be, 'Is the concept helpful?'" (M-24.1)

The belief in reincarnation is one that bafflingly persists in the *A Course in Miracles* community. It's baffling because ACIM states that it cannot be real. And it's baffling because in the experience of the Holy Instant, the experience central to understanding ACIM, you know that it cannot be real. Yes, ACIM also says it may be a helpful concept if looked at the right way. It goes on to say that if it's comforting to the believer its helpfulness is obvious. And that you can emphasize the aspect of the concept that leads one to understand that there is more to existence than this passing life. But those are very slim aspects of the concept to find helpful. They could only be temporarily helpful at best.

I have yet to run across a student who looks at the concept of reincarnation in a way that is comforting or helpful. Always they speak of it with guilt and fear. Either they are unhappy and fear having to repeat life in a body. Or they feel that they will never see the end of guilt. How many lifetimes of guilt do they have to undo? How many lifetimes will it take to undo the guilt? How can they stop from making more guilt in this lifetime? Guilt is built into the concept of reincarnation.

One of the most difficult questions for students of ACIM to answer is "What happens to me when I die?" It is difficult to answer because that which asks does not exist! "Eternity", as ACIM uses the word, is not "endless time" but "timelessness". Eternity is outside of time. It has no beginning and no ending. It simply is. That Which is eternal within you is not touched by the story that you have for yourself in time. Peace is attained by becoming aware of the Eternal within you and focusing on It as you let go of the story that you have for yourself in time. When you do that you stop having questions about death. That which would be concerned with death has already fallen away from you when you are aware of the Eternal within you.

"Reincarnation would not, under any circumstances, be the problem to be dealt with now. If it were responsible for some of the difficulties the individual faces now, his task would still be only to escape from them now." (M-24.2)

The trap is the belief that there is something out there in the future to be attained. The Eternal is within you now. You are only unaware of It. Your obstacles to peace are beliefs in your mind now. If you are unhappy now the source of your unhappiness are thoughts and beliefs in your mind now even if they seem to be about the past, of this life or of another life. This is why you can undo them now. If the source of the thoughts truly was in the past then you would not be able to undo them. The source of anything you feel now is a belief in your mind now.

"The ego teaches thus: Death is the end as far as hope of Heaven goes. Yet because you and the ego cannot be separated, and because it cannot conceive of its own death, it will pursue you still, because guilt is eternal. Such is the ego's version of immortality." (T-15.I.4)

Reincarnation is a very comfortable belief for the ego (personal thought system) because it is the belief that guilt is real. Though students may say that they understand that guilt is not real and that the problem is that believe in it, there is no way to avoid feeling punished as they contemplate an indefinite number of future lifetimes to undo an indefinite number of past lifetimes of the belief in guilt. This is just guilt and punishment in disguise. In fact, all you have to do is deal with the feelings of guilt that come up now. Feelings always reveal your true beliefs. So look at them with the Holy Spirit and undo them. In time you will realize that you always come back to a single core belief – that there is a power over you (a god) that judges you and that you have to live up to. As you correct this illusion again and again in its many forms you will eventually undo it. The ego will always tell you that you are guilty. But you will no longer believe it so the idea will have no power over you. This is something that you can accomplish in this lifetime.

17. A Follow-up to "Death, Reincarnation, and Guilt (April 24, 2015)

I knew my last article was on a loaded topic: reincarnation. I did receive some positive emails. But I felt that many of the comments on the article at my blogsite, via email, and in discussion with clients missed the central points of the article. This is a common phenomenon! I learned a long time ago that everyone reads through their own filters. But I want to clear up some of the issues that came up in the comments and then I'll be done with it. When I write an article all I can hope is that the readers read it with the Holy Spirit and get something useful out of it for where they are now in their process, even if it's not what I intend for them to get.

The point of the article was how the belief in guilt persists through the concept of reincarnation. As long as you believe in guilt the ego (personal thought system in your mind) will provide stories for your guilt, whether they are from this lifetime or from another. As long as you want to go in search of guilt in your mind it will provide stories from this lifetime or another lifetime. When you work out the guilt in your mind you will not be interested in these stories any more. The ego in your mind will still have them. But you won't attend to them because you will see that they are not true.

Stories of guilt in your mind are not really the source of your guilt. Your belief in guilt gives rise to the stories. The value of looking at these stories is that they bring your belief in guilt to your conscious awareness. This belief takes many forms. But each time as you drill down to the source of guilt you will arrive at the same underlying belief: that there is a power outside and over you (a god) taking your measure and judging you. This, ultimately, is the only belief that you have to undo. It is what holds guilt in place. It is what makes you fear Truth. Eventually you will not be deceived by the many forms guilt takes. Instead when guilt comes up you will go right to undoing your underlying belief in a judgmental god. (My book, *Releasing Guilt for Inner Peace*, explains all of this in depth).

There are some who believe firmly in reincarnation and I have no doubt that, if they are willing, the Holy Spirit will use that belief in a way that will help them undo guilt now. But there is no reason to despair over the idea of reincarnation. Nor is there any reason to adopt the concept if it fills you with fear or does not make sense to you. The other important point that I made in the last article is that it does not take lifetimes to undo your belief in guilt. It just takes willingness *now* to look at guilt when it comes up naturally.

Sometimes when you study something like ACIM there are concepts beyond your ability to understand. If you cannot understand Eternity as timelessness or existence without a self then accept that you do not understand Eternity and True Being (God) yet. Understanding will come as you are ready to understand. You don't have to adopt concepts that scare you or that do not make sense to you in the meantime. It is a more helpful practice to keep your mind open to the Holy Spirit. It will bring you the concepts or experiences that you need to understand. (And, yes, for some it may be reincarnation but not if it scares you or does not make sense to you. If you feel despair you are listening to the ego, not the Holy Spirit!).

The concept of reincarnation was used by the Voice she called "Jesus" to motivate Helen Schucman to be a channel for and scribe of ACIM. When you read about a person's specific experience with the Holy Spirit (or "Jesus") what you want to take away is *that* they were answered, not necessarily *what* they were answered. The Holy Spirit speaks to your mind and the unique way it works. It meets you where you are in the process. [For more on this, see *The ACIM Mentor Articles*, #182. *The One Limit to the Holy Spirit's Guidance* (June 26, 2007) and ACIM Mentor Articles, Volume 2, #75 *Ask: What makes the Course different from other specific answers?* (May 11, 2012)].

For those who have had past life experiences but who are made fearful by the concept of reincarnation I offer you two alternative ways of looking at those experiences. The first is that as each of us in our seeming-individuality are figures in the "dream" of one mind then past life experiences are really just "memories" of other dream figures in that one mind's dream. In other words, you did not *personally* live those lives. You are just remembering something in the collective dream. This is why many different people can have past-life experiences of being the same historical person.

The other view is one that comes from my own experience. I, too, have had past life "memories", three in total, two of them under hypnosis over 20 years ago. Right away I recognized that they were analogies for what I was experiencing at the time. For example, while I was dealing with what I perceived as a painful rejection one of the regressions revealed how in a past life this same person had "stabbed me in the back" and killed me. The "memories" in these regressions seemed to me to be just like a dream I have at night that produces analogies to what I am experiencing awake. They were stories from my subconscious built around my feelings.

Beyond specific stories for guilt the concept of reincarnation reinforces guilt by emphasizing your identification with a self. It can therefore only come from the ego, which is the thought system for you as a self. The concept is an attempt to give an attribute of Reality – immortality – to the ego to make it seem real. For this reason even if the concept is helpful for some temporarily it will eventually fall away when they recognize it as an obstacle to complete peace.

18. Unconscious/Subconscious (May 1, 2015)

Lately I've received some questions about the terms "unconscious" and "subconscious". Students want to know what we are talking about when we talk about unconscious thoughts and beliefs. Unconscious thoughts and beliefs are thoughts and beliefs in your mind but out of your conscious awareness. We refer to them as being in your "subconscious", or below your level of conscious awareness. You can only hold a limited amount of what is in your mind in your conscious awareness. The rest is in your subconscious.

Some of what is in your mind that you are not conscious of is there through your denial. These are thoughts and beliefs that you find frightening or painful. These include, but are not limited to, memories. Beyond specific memories there are beliefs that you have internalized and find too painful to look at, like the belief in intrinsic guilt, fear of a god outside of you that is going to punish you, unworthiness, the belief that you are "bad", etc. Some people repress these thoughts more than others. Sometimes you are aware of these thoughts but not always aware of how deep they go in your subconscious and how they drive you. These are your "obstacles to peace", the "darkness" in your mind that *A Course in Miracles* says you must bring up to "light", or conscious awareness, to dispel.

When beliefs are integrated into your way of thinking they end up in your subconscious because there is no reason for you to hold them in your conscious mind. Not all of these are negative beliefs. Even helpful ones eventually end up in your subconscious as they are integrated.

Some thoughts occurring in your mind happen so fast that you are not conscious of them, nor do you need to be. Intuition works this way. Intuition is your mind making unconscious connections and seeing patterns so quickly that it results in you feeling immediately that you know something about someone, something, or an event. Connections (negative, fearful, guilty) made by the ego (personal thought system) may show up intuitively. Your mind may also make neutral intuitive connections that merely make an observation. And helpful communications from the Holy Spirit (awareness of Truth in your mind) may show up intuitively.

Your subconscious is not something outside of you that drives you. Nor is it a mysterious force within you. It only seems mysterious when you do not understand it. But when you understand that you have thoughts and beliefs in your mind of which you are not aware you can choose to become aware of them. When you say that you did something unconsciously it is an *explanation*, not an *excuse*, for dysfunctional behavior. You can take responsibility by becoming aware of what is going on in your subconscious so you are not blindly driven by it. You do this by being willing to know what is going on in your own mind. You can say to the Holy Spirit in your mind, "I am willing to see what thoughts I have hidden in my mind that caused this feeling/behavior/attitude."

You were born into a state of consciousness that denies God (True Being). But Reality cannot be wholly denied. So beyond all of the thoughts and beliefs in your subconscious there is always God, whether or not you are consciously aware of God. Do not underestimate the ego's (personal thought system's) resistance to you looking into your subconscious. It is heavily invested in you not learning that God is in your mind. When you look into your mind and learn how it works the ego will be threatened. It will tell you that you will find horrible things if you look within your mind: You will find out how evil you really are. This is how it protects itself from you. But you can only fully take responsibility for yourself when you know what is going on in your mind. And you can only find God by looking into your mind.

You do not have to root out every thought and belief in your subconscious. Just deal with what comes up naturally and what you learn will eventually generalize and undo unhelpful thoughts and beliefs. All feelings are caused by thoughts and beliefs. So if you don't like how you feel, and you are not consciously aware of the thoughts and beliefs that cause the feeling, willingly ask yourself what beliefs are in your subconscious. I guarantee that they are never so bad that you cannot deal with them. It is only their being hidden, and the ego's fear of being undone, that makes them seem frightening. They are, in the end, only *beliefs*, not facts.

19. A Spiritual Atheist? (May 8, 2015)

I've always had trouble answering the question, "Do you believe in God?" First of all, "believing" to me means "accepting a concept without evidence". If I have evidence then I*know* instead of *believe*. I *experience* God so I *know* God. Also, more often than not, when people say "God" they mean a judgmental being with power over them that made the universe of form and that has power over it. They are not referring to the one benign Being that is Reality beyond this seeming-reality and that has nothing to do with this seeming-reality. So I know what they are asking about is not what I experience. I don't believe in a god as that concept is usually held so I would be an atheist as far as they are concerned.

But of course most atheists would not consider me an atheist. I'm a spiritual teacher for heaven's sake! But I've always respected atheists for their honesty. They do not experience anything beyond this world and they do not pretend that they do. They do not say they "believe" – accept concepts – to fit in or out of fear that there may be something out there judging them. The universe of form runs on certain physical and mathematical laws. And the physical evidence is for some kind of evolution. Physics and evolution are not ideas to "believe in", either. You either accept what the evidence shows or you do not. I understand atheists accepting facts as they appear. As far as the universe of form goes physics and evolution are the manifest story. I just know that there is Something beyond the universe of form because I have experienced It. This is what would make me not an atheist in the eyes of atheists. If it were not for these experiences I would be an atheist.

I do not confuse with the universe of form the Reality that I have experienced beyond form and Which I prefer to call "Truth" rather than "God". This is what makes me not religious. Religion spiritualizes the universe of form by giving some aspects of it spiritual relevance. I have spent my life sorting out not-Truth (form) from Truth (Formlessness) so that my mind can transcend not-Truth. I seek to maintain in my awareness the experience that transcends form rather than to spiritualize form. This is what makes me spiritual rather than religious.

There are some who accept what science and math and the physical evidence reveal about the universe of form and also believe that there is an Intelligence, or Mind, that set the physical universe in motion according to physical and mathematical laws. Some of them call this Intelligence "God". In *A Course in Miracles* this Intelligence or Mind that made the universe of form would be called the "Son of God". But beyond the "Son of God" is what ACIM calls "God" – Formless, Infinite Being. So what many consider "God" for students of ACIM is the "Son of God" and "God" is not a god at all to students of ACIM.

20. The Only Teacher to Follow (May 15, 2015)

A Course in Miracles is a self-study course for inner peace. It is an inward path that does not require you to be involved with other students. It is meant to be studied with the Holy Spirit (awareness of Truth) in your own mind. ACIM is not a passive path. You must have some self-starter qualities to truly benefit from ACIM. You must have some trust in your own discernment and critical thinking. You must use your own experience and common sense.

When you begin ACIM it can be helpful to study and discuss the practice of ACIM with other students, especially with those who are more experienced. But helpful study and practice with others will reinforce, not replace, your awareness of the Holy Spirit within. Unfortunately I've heard of three ACIM groups that are cult-like in their approach to teaching. And I'm sure that they are not the only groups like that out there. These groups ask their members to follow their leader or leaders rather than the Holy Spirit within. And in this process the members give up their power to the leader or leaders of the group. So if you are ever concerned that you could become involved with a cult or cult-like group here is a simple guide to choosing healthy, helpful teachers of ACIM:

A healthy, helpful teacher of ACIM will lead you inward to the Holy Spirit within you. "Holy Spirit" is the label given to the thought system in your mind that is aware of Truth, whether or not you are conscious of It. You can, and must, choose to become conscious of this thought system if you want to remember Truth and be at peace. The Holy Spirit within you is the *only* Teacher for you to follow if you want true peace. Only It can take you through the unique highways and byways of your mind to Truth. It may lead you to teachers in the world (in person, over the phone, through writing). But these teachers' job is to reinforce your awareness of the Holy Spirit within you through validation and the undoing of blocks (guilt, fear). If he or she is a true teacher of Truth you will feel in charge of your relationship with them. Even if you want to give them power over you they will never accept it. So:

Do not trust a teacher who says "follow me". You want teachers who say "follow the Holy Spirit within you" and who help you to do so.

Do not trust anyone who says "my way is the right way and any other way is wrong". Every path unfolds in its own unique way. Learn to trust the unique unfolding of your own path from within.

Do not trust anyone who says they know what the Holy Spirit wants for you. Only you can hear the Holy Spirit for you.

Do not trust a teacher who uses "should/shouldn't", "right/wrong", or "good/bad" statements about your behavior or thoughts. These increase guilt in your mind. ACIM is a path of undoing guilt so you can release yourself to Truth. What you want are teachers who suggest behaviors and thoughts that undo guilt and fear and increase your peace.

Do not trust a teacher who asks you to change to conform to their standards or to their group. For example, they may ask you to dress a certain way, to speak a certain way, to take a new name, etc. A true teacher of Truth knows that an awareness of Truth leads to transformation from within that shows up not as conformity but as authenticity.

Sometimes people hope that following someone else will be easier. They hope that someone else will do the work that only they can do. If you want peace no one else can hear the Holy Spirit for you or undo your obstacles to peace for you. These are within you. There is no way to peace faster than the process ACIM teaches. It teaches you to go directly to the only Help (Holy Spirit) that works. And it teaches you to deal directly with your obstacles to peace (guilt/fear) where they are, within you. Because it is a short-cut it *is* intense and not for everyone. But for everyone who wants peace there is a path.

Peace will only come to you when you are willing to feel empowered within. If you find that you are looking for someone to follow, or you are already following someone, then I suggest that you are not yet ready for a true spiritual path. Before you can embark on a true spiritual path you must feel worthy enough to be empowered. You can prepare for a true spiritual path through psychotherapy or other forms of self-help that help you grow your self-worth.

21. Trust Your Own Path (May 22, 2015)

If I had my way (oh, there's so much I could say after this!) no one would be able to read spiritual material or to listen to spiritual teachers that are more advanced than they are. It seems to cause so many problems. And of course the problems are not in the material but in the readers and listeners.

I'll say again what I've said often lately: this path has not unfolded in the way that I thought it would. I have gone along for a ride that has taken some surprising turns. Of course the way I thought it would unfold was shaped by what I read into others' experiences. It was not necessarily what the writers intended.

Sometimes I misunderstood what others shared because I was not yet at their level of awareness. Sometimes I didn't have their experience and felt I must be failing or missing something. And sometimes others simply used different words to describe an experience we shared. Often I reached a point where I'd say, "Screw what I've read! What has my *experience* taught me?" For me, experience always trumps concepts. So eventually I did accept that I know nothing. I just have to sit back and let this journey to peace unfold as it will without judging it.

I missed miracles because of my guilt and expectations. In guilt I felt I was always falling short. In guilt I couldn't see that I was in a process because I was so certain I was somehow wrong or off. I focused on what I lacked, not the peace, the insights, the everyday and higher miracles, the Revelations that I had experienced. I wasn't sufficiently grateful for those because they weren't "enough". Unconsciously I was afraid that they were all I would experience because I was afraid that they were all I deserved. So even when I came to accept that I was in a process I would still have horrible bouts of resisting this awareness. I wanted *peace now, damn it*, because unconsciously I was afraid it would never arrive.

Expectations meant I often looked in the wrong place for results. The biggest example of this was my expectation that the ego (personal thought system) would change. Of course it didn't so I felt a failure. But then peace came to stay and the ego was still in my awareness. That's when I realized I had been looking in the wrong place for peace. Peace came to me, not to the ego. Of course! The ego isn't me. Isn't this what I was learning? Now it seems obvious.

There were so many big and little expectations, some of them not consciously held by me, that have been undone or have fallen away. So I say to you: Read or listen to others' experiences with interest but not with expectations for yourself. Keep your mind open and let your path unfold. Some experiences you will understand right away. Some you too will experience in time. Some you will never experience. Trust the unfolding of your own unique path from within you. Be with the Holy Spirit (the awareness of Truth in your mind) where you are right now. You are now where you have to be to get where you are going.

22. A Different Approach to the Body (May 29, 2015)

Last week I wrote about how I learned to put aside expectations that arose from spiritual study and to allow myself to be led from within. An example of this would be how I was led to an approach to the body that was different from what I read in *A Course in Miracles*.

When I first became a student of ACIM I was, like everyone, filled with guilt (but didn't know it). So I read ACIM through a filter of guilt. I read a lot of love and release (forgiveness) in ACIM, too, but in many ways I felt condemnation when I was reading. I vaguely knew this was coming from me but my belief in guilt was so strong that I couldn't look at this directly for many, many years. One of the topics over which I felt tremendous guilt while reading ACIM was the body, especially when it came to physical illness.

ACIM teaches that the universe of form, which of course includes bodies, was not made by God. Therefore, the body is not real. However, I experience a body and denying that I experience the body would denigrate the power of my mind. So I do not have to deny the experience until that happens naturally. The body is only an idea in the mind and everything that happens in the body, including reflexes, instincts, illness, etc. is actually a choice of the mind. The body is neutral and in its neutral state it manifests perfect health. Illness in the body is caused by the guilt and fear of God I experience in my identification with the body. So if I do not identify with the body it will manifest perfect health. [You can read in detail what ACIM teaches about the body and illness and physical healing in *The ACIM Mentor Articles, Volume 2, #76. ACIM and Body Disorders* (May 18, 2012)].

However, from the beginning I was often told something else by the Holy Spirit in my mind as I read ACIM. Sometimes I would think that I was only being given an interpretation. But later I'd discover that it was not only an interpretation. I was experiencing something very different from what ACIM said. For example I would read in ACIM that illness in the body is caused by my identification with the body. In my guilt I would feel fearful when I read this. But later when I would think of those passages the Holy Spirit in my mind would explain that I experienced illness because of my identification with the body. This, of course, makes perfect sense. I would not experience illness otherwise. The clarity with which I experienced this made me think that my original, fearful interpretation was being corrected. But later I'd come across the same passage or one like it and I'd see that I was given more than an interpretation. I was given a whole other approach. This happened often when I read about the body and illness. And it only happened when I read about the body and illness. No other topic in ACIM was changed for me.

ACIM says that using form (medicines, treatments, etc.) to heal the body is "magical thinking". The body can only be healed by the mind. But the Holy Spirit told me that the remedies for form are at the level of form. Cause and effect applies at the level of form. Genes, environment, attitudes, behavior, choices, and energy all affect the body at the level of form. So at the level of form medicines and treatments are not "magic". They are manifestations of the choice to be relieved of physical symptoms at the level of form. The Holy Spirit told me that I am mind and that "magical thinking" is not thinking that medicines can help the body. "Magical thinking" is the belief that healing the body would heal mind. You can see that there is a big difference here.

Once when I was thinking about sickness the Holy Spirit explained to me that when a lion takes down a gazelle it is not personal. The lion is only trying to survive. It's the same with a virus, like a cancer or a 'flu. The virus is only another organism in the world. It is not personal when it attacks a body. It's only doing what viruses do to survive. So a virus is not "wrong" or "bad". It's neutral. It has no meaning in itself. It's just part of the experience of the world. The whole experience of the world is one of guilt and fear. Illness is not a special case of this. The body does not have a neutral state of perfection. The whole of the universe of form, as the opposite of Perfect Truth, is inherently dysfunctional. This dysfunction is not wrong or bad. It is just the way that the opposite-of-Truth is. Again, this is very different from what ACIM teaches.

What ACIM had to say about the body and illness always felt off to me. However, the Voice of ACIM was always consistent to me so I never felt that Helen had let in other voices or her own ego. So for a long while I assumed that the "off" feeling was just a projection of my own guilt. This other, clear approach that I have received from the Holy Spirit came over a very long time because in my guilt and fear my mind was closed. It also confused me. *Was* it different from ACIM? Fear made it hard for me to sort them out. I expected that when I was less fearful and therefore open what ACIM teaches would become clear to me. And it did (see link above) but it still felt "off" to me. I thought I must still be blocked. It took me a long time to see that I had actually been led to a different approach.

When I asked the Holy Spirit about the difference between ACIM and where I have been led I was told that Helen had a different goal from my goal. I cannot speak to her goal. But mine has always been to know Truth and be at peace. Helen was told that if she healed the body of illness by simply choosing against illness it would demonstrate the power of mind. She would learn that the mind decides how the body feels. She would learn that she is not the victim of the universe of form. Last year during a brief illness I caught a glimpse of the level of mind where the choice of illness is made. When I saw this I simultaneously saw that that level of the mind is not real, either. The body, illness in the body, the part of mind that causes responses in the body – all of that is not-Truth. I was not led to change that level of mind to heal the body. I was led to let it *all* go. All along I've been led to detach from the body – indeed, all of not-Truth - not to seek to change my mind to heal the body.

When I translated ACIM into plain, everyday language I kept its message about the body and illness the same though it conflicted in many ways with what I was learning directly from the Holy Spirit. In fact, that was when I began to enquire into the difference. But it was not my place to change ACIM's message. What I teach now is what I have learned directly from the Holy Spirit. When students contact me to learn how to heal the body by changing their minds I direct them to other ACIM teachers whose interest seems to lie in that direction.

This approach to the body is still unfolding for me. I will continue to be led from within rather than from a book or another person in the world. Teachers and teachings are not ends in themselves. They are means to my goal of being aware of Truth but only when viewed through the Teacher of Truth (Holy Spirit) in my own mind.

23. More on A Different Approach to the Body (June 5, 2015)

Last week's article, "A Different Approach to the Body", resulted in a wave of comments and questions at my blogsite and in my email. The central point of the article was to give an example of how one should be led from within rather than from a teaching in the world. However, the comments and questions I received were largely about the example rather than the central idea. Here I will attempt to clear up some points that seemed to confuse some students:

First, I did not mean to imply that the different approach to the body to which I was led by the Holy Spirit (the awareness of Truth within me) was *wholly* out of line with what *A Course in Miracles* teaches. Some sent me quotes from ACIM that were in line with what I teach. However, if I stopped with those passages from ACIM I'd be disregarding significant portions of what else ACIM teaches. So, yes, much of what I teach about the body is in line with ACIM. But I've also been led away from its core teachings about the body. ACIM puts a lot of emphasis on how the mind causes illnesses in and is the source of healing the body. My awareness of Truth (Holy Spirit) has led me to see form as all one illusion and to disregard it as a whole. This includes the level of mind that makes decisions about the body's condition.

Second, this part of my article confused many. They could not see the distinction I was making:

"For example I would read in ACIM that illness in the body is caused by my identification with the body. In my guilt I would feel fearful when I read this. But later when I would think of those passages the Holy Spirit in my mind would explain that I experienced illness because of my identification with the body. This, of course, makes perfect sense. I would not experience illness otherwise."

Here's the distinction: ACIM says that illness in the body is caused by one's identification with the body. If one withdraws their identification from the body, the body will be healed:

"The idea of separation produced the body and remains connected to it, making it sick because of the mind's identification with it." (T-19.I.7)

"The body, valueless and hardly worth the least defense, need merely be perceived as quite apart from you, and it becomes a healthy, serviceable instrument through which the mind can operate until its usefulness is over." (W-135.8)

What I have learned from the Holy Spirit is that like all form, the body is limited, changeable, and open to manifestations of dysfunction in many forms. This is so because the experience of form is the opposite of eternally perfect, limitless, formless Truth. Medicines, treatments, etc. for the body are available at the level of the body (form). I only experience illness when I identify with an ill body. However, as mind I can detach from the experience of the body, whatever its condition, and watch it in the recognition that it is not real and is a passing experience.

So, to sum up: ACIM teaches that illness in a body is caused by the mind that perceives itself in that body. It teaches that one only has to choose to not be ill and they will not experience illness or a manifest illness will disappear.

What I have been taught is that illness in the body is the result of causes (genes, environment, attitudes, behavior, lifestyle choices, energy) at the level of form. Some causes (attitudes, behavior, choices, energy) can change if one changes them and this may result in illness not manifesting, being mitigated, and perhaps healing. One's willingness to have the body be well results in their becoming aware of the appropriate medicines, treatments, diets, etc. at the level of form.

The significant distinction here is that ACIM teaches that the body can be perfected by one withdrawing their identification from it. Where I have been led is to see that one can withdraw their identification from the body and experience detachment from its conditions. But the body continues on as inherently limited, occasionally or chronically dysfunctional, deteriorating form that eventually ceases to be animated ("alive") and decays if it is not preserved (mummified, etc.) or destroyed.

Why is this distinction important? Because ACIM's way kept me focused on the body's condition as an indicator of my state of mind. The way I have been led has allowed me to be at peace no matter the condition of the body. I accept that the experience of form will never be perfect. This sets me free to detach from it and to focus on mind instead of the body. The result has been for my awareness of Truth and peace to be my focus as the body falls into the background of my experience.

For me, anyway, ACIM's way blurred the line between Truth and illusion; between Formless Mind and form-bound thinking. The way I have been led has made the distinction between Truth and illusion clear to me. Any concern with form is limiting.

Third, ACIM does *not* say that the goal is to heal your mind to heal the body. [Again, You can read in detail what ACIM teaches about the body and illness and physical healing in *The ACIM Mentor Articles, Volume 2*, #76. *ACIM and Body Disorders* (May 18, 2012)]. Nor was I suggesting that this is what ACIM teaches. What it does teach is a result of health for the body as the mind is healed. In other words, physical healing is not the goal for healing the mind, but is a side effect. Where I have been led is to attend to mind and let the self (body, personality) be as it is without judging it. This is how I detach from it. And I have experienced a mind growing in its awareness of Truth and peace while the body continues on with many of the typical issues of middle age. My experience seems to be in line with other spiritual teachers, mentioned by some readers, who no longer identified with a self and yet whose bodies died of illness. (I do not yet claim to not identify with a self at all. But it is harder to find).

Having written all of this, I hope readers will eventually come to realize that *we are talking about nothing*. Attend to the body and it will grow in your awareness. So will guilt and a feeling of vulnerability and fear. Attend to Truth and It will grow in your awareness. So will the awareness that you are whole and perfect in Truth and that the body is nothing.

24. Ask: What does ACIM say about visualization and wanting things in the world? (June 12, 2015)

"...I want to ask you as an ACIM student, a new one, what is the perspective of the Course *about the technique of visualization, very used in New Age books like a means for getting what we want. And what is the perspective of the* Course *about wanting something like a successful career, money, financial freedom, fitness goals, academic goals, etc. Are they bad? Is it inappropriate to wish them and go for them?..."-* FG

A Course in Miracles teaches that lasting peace and happiness comes only from an awareness of Truth (what it calls "God") within you. Using techniques of any kind to manifest what you want in the world to make yourself feel whole, happy, secure, at peace, etc. is a misuse of the mind. This misuse is misguided, not "wrong" or "bad". It comes from the mistaken belief that you need something outside of you to feel whole.

ACIM also recognizes that you are not yet in touch with your inherent wholeness in Truth. So it teaches you to use your goals in the world as the means to become aware of the Truth within you. Instead of ends in themselves your goals become means to the goal of peace. Every situation becomes a classroom where you can learn of Truth from the Holy Spirit (the part of your mind that is aware of Truth) within you. So you do not have to give up your desires in the world. Instead, share them with the Holy Spirit in your mind. Then they will be the means to peace rather than obstacles to peace.

25. Ask: Can you address the discrepancy between daytime "dreaming" and nighttime dreaming? (June 26, 2015)

"...I was wondering if you could address in one of your articles the seeming discrepancy between our daytime 'dreaming' in which we more and more frequently turn to Jesus or the HS to help us remember Truth and our nighttime dreams in which (in my case anyway) it is as if the Course *never entered my life. This has puzzled me for a while..."* - LG

This seems to be common among *A Course in Miracles* students, although some students do tell me they call on the Holy Spirit or Jesus in their dreams. For myself, it is very rare that my spirituality comes into my dreams at night, at least as far as I remember.

Dreaming at night is really just our mind's way of blowing off steam. For some it seems to be more of an avenue to self-awareness than for others. For myself, some dreams have been significant and I recognize that right away on waking. Other than that I usually only pay attention to them when I recognize a reoccurring theme. Then I know something in my mind is being revealed to me.

However you dream, just accept that as natural to you.

26. Ask: How can my personal desire become a means for peace? (July 3, 2015)

"Your response to a student's recent question re. visualization included the following: [The Course] *'teaches you to use your goals in the world as the means to become aware of the Truth within you. Instead of ends in themselves your goals become means to the goal of peace.'* How would you apply this to my desire to get a sailboat?...because I did truly enjoy every aspect of owning one. I know that getting a boat will not bring me peace but I still would love to get one... How could this personal desire for a sailboat become a means to my ultimate goal of peace?"* – ES

Some of our desires and preferences are just expressions of personality. They are neutral in themselves. We are not always looking to them for salvation (wholeness, peace), in which case they *would* be obstacles to peace. If you feel moved to act on this desire simply bring the Holy Spirit (awareness of Truth in your mind) with you in the process. Let It be your partner in decision making and in any actions you take. Then the situation will be a means to be aware of the Holy Spirit. As your awareness of and trust in the Holy Spirit grows so will your peace.

27. Ask: Why do I feel guilty after setting boundaries with my mentally ill brother? (July 10, 2015)

"My brother, let's call him Sam, (71 y/o) is brain damaged from an industrial accident 40 years ago. He functions somewhat but has very little "common sense" and has fanatical ideas of about God speaking to him and telling him to fight ISIS and have a new baby Jesus with a woman, etc...He has gone off his anti-psychotic medication so that is contributing greatly to his fanatical ideas... Off meds results eventually in a breakdown (deep depression) which has happened several times over the years, and the signs are there again. The family will then have to bail him out in many ways since he ends up in a mental hospital, without funds, without a place to live, and an inability to survive alone etc. He feels it's his own business that he is off meds but obviously it is affecting many of us...he attacks me in emails, I mostly ignore it...So, I know to do my forgiveness work and let Holy Spirit do the rest. That work is constantly with me whenever thoughts of Sam come up. Maybe that answers the esoteric part of this, but I feel a responsibility to my brother, as a Son of God, but especially as a sibling. What does ACIM say about the mentally disturbed? Right now, after this past week of frustration with him, I am disengaging from him, just responding to emails of inquiry on non-hot subjects and I continue to send him Light and Love. I still feel guilt there though, so something isn't right yet! More forgiveness work. Any light you can shine on this?..." – JP

You have a social-moral responsibility for the physical care of a mentally ill member of your family. It is not fair but that is the way of the world. And that is where your responsibility for "Sam" ends. You cannot change the mind or behavior of what are considered healthy adults in the world so you certainly cannot expect to do so for the mentally ill! Beyond encouraging him to take his medication there really is nothing else you can do for him but let him know that you love him. But loving him does not mean putting up with abuse from him. You have taken wise action by putting up boundaries with Sam to keep yourself away from his abuse and engaging with him on a limited basis. Now you need to extend those boundaries within yourself so that you stop taking more responsibility for him than is really yours.

You need to ask yourself why you feel you have more responsibility for Sam than you do. Who says so? Where did that idea come from? How deep does it run? Is it based on fact or on false ideas? Do you take responsibility that is not yours in other areas of your life? This may be part of a larger pattern. When you have worked that out and released (forgiven) yourself from a false sense of responsibility you will find that the guilt falls away.

If you find yourself resenting the time, money, and energy that you have to put into your social-moral responsibility toward Sam then you need to look at what stories you tell yourself about the situation. For example, that it is wrong and that you are a victim. You react to the story you tell yourself, not to the situation, which has no meaning in itself. So it is the story in your mind that you have to forgive (release). So sort out the story ("I'm a victim of my brother." Or "I'm a victim of this situation." Or "This is my punishment for..." etc.) from the facts ("This body has a social-moral obligation to take care of that body. This has no meaning. It is not personal. I am not being attacked. I am not being punished." Etc.) When you release (forgive) the story you will be freed from resentment.

28. Ask: What steps can I take to overcome this fear of loss? (July 17, 2015)

"My best friend and husband died suddenly one night a little over 3 years ago and your help was wonderful...the fear and pain of that sudden "loss" opened up a door to the Truth and I was able to move forward...However at the present time, I fallen back into the trappings of the dream. With T gone and no family I've put all of my security and sense of well-being into the two Pugs we were raising together and our home...I see that I've come to believe my safety lies in having these things around me, this while studying every day and going into silence almost as consistently...

Each time something "happens" to threaten whatever illusion I've put my faith in, obviously, I quake with fear and run to the Course. *Now it's one of the dogs. I can't believe what happens whenever something seems to go wrong with one of them...And with my years of studying I have felt the feeling of dark terror so much less than I did that when it does come I feel as though I might die. And then I remember that what is frightening me so isn't these "things" at all. And then the fear really comes.*

My question is whenever I take anything in the dream seriously, do I bring those thoughts to the Truth in my mind? I do this, but with my head bowed in shame for being duped yet again, for taking it all seriously and making it real. How do I laugh gently at these things I believe are so real and threatening. How do I get to look at the dream battle field from above?

The Course *says it is never talking about form or to the dream figure reading its words, that the decision maker is the one who will lift the veil... My real question is...What, if anything, can the dream figure do to help the decision maker change its mind? I've reached a point where I feel like I'm banging my head against a huge iron door with the decision maker on the other side and there's nothing I can do to get in touch! And I know the more I believe it's impossible that is exactly what I will experience.*

...What's next? I guess I'm looking for steps... I've got one foot planted firmly in the dream and the other tentatively dipping it's toe in Truth and I feel lost." – SB

First, let me clarify that you are the "decision maker". This is not a term in *A Course in Miracles* but it was one coined by Ken Wapnick to describe your mind in its split between Truth and illusion. The "dream figure" is the body/personality/ego (personal thought system) with which you as the decision maker erroneously identify. You have the choice to continue to identify with the dream figure or to grow your awareness of Truth. And what you describe indicates that you are smack in the middle of the process of choosing Truth over illusion. For a long time we students of ACIM vacillate between the two thought systems in our mind as we learn that Truth is more valuable than illusion. It is as though we have two competing realities. This is simply how this process works. You are not failing when you find yourself back in ego. It just means you have not fully realized it has no value for you. And identifying with the ego is not "wrong". It is simply not Reality. Whether or not you want Reality is up to you. There is nothing and no one who says you have to choose It.

Two statements that you wrote explain why, instead of just going back into the ego (personal thought system) and being uncomfortable for a while, you experience such fear. One was your statement that you are aware that what frightens you is not the fear of losing things in the world. I assume that you mean that you are aware that your real fear is fear of Truth. And this fear makes you even more afraid. This indicates that you feel guilty for your fear of Truth. The other statement that you made was also of guilt: the shame you feel for being "duped" again by the ego. These statements reveal that you still believe that there is a god that holds you to a certain standard that you are failing. No wonder your fear is so extreme! And no wonder you keep turning back to the ego. You may not like the ego but it must feel safer to you than a disappointed god. You are experiencing one of the very reasons why for a long time students continue to turn back to the ego.

So what you must do now is root out that belief that there is something outside of you with power over you (a god) sitting in judgment on you and who is waiting to punish you for not being perfect. That god does not exist. It is a construct of the ego and your conscious and unconscious belief in it is the source of your fear. While you do this you want to remind yourself that the Truth goes on within you, whole and perfect, no matter what you seem to do or to not do in the universe of form. Remind yourself of these facts every time your fear of loss comes up.

If you want to know in more detail where guilt comes from, how it is maintained in your mind, and how to release it you may be interested in my book *Releasing Guilt for Inner Peace*. It is only in digital form and you can find it at www.amazon.com (Kindle) or www.lulu.com (PDF or ePub).

29. Questions for Deeper Study and Practical Application (July 24, 2015)

Studying is more than just reading. It is thinking about what you read. Early on in my study of *A Course in Miracles* I found I was asking questions while I studied that would help me to take the ideas in deeper. This was especially important for me as a student of ACIM because ACIM gives so many words and concepts new definitions. The questions were like this:

1. How do I think of this concept now? What do I feel about it?
2. How is this concept being used here? Is it different from how I'm used to using it?
3. If I accepted this concept (or how it is being redefined) as true how would that change how I feel about myself?
4. If I accepted this concept (or how it is being redefined) as true how would that change my relationship to the world?

For example, ACIM was not the first place that I read that God is within rather than an outside being. But it was as a student of ACIM that I realized that I had to integrate this idea or ACIM would have no real effect on me. So:

1. How do I think of the concept of "God" now? What do I feel about it?

Traditionally, I think of "God" as a paternal, authoritative being outside of me that sits in judgement on me. This is a frightening idea to me. It makes me feel ultimately powerless and angry. And I feel guilty for feeling that way.

2. How is the concept of "God" being used in ACIM? Is it different from how I'm used to using it?

In ACIM "God" is the one Being That is. God is my True Being. Yes, it is significantly different. God is not another being sitting in judgment on me. There is no separation between us.

3. If I accepted as true that God is within me how would it change how I feel about myself?

I would feel completely empowered. I would feel whole. I would not fear "sinning" and being punished by some outside being. This concept is so staggering that I don't think I can even see all the ways that it would affect me. But it would all be positive.

4. If I accepted as true that God is within me how would it change my relationship to the world?

I would feel I could do anything I wanted. I would feel always safe and secure. I would feel wholly empowered.

I did not ask myself these questions to force myself to accept the concepts, only to understand them better. Nor did these questions cause me to immediately shift in a new direction. But they helped me to see what had to be accepted and the shift that had to be made. Often they made me see how much my mind had to change to align with Truth. So they helped me to formulate the correction that I had to bring into my day-to-day life to bring about the change. I realized I had to pay attention when I found myself falling into the old way of thinking and correct it to the new way. For example, let's say I was driving and I saw a bumper sticker that said, "God loves you." My initial feeling would be to try to convince myself that something outside of me loved me. Then I'd catch myself and think, "God is not outside of me. God is my True Being. So what does 'God loves me' mean to me now?" I'd realize that "God loves me" was an unnecessary statement. God is Love and is my True Being. That was a radical change in how I thought about the word "God".

Deeper study led to practical daily application. This eventually led to the necessary shifts and integration of the concepts into my experience.

30. Getting Past the Ego's Response (July 31, 2015)

Back in the day when I was a political junkie I'd occasionally read an editorial or an opinion in the newspaper that would get me so fired up I'd dash off a letter to the editor in response. But before sending the letter I would go back and re-read the original offending article to be sure my response was as sharp as possible. And many times, much to my embarrassment, I found that the original article was not offensive at all. Sometimes it was even on my side and my response said the same thing it did. After expending my emotional response the original article would read completely different from the way I originally read it. Fortunately, because I didn't send the letters before re-reading the original articles, my embarrassment was limited to myself.

After this happened a few times I finally caught on: My emotional response to something early in the article blinded me to the rest of the article. In my expectation that I would be attacked I read attack. I was experiencing how the ego always speaks first. It not only speaks first but its response is always emotional and defensive. I learned to step away when I read something that evoked an emotional response in me. I'd let my own response run its course and then go back and re-read the article later. Needless to say after a while I wrote far fewer letters to the editor.

This lesson came in handy as a student of *A Course in Miracles*. Much of ACIM seemed loving to me, but there was also much that I felt condemned me, too. I was reading through the filter of the guilt in my own mind. I would have fearful and sometimes angry responses that closed my mind and blinded me to what followed. I was defensive because I expected to be attacked and condemned. This is why later I'd read something in ACIM that would release me from guilt and fear and I'd feel like I never read it before. Each time I read ACIM it was a new book! As layers of guilt and fear peeled away ACIM became more charge-neutral (matter-of-fact) and more loving. I began to read its parts through its whole message rather than as isolated, unconnected concepts.

It took another long while but eventually I learned to extend this lesson beyond my emotional responses to what I read. I learned to take a moment when I had an emotional response to something I heard from another, whether in person or on the radio or TV. I was always amazed by how much I didn't hear once my emotions were engaged. I had nothing to lose but embarrassment by taking a moment to let the emotions and defensiveness pass before responding.

My emotional responses were very revealing. They taught me that I expected to be attacked and condemned because I felt guilty. The specific form of what upset me showed me the specific form that guilt took in my mind so that I could undo it. I was never grateful for the upset. But I learned to be grateful for the opportunity to see what was going on in my own mind.

31. Putting Aside the Alienation (August 7, 2015)

Living in the limelight
The universal dream
For those who wish to seem
Those who wish to be
Must put aside the alienation
Get on with the fascination
The real relation
The underlying peace

- Limelight [Rush (Chronicles)]

A recurring theme with students on a spiritual path is the personal alienation they feel while still being aware of a sense of Wholeness and Peace beyond. And this is the choice before you: seeking for connection with others as a person or resting in the Wholeness and Peace that is always here within you. Your choice is to live in a lack that will never be filled or to accept the Wholeness That *is*. You cannot have it both ways.

The real question is why, when you are aware of Wholeness and Peace, you still go back into a feeling of loneliness and lack and a desire for connection to fill the loneliness and lack. The answer is simply that you are used to being a self and when Peace comes it does not come to the self or its thought system (ego/personal thought system). You are used to seeking through the self for fulfillment and when you find that you no longer need to it is baffling even when it is also a relief. The habit of seeking—the habit of being a self— takes some time to undo. And there is often a sense of loss, too. You may have enjoyed seeking. You may have enjoyed "doing". When you find all of that is unnecessary it is like the sudden quiet when a loud machine has been shut off. Yes the clamor was annoying but you had adapted. The sudden emptiness is shocking.

Much of this process comes down to acclimating to – getting used to – just *being* and being whole in Being. It is a process of learning to be without the empty, limited, always-seeking, always-doing self. Instead of seeking for love and connection with others, you learn instead to come from the Love (wholeness) already within you to remain aware that It is already here.

A spiritual path is not going to lead to an emotionally (ego) satisfying sense of connection with others. If it does, you are coming from ego, not an awareness of Truth, so the effect is temporary. An awareness of Truth offers so much more than emotional satisfaction. It lifts you out of the need for emotional satisfaction, which is a lame substitute for true Wholeness.

32. You Do Not Need to Repress the Self's Emotional Needs (August 14, 2015)

My last article about the egoic experience of personal alienation as one grows in their awareness of Truth seemed to cause some confusion and perhaps led to upset for some readers. I was not prescribing a course of action in that article. Instead I was describing what occurs naturally when one becomes aware of Truth and of their wholeness in Truth. It was therefore for those readers who have attained this experience naturally. It was not meant to suggest that those who have not attainted this experience naturally try to force detachment to occur through repression or denial of the self's emotions or emotional needs.

So let me paraphrase that article another way: As your awareness of Truth grows and you find yourself feeling whole in that awareness the ego (personal thought system) will still persist in telling you that you are not whole and that you need to connect with others to be whole. Your choice is to accept the wholeness that you are experiencing or to continue to listen to and believe that the ego speaks for you.

At no time are the self's emotional needs "wrong" or "bad". Lack is simply the experience of the self. And the self is not reality so nothing about the self has any real meaning. You simply mislead yourself when you think that the self's experience of lack is your experience of lack. However, you will be driven by lack until you experience wholeness in Truth and naturally detach from the self.

At no stage do you need to deny the emotional needs of the self. You will naturally detach from them when you experience wholeness in Truth and realize that the self is not you. This will not result in you repressing or denying emotions. This will result in you releasing yourself from defining yourself by them. The self will continue to have needs and to seek to fulfill them. But you will not define yourself by the self. You will merely observe it without judging it because you will recognize that it is nothing.

If you cannot understand how this can be then you have not yet experienced the detachment that will make this clear to you. You must first focus on growing your awareness of Truth. Then, in time, detachment from the self will come naturally and you will understand.

On a lighter note it was pointed out to me that my quote of the song from Rush was wrong. "The underlying peace" should be "the underlying theme". Oh, well. I heard what made sense to me…

33. "What could you not accept…?" (August 21, 2015)

The level of form is one great story; one tapestry of interconnection. Nothing at the level of form lives in isolation from the rest of the level of form. Everything that happens affects everything else. When something happens at the level of form there are multiple contributing factors. There are causes and effects and effects which became causes themselves all playing on each other. The attitudes, behaviors, choices, and energy of the self with which you identify all play into this one grand story. And everything else happening at the level of form plays into the self's seemingly-singular little story within the grand story.

All of this happens apart from Truth (God). It is the opposite of Truth, so it is without meaning because Truth cannot have an opposite. Therefore it is an "illusion" or "dream". Its interconnectedness is not the Oneness of Truth, Which is not made up of discrete parts joining, but is the same throughout.

When you (mind) change, the self's attitudes, behavior, choices, and energy change, thereby affecting the self's relationship to the rest of the universe of form. In response, the universe of form changes in relationship to the self. These changes of mind can be within the self's thought system (personal thought system/ego). These would be changes of mind in the context of the self-as-reality. Or they can be caused by an awareness of Truth. These changes would be the process of self (form)-identification falling away.

So Truth never enters into form directly to change it. Your awareness of Truth indirectly has an effect on form. And this is, again, always without meaning in itself. Any meaning you see in it comes from you. And you only have two choices of perspective: the ego/personal thought system or the Holy Spirit, Which comes from your awareness of Truth.

"What could you not accept, if you but knew that everything that happens, all events, past, present and to come, are gently planned by One Whose only purpose is your good?" (W-135.18)

So this quote does not mean that the Holy Spirit goes out into the world and makes things happen "for your good". The Holy Spirit's "plan" is an *interpretation*. The Holy Spirit lovingly interprets what happens in the universe of form for the peace of your mind. The personal thought system in your mind may not like what happens in the universe of form. It may judge things as "wrong" or "bad". But the Holy Spirit in your mind sees everything as a lesson. It will always interpret what happens in a way that leads to your lasting peace and happiness. And its interpretation will always make sense to you where you are right now.

34. Ask: Any insights on accepting not having the partner and family I want? (August 28, 2015)

"I am 39 and single, childless. I have spent the last 15 years doing everything (and at times letting go) to find a partner (and be the best I can be and absolutely everything under the sun) and have a family. This has not happened. I am a few months shy of 40, and am accepting the painful truth that it hasn't and probably will not happen (I am not prepared to have a child on my own). It is so hard not to judge this as 'devastating' and 'wrong'. I can't even judge it as 'for the best' or 'meant to be'. I can't seem to connect to the HS in my mind at the lesson or truth of this. There is shock, grief and denial. I've been able to accept spiritual understanding with so many things, but not this. In saying that, I am definitely in a process right now, and am quite certain I will come out the other side- I always do. Insights?" - HE

The first thing you need to clarify for yourself is that what does or does not happen in the universe of form has nothing at all to do with God (True Being). I say this in case you feel some anger toward the Holy Spirit for what has nothing to do with the Holy Spirit. This anger could be why you are unable to connect to the Holy Spirit lately.

Also your statement that you have been "the best I can be" may indicate that you believe that you have to "earn" what you desire from some power over and outside of you (a god). That god does not exist and the universe of form does not function as a system of reward and punishment.

The universe of form is an expression of the idea of not-God. It is an idea that was over as soon as it was thought. And it is meaningless because the opposite-of-God is not possible. But the ego (personal thought system) in your mind, which is part of that idea, teaches you that form is reality and therefore meaningful. It teaches you that you are part of form (a self, or body/personality) and to seek to fulfill your sense of lack through form. On the other hand, the Holy Spirit (awareness of Truth) in your mind teaches you that you are already whole in Truth and to just observe the unfolding story of the universe of form.

It has been my observation, of this self's life as well as of other selves' lives, that a self's deepest authentic desires generally express the role that self will play out in the story of the universe of form. However, that does not mean it will play out exactly as one assumes or in the time frame one would like. For example, for much of this self's early life it thought it wanted to raise children. This self is a nurturer and the natural assumption was that the desire to nurture would be satisfied by raising children. But this self nurtured in other ways and realized she didn't need to have children to be fulfilled and does not regret not having children.

Also, this self always wanted to be married. She wanted to experience a life-long commitment with another. But she didn't meet her mate until she was 30 years old. So the lesson is to trust the unfolding for the self and to open your mind to the possibility of the self's desires being fulfilled in ways you perhaps have not considered. Where the Holy Spirit comes into this is in living present in the wholeness of Truth. When you know that you are whole in Truth you stop looking to the self's unfolding life for wholeness. This frees you to trust and watch the unfolding for the self.

35. Accepting What Is and Accepting what Is (September 4, 2015)

This week's article follows up on an earlier article about living in the flow of the universe (#13) as well as last week's "Ask ACIM Mentor" article. When you accept What is—that only the Truth is true—it follows that you also accept what is at the level of form without resistance or judging the self's role in the unfolding story of the universe of form. When you find your wholeness in Truth you stop living through the self so you accept it as it is and just watch it unfold.

The play/movie "Amadeus" always comes to my mind when I think of an example of how miserable a life is when one does not accept it as it is. The story is a fictionalization of the relationship between the genius composer Wolfgang Amadeus Mozart and the composer Antonio Salieri. In the story Salieri as a young boy is so moved by beautiful music in church that he makes a deal with his god: He will devote his life and his chastity to his god if his god will give him the ability to make beautiful music. Salieri indeed goes on to become a composer and is talented enough to rise to be the composer to the Austrian emperor's court.

Then one day Salieri hears the beautiful music of Mozart and knows that only someone touched by his god could make such "forgiving" music. He is eager to meet the man whom his god has blessed. But in the story Mozart is depicted as vulgar, uncouth, and undisciplined. *This* man is blessed by god? Salieri is appalled and feels mocked and abandoned by his god. He vows to take revenge on his god by destroying Mozart, whom he sees as his god's favorite. He does everything in his power to obstruct Mozart and he terrorizes Mozart with visions of his late disapproving father. When Mozart is dying (kidney failure) Salieri can't resist taking an opportunity to be touched by his genius and helps him finish his final composition (Requiem). Mozart dies in poverty and is buried in a pauper's grave. Salieri's obsession with Mozart lands him in an institution and he ends his life lamenting his own "mediocrity".

Salieri made a deal with a god that existed only in his own mind. Even if there was such a god the deal was all one sided – Salieri alone decided the terms of the deal. For this deal with an imaginary god he made sacrifices no one asked him to make. When things didn't turn out the way he demanded he destroyed his own life as he tried to destroy another. He never saw that it was his own arrogance and resistance to *what is* at the level of form that led to his sense of persecution.

Now imagine if instead Salieri knew *What is*—that only the Truth is true. He would have found wholeness in Truth. So he would not have needed to seek through the self's life in the world for wholeness. He would've accepted the self's talents and limitations, without judging either. When Mozart came along he would've felt blessed to be around to hear such music rather than feeling deprived because the music didn't come through him. Instead of judging Mozart he could've used his power to assist Mozart in getting his music out to the world. Salieri would've understood that his love of music was for playing out the role, not of a composer genius himself, but of facilitating the genius of another (Mozart). How much more harmonious and peaceful would Salieri's mind have been if he had accepted the self's role rather than insisting that it play out the way that he decided it should?

36. Why It Is Important to Accept the "Dream" As It Is (September 11, 2015)

A Course in Miracles teaches us that Reality is formless, eternal Being extending without limit. It likens our experience of Reality's opposite—a universe of time-bound, limited form—to a "dream". It isn't real but it sure seems real when you think you are in it.

Sometimes students ask, "If it's a dream, why can't anything be true? Why can't reincarnation or unicorns or a ten-thousand year old earth or humans with wings or human civilization as the result of beings from other planets, etc. be true in the dream?" What they imply is that since it is a dream it can be anything one wants to dream it is.

Very simply, the dream cannot be anything but what it is because it is over. The "dream" *is* what the "dream" *was*. When ACIM says you are always looking at the past it means this on two levels: As a self you look at the present through the filter of your personal past. But on another level the entire experience of the universe of form is over or "past". The idea of the opposite of Reality was over as soon as it was thought because Reality's all-encompassing nature makes an opposite of It impossible. Only within the idea, the "dream", does the idea seem real and present. And when you think in terms of an "I" and of changing the universe of form you think you are a figure in the dream, that it is reality, and that it is happening now. You are not aware that you are the dreamer of the dream, that it is a dream, and that it is over. And when you do eventually realize that you are the dreamer of the dream you no longer care to change it because, not only is it over, it was a *dream*. It was nothing.

Think about the last time you had a dream while sleeping. When you woke up I bet you thought it was funny or sad or frightening or weird, etc. But I bet you didn't spend any time at all on changing it because not only was it over but it wasn't real. You will eventually realize this about the universe of form. Until then it is important to accept the dream as the evidence within it reveals it to be because otherwise you are fantasizing about the dream within the dream and you are twice removed from Reality.

37. Deal at Your Level of Awareness (September 18, 2015)

Often when I answer in my newsletter/blog a question from someone experiencing an upset in their life they explain that they have tried and failed over and over again to forgive the situation as just a projected image in their mind. This effort would seem to be in line with *A Course in Miracles* but in practice it is not helpful. If your awareness has not grown to the point where you see something as just a projected image trying to forgive it leads to repression rather than to release (forgiveness).

What shows up at the level of form is the result of cause and effect at the level of form. The mind in which this occurs is the one split mind, which ACIM calls the "Son of God" or the "dreamer of the dream". What you experience as "you" having the upset is a figure in the dream. Your mind is ultimately the one split mind (dreamer), but that is not how you experience it. You experience it as though it is the figure in the dream. And you have to deal with the thoughts in your mind at the level at which you experience them. It is not helpful to pretend you have an awareness that you have not yet attained. So my answers address how the writer experiences their problem at the level of form. I deal with their projected interpretation of what they see rather than with the image itself because their upset is in response to their interpretation, not to the actual image.

For example, sometimes I get emails where someone writes something like: "I just learned that my sister has stage 3 cancer. Since she is an image that I project I have tried and tried to forgive this but her cancer persists. I want to know what I'm doing wrong. How did I cause this? What thoughts do I have to forgive to heal her?"

At the level of form the writer is not responsible for all of the forms that she sees. She did not think her sister into cancer. Logically, how could that be? She does not live in a vacuum with her sister. What about everyone else in her sister's life? Did they contribute to her having cancer also? If this were the case then everyone who ever saw the image of her sister would have to heal whatever it was in their mind that caused her cancer so that she could heal! And what about her sister's own mind? Didn't that contribute also? The writer is not responsible for the cancer but for what she tells herself about the cancer and its effect on her sister and her own life. These stories are what determine her experience of peace or conflict.

When you do rise in awareness and become aware that you do project what you see you are no longer identifying with the figure in the dream. You are the "dreamer of the dream". You realize you are the one split mind and that you project *the whole dream* not just individual parts. And you also *see that it is nothing*. In other words, forgiveness and the awareness that you are the dreamer occur simultaneously. The "dreamer of the dream" is the level of awareness that *is* forgiveness. Until you have that awareness, concerning yourself with what shows up rather than just with the meaning (interpretation) that you project onto it only increases guilt. Form is still real to you and you think that it has meaning. So deal with undoing the meaning that you project onto the images that you see and eventually you will realize that what you see has no meaning in itself. It is nothing. All the meaning that you see you give to it. This will help you to see that there is no justification for guilt. And as guilt falls away your awareness will transcend the dream and forgive it.

38. "Separated from God" (September 25, 2015)

A Course in Miracles says that your one problem is that you feel "separated from God" and that you feel guilty for this. But it's fairly common for students to tell me that they have a hard time getting their minds around this concept. They don't go around thinking "I've separated from God and I'm bad for this" and they even believe in God. The concept is too abstract for them to grasp.

The belief in separation from God is largely unconscious and it is the source of all guilt. It is actually the consciousness into which you think that you are born into in your identification with a self. The concept is there at the core of the ego (personal thought system) in your mind. It is the idea that "proves" that the ego is real and that also protects the ego by keeping you from looking inward. You are not meant to see it consciously because then you'd be motivated to undo it and therefore undo the ego. Because the belief in guilt is the consciousness of the world, the world reinforces guilt, overtly and covertly. Rather than question this experience of inherent guilt the world's (ego's) religions try to explain it with concepts like "original sin". They reinforce guilt as valid and true. (All of this I go into in depth in my book "Releasing Guilt for Inner Peace").

So, practically, what is really meant by feeling "separated from God" and how does this lead to guilt? Since God is your True Being then to think that you are "separated from God" means that you are not aware of your True Being. You are not in your natural state. Perhaps it is easier to understand that you are unhappy and conflicted and just uncomfortable in general because you are not in your natural state rather than "separate" from some abstract concept of a god.

If you think of "separated from God" as "not in my natural state" then where does guilt come into it? Since you are not in your natural state you feel that something is "off" or "wrong". And, to preserve itself, the ego (personal thought system) tells you that this feeling is because you are inherently "wrong"; you have done something "wrong". And if you did something wrong there must be something against which you did something wrong. In your unnatural state of identification with the ego your True Being seems outside of you. The ego tells you this Being outside of you – this "god" – is that against which you did something wrong. In your identification with the ego you fear your True Being as though It is something else: a god outside of you with power over you and which sits in judgment on you. No wonder you do not want to approach your True Being!

So guilt is the ego's distortion of your discomfort when you identify with the ego. And the ego makes a god out of your Reality but telling you that It is outside of you and sits in judgment on you. This distortion is to protect the ego from your looking inward into your mind and looking past the ego. It tells you that if you look inward at all you are not to look too far or you will find out how truly "wrong" you are. But, of course, if you do look inward, after you get past your belief in guilt, you realize that you are uncomfortable not because you are guilty but just because you are not in your natural state. And that's easy to remedy by welcoming your True Being back into your awareness. This is the "one solution" to your one problem. This is the "Atonement" or correction of your perception that you are separate from God, which *A Course in Miracles* teaches.

39. Unfolding Detachment (October 2, 2015)

Once upon a time as this mind's awareness of Truth grew the natural result was that this mind came to experience that it was "in the world but not of the world", as the popular phrase goes. This meant that it felt that it was still a self operating in the world but that it had a growing awareness that its interest was really in Truth. It was a lot like being at a party but standing on the edge of the room and watching the party rather than fully participating in it.

Then this mind attained an experience of detachment that was "not in the world but aware of the world". This meant that it no longer lived through the self to fulfill a sense of lack but that there was still a world in its awareness. This was a lot like being outside of the house in which a party was occurring but still being aware that there was a party.

Now this mind is attaining an awareness that it is "not in a world but aware of a meaningless idea of a world". This is like being in a quiet place and remembering that once it had an idea, far distant now, of a party that was only ever an idea.

In the *A Course in Miracles* community there is a lot of talk about "observing the world" and "observing your thoughts". This practice comes naturally as a mind's awareness of Truth results in it experiencing itself as apart from the world and its own thoughts about the world. At first this detachment is vague but grows as one's awareness of Truth grows. This first experience of observing helps a mind to gain an awareness that the ego's (personal thought system's) thoughts are not the mind. Since the mind can observe them, the mind cannot be them. This practice results in the first two experiences described above. It is done by mind as a "decision maker" or "learner". This is when it still makes sense to mind that it has a choice between Truth and illusion. Mind seems to be making a choice, or a decision, to detach from the thought system (ego) about a self. Mind is becoming aware, very dimly at first but stronger as time goes on, that the self and its world is not reality.

Beyond the decision maker or learner-mind is Mind Itself. Mind Itself observes it all: the ego, the world, the decision maker, the mind's growing awareness of Truth. The Observing Mind is always present. It is not something that a mind practices; It is something that a mind allows. This leads to the latter experience described above.

40. Ask: What do you suggest I do to end unhealthy relationships? (October 9, 2015)

"I have been having some trouble withdrawing from some 'friends' that I no longer feel I want to spend time with. In the past I have felt justified in confrontation and judgment when I felt I was right, but clearly, after 13 years of study that is no longer an option I want to pursue. But, even as I write this I want to list their "sins" and unfairness, proving to you and the Truth in my right mind that they are the guilty ones and I the innocent victim…the bottom line is I feel that they take advantage, been dishonest and without going into more detail are 'friends' I no longer trust or want to spend time with them, however I don't want to hurt them or, as I am so dying to do…tell them what I think is wrong with them. In Truth, intellectually I know that they are characters I cast in my own play, speaking my own scripted dialog and have done nothing that I didn't unconsciously want them to do but in form I feel further contact would be toxic and very uncomfortable for me. In form, they have taken advantage, ignored boundaries I've set and lied to me. But again, on another level I know this whole situation is just another smokescreen to "protect" me from the Love that is still clearly very frightening to me, and so I've seized upon this situation as a "problem" that must be solved but in Truth doesn't even exist… And the Course

never addresses what we should or shouldn't do in the world of form because there is no world of form, however I still clearly believe there is so what would you suggest I do to end the relationship in a kind and loving way?..." –SB

Just to be clear, you do not write the "script"—what others say or do—but you interpret the script. I say this because I notice many *A Course in Miracles* students have a hard time letting go of unhealthy relationships in part because they feel they actually somehow made what shows up at the level of form. At the level of form you do attract and allow certain people into your sphere. But you are not responsible for making those people. Like the self with which you identify they are simply the result of cause and effect at the level of form going back to the beginning of time. What you can affect is the degree to which others are in your life.

Your desire to set boundaries makes it clear that you are no longer so afraid of Love that you want to hold onto these relationships as a "smoke screen". Love is what has led you to a place where you value yourself too much to continue these unhealthy relationships. You can withdraw from these relationships in a couple of ways, depending on the nature of each relationship. One is to be direct and to explain to the other why you no longer want to be in a relationship with them. The other way is to just let a relationship die a quiet death as you no longer pursue it. If the other continues to contact you, then you have to decide if you want to be direct and tell them outright that you find their behavior toward you unacceptable. Or, if you do not want to be so direct, then by not pursuing them and limiting how much you interact with them when they do call or come around they will probably get the message.

I'm not sure why you say ACIM does not address what one should or should not do at the level of form when most of the Workbook and much of the Text addresses this! It's apparent reading ACIM that Helen's problem was not so much her allowing unhealthy others into her sphere as her own unhealthy, attacking mind. But there's really no difference. Your relationship with others is your relationship with yourself. When you remain around others who attack you, you are simply using them to do for you what you want to do to yourself.

41. Ask: Can you give examples of where ACIM says what to do at the level of form? (October 16, 2015)

"I appreciate your last e-newsletter and found the question and your answer very interesting and valuable. However, I also resonated with the questioner's statement that the Course does not address how to deal with issues at the level of form. You said: "I'm not sure why you say ACIM does not address what one should or should not do at the level of form when most of the Workbook and much of the Text addresses this!" Could you provide an example of how the Course addresses what one should or should not do at the level of form, maybe in your next newsletter?" – CT

"This course remains within the ego framework, where it is needed. It is not concerned with what is beyond all error because it is planned only to set the direction towards it." (C-in.3)

I hear often enough that *A Course in Miracles* does not deal with the level of form to assume that the perception that it is an ethereal, impractical teaching must be a fairly common form of ego (personal thought system) resistance to it. But all of ACIM deals with your thoughts, your feelings, and your perceptions, which are all forms. And the Workbook lessons teach you very specifically what to do to deal with those. The Text, as well, is also full of practical advice. What could be clearer about what to do at the level of form than Chapter 30's "Rules for Decision"?

"You may complain that this course is not sufficiently specific for you to understand and use. Yet perhaps you have not done what it specifically advocates. This is not a course in the play of ideas, but in their practical application. Nothing could be more specific than to be told that if you ask you will receive. The Holy Spirit will answer every specific problem as long as you believe that problems are specific." (T-11.VIII.5) (The underlines are mine).

Perhaps what people mean when they say ACIM does not say what to do at the level of form is that ACIM does not give guidance on behavior. This is because ACIM deals with cause, not effect. Behavior is the effect of beliefs, thoughts, feelings, and perceptions. So when you change your mind the self's behavior automatically changes. In fact, there was an example of this in the last newsletter. The writer had been in unhealthy relationships. As she changed her mind and became aware of the Truth within her, her sense of self-worth grew. She found she no longer had a need for dysfunctional, abusive relationships that reflected her former low self-worth. So she was moved to change her behavior: She set boundaries with those who do not treat her with respect. However, some of those unhealthy others refuse to respect her boundaries. So she was further moved to end those relationships.

It may also be the case that some think that "hearing" the Holy Spirit means hearing a Voice from on-high every time they present the Holy Spirit with a problem. And sometimes you do hear It as a still, quiet Voice within. But the Holy Spirit is just the label given to your own mind's awareness of Truth. In the example above, the motivation to set boundaries was the Holy Spirit guiding the writer. Her unhappiness in her relationships was her call for help in a specific situation at the level of form. Her new-found motivation to set boundaries was the specific answer she needed at the level of form.

42. Yes, the Spiritually Aware Set Boundaries (October 23, 2015)

My last two articles discussed setting boundaries in relationships. A common question I get is that if one is spiritually aware wouldn't they not be bothered by others' attacks or negativity. Yes, it's true that when you are spiritually aware you do not have a personal reaction to what others say or do. But that does not mean that you want to be around dysfunction if you have the choice.

First, I want to point out that people who are having problems in their relationships have not yet reached a level of spiritual awareness where they have stopped getting an emotional charge from others' attitudes and behaviors. If they had reached that point they would not need to ask how to deal with their relationships! Boundaries would be automatic. In fact, a sign that someone with low-self-esteem is growing in their spiritual awareness is that they are ready to start putting up boundaries with dysfunctional others. A side-effect of growing spiritual awareness is a healthier self.

But back to the point: When you are spiritually aware you simply have no desire to be around a lot of drama, which is the result of dysfunction. So when you have a choice, you put up boundaries. Even when you are spiritually aware you'd prefer to sit in a quiet place rather than next to a jet engine.

Sometimes you don't have a choice. Or, really, you do, but you are getting something else out of a situation that is of more value to you. For example, you may put up with your bigoted uncle on the holidays because he is part of the family and you want to be with the others in your family. So your boundary is to not have much to do with Uncle Bigot at family events. And you do not seek him outside of family events. Or perhaps you work with someone who is relentlessly negative and judgmental so you limit the time you interact with them to shared projects. You also may have a dear friend whose life occasionally erupts in victimhood drama, even with you, but you work it out with them because you get so much else out of the relationship.

Life in the world surrounds you with so much dysfunction why, when you have the choice, would you not make the choice for a peaceful outside that reflects the peace within? In fact, it's automatic that you seek and create outside what reflects within. It is not a coincidence that those who are more spiritually aware have quieter, simpler, more harmonious outer lives.

And, importantly, the boundaries you set are not only for you. They are a loving way of demonstrating, "I am whole and so are you. I can see there is much more to you than you are now demonstrating." Your boundaries model for others what it is to value yourself and your integrity. They give others the opportunity to look at their own behavior and to grow out of their dysfunction and immaturity. Whether or not they choose to do so is, of course, their choice.

43. Ask: Can the ego be taught? (October 30, 2015)

"...I attended an ACIM *meeting last night and the question arose: Can the ego be taught? My immediate response was 'yes.' Although shortly after I started to question myself, saying inwardly; can a false belief system be taught—can what was never real be taught? But there still was something in me that questions this, believing the* Course *would agree with me. The* Course *speaks of this in rare form, such as these two teachings:* T-4.1.3—Spirit need not be taught, but the ego must be. *And...*spirit cannot perceive and the ego cannot know. They are therefore not in communication and can never be in communication. Nevertheless, the ego can learn, even though its maker can be misguided. *My question is; how is it; what is it, that the ego can be taught, and or can learn?..."* BO

First, let's define what is meant by "ego". The ego is a thought system in your mind that is a part of and is about the idea of the universe-of-form-as-reality. It is about you (mind) limited to a self (body/personality) in a world. The ego is not something that exists on its own. Your mind is its "maker" and it is "making" it anytime it is thinking with it. So it is really your mind, not the ego per se, which learns. It learns either within the context of identifying with the ego, in which case nothing really changes. Or your mind can learn as the "decision-maker", in which case it can learn of Truth. When you choose to learn of Truth then your mind has withdrawn from the ego. And this is real change.

An example of learning within the context of ego-identification is what can occur in traditional therapy, 12-step programs, and other forms of self-help. A mind learns and grows healthier in the context of being a self in a body in a world. This is not a real change in the sense that erroneous ego-identification continues, albeit more comfortably. Many people, if they decide to get healthier at all, stop there. It is still "safe" to them in their ego-identification because they have not let go of the ego.

But sometimes this kind of not-real-change within ego-identification is the first step on the path to real change. Someone whose self-esteem was so low they felt unworthy of Truth (lasting peace and happiness) now feels good enough about themselves to unconsciously or consciously allow Truth into their awareness. This would be the beginning of real change because it would be the beginning of letting go of ego-identification. At the moment that they made the choice, unconsciously or consciously, to allow Truth into their awareness they made the choice as the decision-maker not as an ego.

44. Ask: Does lesson 68 have it wrong? (November 6, 2015)

"During our discussion (in the study group) of Lesson 68:'Love does not hold on to resentment', you made it abundantly clear that you personally could not follow the part about seeing everyone as your friend because trying to do so made resentment even stronger. What mattered, you said, was being in Truth, so regardless how others showed up you would be at peace. And in the event that someone was so dysfunctional, you could set up a boundary and still be at peace. This made total sense to me and suited my own personality. What I can now take out of that lesson is to think how resentment disturbs my peace; how it reinforces my guilt and belief in a false god. What hangs me up however, is that lesson 68 is quite clear when it tells us to see these others 'as my friend', when I know that doing so will be counterproductive. So I choose to ignore it. Is the Course *wrong here? Where else does it give 'bad' advice? Are we free to pick and choose how to interpret it based on what feels comfortable?"* – ES

A Course in Miracles is not "wrong" nor is it giving "bad" advice. This is a good example of what I mean when I say it is important to read spiritual material in context. And it is also a good example of why it is important to read spiritual material with the Holy Spirit (your awareness of Truth).

The context of ACIM is Helen Schucman's mind and her relationships, particularly the one she had with Bill Thetford. Reading the Text and Workbook it is abundantly clear that she held onto a lot of dark thoughts about others. She was full of resentments and stories of victimhood. This seemed to be her primary issue in relationships with others. And it was the way her obstacles to peace showed up. She was being asked to be open to a new way of looking at others. Asking her to look at others as her friends rather than as her enemies probably worked well for the way her mind worked.

But it didn't work that way for this mind. Focusing on seeing others in any way kept me in ego (the personal thought system). I tried for many, many years to apply ACIM as written and found it did not work. Finally, I said to hell with it. I was no longer going to try to "see Christ in others" or to forgive as ACIM teaches forgiveness (to see it is not real). It wasn't working. I decided to focus on what did work for me: Communing with God daily and my companion-like relationship with the Holy Spirit. After focusing on these for a while, lo and behold, forgiveness came! Instead of seeing Christ (Truth) *in* others I found I could be aware of Christ's Presence no matter how others were showing up. My awareness of Truth with me always led to my letting go of the ego and its world. It led to forgiveness.

When I was finally tired of stubbornly applying ACIM in a way that never worked for me I was open to the Holy Spirit giving me a new approach. The reason I wasn't open earlier was because in guilt I was very rigid about ACIM. Like many students for a long time I thought doing ACIM right was the goal rather than that ACIM was simply an instrument that the Holy

Spirit could use to reach me. If I'd understood that the Holy Spirit was the point I would've been a lot gentler with myself and brought my problems applying ACIM to the Holy Spirit much sooner.

You are always free to read ACIM however you want! There is no "right" way or "wrong" way to read it. But there are helpful and unhelpful ways to read it. You only have the choice of two teachers as you study: the ego or the Holy Spirit. I tried to apply ACIM with the ego for a very long time. The clues that I was studying with the ego were in how it wasn't working and how my guilt increased with my sense of failure (not helpful). The ego is a rigid, judgmental teacher. The Holy Spirit is the Gentle Teacher. It will always help you find what works for you and It will never increase your guilt (helpful).

45. Ask: Can you clarify the term "magic thoughts"? (November 13, 2015)

".... Could you please clarify the use of the term 'magic thoughts'?..." – TB

A Course in Miracles uses the concept of "magical thinking" in two ways. One form of magical thinking is the belief that anything outside of you can make you whole and at peace. For example, the belief that if you just had perfect health or the right partner or enough money or if that person would change or if everyone just believed as you do, etc. then you would be at peace. ACIM includes in this form of magical thinking the idea that sickness is a form of problem solving. For example, using illness as a way to get attention, to be a victim, to avoid a situation, or as self-punishment to mitigate God's punishment of you, etc. The belief that the things that illness would get you "saves" you is a form of magical thinking.

The other form of magical thinking in ACIM is the belief that change at the level of form is caused at the level of form. For example, the use of medications or other treatments to reduce the symptoms of or to cure an illness in the body. ACIM says that this is magical thinking because only changing your thinking can change the body.

For those readers who have followed my teaching in one form or another for a while I will head off some inevitable questions by clarifying that yes, I teach only the former not the latter, despite what ACIM teaches. What I have been taught by the Holy Spirit is that thinking that healing the body is any true healing of me (mind) is magical thinking. Physical healing does not heal the mind of the perception that it is a body – the fundamental error of mind that needs to be corrected or "healed". This is in line with what ACIM teaches in part. But the Holy Spirit has taught me that remedies at the level of form *are* at the level of form. Medications and treatments are how solutions to bodily ailments show up when one is ready for physical healing. Just as, if my house has plumbing problems I need to call the plumber or if my car isn't running properly I need to take it to a mechanic. The body is not a "special case" of form that is fixed somehow by a change of mind where other forms of disorder in the universe of form are fixed at the level of form. This is where I have been led away from what ACIM teaches.

46. Ask: Does the Holy Spirit speak quickly and first? (November 20, 2015)

"...My question is...does the holy spirit speak quickly and first with lightning speed? I find I feel this voice may be the correct voice since it sounds definite and inspired. The answer almost seems to come out of nowhere and not even have thinking involved, just a kind of knowing..." - AB

"The two voices speak for different interpretations of the same thing simultaneously; or almost simultaneously, for the ego always speaks first." – T-5.VI.3

"The ego always speaks first…The Holy Spirit does not speak first, <u>but He always answers.</u>" – T-6.IV.1.3

As a rule, it is the ego that speaks with lightning speed. This is especially true when you look on a person or situation or you are seeking an answer. But sometimes when your mind is quiet and relaxed you may hear the Holy Spirit spontaneously. You may hear words or you may have unformed thoughts that seem to rise up into your conscious awareness and take form there.

It takes a while to sort out the Holy Spirit and the ego (personal thought system) because the ego will try to mimic the Holy Spirit. You can recognize the difference in this way:

The Holy Spirit's answer is quiet and you do have a sense of deep "knowing". Its response is without emotional charge (although *you* may react emotionally afterward). The Holy Spirit never judges. It observes and it may explain. The Holy Spirit never inspires guilt. It inspires liberation from guilt so you have a sense of release or relief.

The experience of the Holy Spirit is "light", both in the sense of illumination and in not bearing any weight. It inspires a sense of "lifting".

The experience of the Holy Spirit quiets your mind, at least for a moment.

The ego is usually emotional, but it may try to mimic emotional neutrality. However, you can recognize it by the content of its response. It will be judgmental or evaluative (good/bad, right/wrong, better-than/worse-than, etc.). It always leads to increased guilt and fear.

The experience of the ego is dark and heavy, but when you are used to it you may not recognize this until you experience lightness. It either maintains or increases your sense of being burdened. It maintains or increases the chatter in your mind.

47. Ask: I fear that if I continue with my Course studies I will lose the memory of my husband… (November 27, 2015)

"…I contacted you almost 4 years ago when my husband of 20 years, and the kindest, most supportive and best friend I've ever had, died suddenly and unexpectedly in his sleep at the age of 43. I contacted you soon after and asked your thoughts about seeing a world famous medium and you said I should do whatever might help. I have received many messages of support from him since then in the form of readings from various mediums, a host of coincidences and even sightings in my daily life. These have been a great help in my embracing our eventually being reunited when I die. That said, I can't apply the Course *teachings to everything else and not this. If everything I experience here is what I've asked for that means all of my husband's messages are coming from me and not him and that is crushing me. Literally. And now, the personal thought system is constantly telling me that if I continue with my* Course *studies, my husband will disappear from my memory because he was nothing but my own projection and that when I die I will not remember him and will never see him again and this, more than anything else, has interrupted and stalled my progress…Ken (Wapnick) said that the thoughts of love we have here are but shadows of what is beyond and you explained that Tim was a manifestation of the Love that I am. It's all so confusing to me. Obviously I can't go back, but I also do not want to give up the hope that I'll see my husband again…"* – SB

Only the Truth is eternal and unchanging. If you have something and lose it, it was an illusion. You seem to feel that either your husband was the source of your well-being or your relationship with him was the source of your well-being. If your well-being falls away when he is gone then it is not real, lasting well-being. It is an illusion of well-being.

But the good news is that you do have a Source of eternal, unchanging well-being within you. You won't let go of your husband as long as you think he is the source of your well-being. You will let him go naturally when the Truth is true for you and you know that you can rest in Its eternal peace. There is no reason for you to feel guilty for your mistaking the source of your well-being. The Truth in you goes on whole and perfect, untouched by this. The path to true Peace, for everyone, is one of holding onto idols while growing your awareness of Truth. No one releases idols until they see that they do not work and they are aware of What does work. Your having an idol simply means that you are not yet aware enough of Truth to not have an idol. Growing that awareness is a process.

You also do not have to fear that you will lose idols that you are not ready to release. Nothing can be taken from you. What falls away does so because you are ready for it to do so. However, it is true that you will not continue on a path that you do not believe will bring you the unchanging peace that you seek. When you find yourself fearing that you may lose the memory of your husband as the source of your well-being remind yourself that this will fall away only when permanent Peace has come into your awareness. At that point you will not experience any loss. You will then remember your relationship with him, not as an idol that was the *source* of your well-being, but as a *manifestation* of your eternal well-being. There will no longer be any fear associated with this memory.

48. The Value of Self-talk (December 4, 2015)

I used to have episodes of panic attacks. After the panic attack subsided I'd remain in a heightened state of anxiety for days in dread of more panic attacks. This heightened state of anxiety led to more panic attacks, more anxiety, more panic attacks, etc. It was a vicious cycle.

Eventually I learned that the primary cause of my panic attacks was some small change in my body that I would pick up subconsciously and that would lead to fearful thoughts just below my conscious awareness. These thoughts would lead to the rush of adrenaline that fueled the panic attacks. For example, I noticed I often had panic attacks at the beginning of Fall. When I paid attention I became aware that there was a very slight thickening feeling in my bronchia. I was experiencing a small allergic response. I would subconsciously pick up on this and I'd have thoughts just below my conscious awareness that I was suffocating. But even after I discovered this I felt powerless to do anything about it. I tried talking to myself about what was going on, for example, "This is just a mild allergic response. I am not suffocating. My bronchia are just swelling a little. This happens every Fall. I never suffocate." Etc. But this did not lead to an *immediate* reduction in adrenaline and panic so I didn't pursue it. Until one day I did. I just kept talking calmly to myself about what was really occurring just as I would to a friend having a panic attack. And lo and behold I found that talking to myself about what was really occurring eventually did reduce the adrenaline and therefore the panic. It wasn't immediate. It took a few minutes, but it worked. The adrenaline would go down and the panic would subside.

This lesson in persistently correcting thoughts and giving them time to work is something I've taken with me into this process of attaining peace. Originally I let the ego's (personal thought system's) thoughts run on and on and felt helpless to do anything about them. I learned that arguing with the ego only made its guilty, fearful thoughts more real to me. But when I persisted with correcting thoughts, rather than arguing with the ego, I found relief. Guilt and fear did not subside *immediately* when I corrected the thoughts that induced them. But they did subside *subsequently* if I was persistent in correcting the thoughts. I learned to not let the ego have the last word. If it said something that I could not dismiss but which I feared, I corrected the thought so that it did not remain the last thought in my mind.

The ego gets to you by repeating the same false, negative, guilty, fearful thoughts over and over again. You hear these unconsciously or consciously and you believe them. So you have to do the same thing with the facts. You have to counter with facts the ego's thoughts over and over again until the facts undo them. You must correct the ego's thoughts with thoughts that you believe. If you do not believe in what you say to counter the ego it will not work. And the correction must be specific if the thought is specific. General thoughts will not correct specific thoughts. So, for example, if the ego says you are an idiot for making a social faux pas do not say "The ego is an illusion. Everything it says is false" unless you can see that the ego is an illusion and everything it says is false. Say instead, "I didn't commit a sin; I just made a simple human mistake. There is no god outside of me that will punish me for this. I'm not perfect as a person and I never will be. I am perfect in Truth." More than just saying this, *think about* the meaning of what you say. Sometimes you may have to repeat correcting ideas many times before the ego will stop using specific circumstances for attack. But self-talk does eventually work. If it wasn't a useful tool the ego wouldn't use it!

49. Beyond Managing Mere Moods (December 11, 2015)

This mind is grateful that its current stage of awareness of Truth coincided with this body's peaking in peri-menopause because otherwise it would be a neurotic mess. If peri-menopause had happened earlier in this mind's developing awareness of Truth this mind would be totally distracted by the physical, psychological, and emotional effects of the wild and unpredictable surges in hormones that are the natural process of this stage of the body's life. The body would require hormone replacement therapy at minimum and perhaps anti-depressants and anti-anxiety medicines. This time of life for the body coinciding with this stage of growing awareness of the mind has in fact helped this mind to hone its detachment from the body, the self, and its story. It has helped it to see that there is no real difference between a "good" mood and a "bad" one in that they occur in the same self-identified part of mind. It has helped this mind to see all moods as one single experience – the human experience – so it can let go of them all as one. And it has helped this mind to see how much time it spent before managing mere moods and mistaking that for "spiritual" work.

Not all of the body's moods when it was younger were caused by hormones. Many moods were the result of this mind's conscious and unconscious belief in guilt and were only sometimes exaggerated by hormones. But this mind does now see that it was not always aware when hormones were in play. In any case, being self-identified, this mind believed the body's feelings and the thoughts that they induced were its reality. Its efforts were all toward managing these moods. It used spirituality to feel better or to feel good. In fact, it thought that was the point of the spiritual process. It was endlessly trying to find the right thought, the nicer thought, the good thought, the loving thought, etc. that would fix or change the body's mood. It wasn't until peace came to stay in its awareness and the body and the ego (personal thought system) didn't change that this mind realized that it had been using the wrong gauge for measuring its awareness of Truth. The moods of the self are irrelevant. Managing the self's moods is a distraction from true Peace because nothing about the self has anything to do with Peace. A "good" mood is not inner peace and a "bad" mood is not inner conflict. The mind can be at peace and observe that the self is in a "bad" mood. The shift this mind needed was not in mood but in where it rested within itself: in Truth rather than in the body.

This mind has come to accept that this self will never be lastingly happy. This mind has a deep, abiding contentment despite this so this fact is nothing. True Peace comes from the awareness that Truth *is* and It is completely untouched by anything in the universe of form. Of course what motivated this mind to pursue an awareness of Truth was the desire for personal happiness and peace. How could it be otherwise when the self was all it thought it knew? It had to learn that there was more to mind than ego. It had to undo its belief in guilt, which is what made the ego real to it. And then it found detachment from the ego and the self. This mind can manage the self's moods or it can rest in Peace and just watch the self's moods. But it can't do both.

[Let me head off some emails by saying that in the first paragraph I am not saying it is "wrong" for women to use HRT, anti-depressants, and anti-anxiety medicines in peri-menopause. I advocate for the judicious use of medication that will make anyone physically or psychically less distracted by the body and its processes and disorders. I have been able to (narrowly) avoid them only because of the detachment I have attained after more than 30 years in this process. You cannot pretend a detachment that you do not have. You cannot pretend an awareness that you have not attained. There is no value in being in pain or so uncomfortable that you do not have any quality of life].

50. The Present and the Process (December 18, 2015)

First, this mind believed it was a self in a process toward the goal of peace. Then one day it had an experience while meditating that *Truth is right here*. It was the Holy Instant and It was breathtaking. This mind realized that in meditation, and in everything else, it always *reached for* Truth. And in that reaching it *over-reached* Truth and missed It because *Truth is right here*. It was like when the self looks for the mustard in the refrigerator but does not see it because the mustard is right in front of it and the self is looking past it to find it.

And then the awareness of the immediate Presence of Truth was gone. Each day in meditation this mind tried to be present and experience the Truth again but could not. It could remember the experience but not conjure it. How long did this go on? Months? Years? Then it happened again and this mind would think, "This is it. This is all I need to experience. This is all I need to remember. Stop reaching. It's here now." And then…It couldn't make it happen again. More months, maybe years, before this mind had the experience again. But then, over a long, long time, it began to happen more often. And this mind began to take the awareness that "Truth is here now" into the unfolding of each day. "It's here," it would remind itself throughout the day and it would just be with It. If this mind couldn't experience Truth it still reminded itself that Truth is here. This mind does not need to experience Truth for Truth to be.

Over a long time this mind re-trained itself to stop reaching, to stop thinking in terms of a goal, to just stop and be present to Truth. If this mind reached for peace it missed peace because peace is here. If this mind set up peace as a goal it would obtain in the future it put distance between itself and peace because peace is here now. And, over that long time, all that reaching and goal-setting diminished until it finally ceased. The Truth is here now and so is this mind. This mind no longer has anything for which to reach.

But there is still something in this mind that is in a process and that still seems to be learning. This mind has come to understand that actually time was over for it many, many years ago when it first allowed Truth into its awareness. Since then all it has been doing is *accepting* this fact. And now that it has accepted it, it can see that the self and its story was only ever an *effect*. Originally the self's life in the world was an expression (effect) of the idea of not-Truth. Then, when this mind allowed Truth into its awareness, the story of the self became an expression (effect) of the-undoing-of-the-idea-of-not-Truth. And that part of the story is still going on. But this mind is learning to no longer confuse itself with the story. The unfolding story of the self is just an idea in its mind that it observes while it rests in the present in peace.

51. The Two Visions (December 25, 2015)

A Course in Miracles talks about two "visions", "sights", or "perceptions". (In my translation into plain language I used only "perception" for clarity). This "seeing" is not done with the body's eyes. It is an inner seeing. It occurs in the mind from one of two unconnected places in your mind. It is much like these two visions are two different platforms in your mind. One platform, the lower platform, is in the world. On that platform you are very involved with the world. You can move around on that platform and look at the world from different angles, but all of those angles are on the same level. The change in view is not a real change. It is simply a different angle on the same thing. For example, you learn something new about someone and you "see them in a new light". Outwardly they have not changed, so you do not "see" them in a new *physical* light. You see them from a new point of view *within your mind*. Your inner vision of them changed. You stood in a different place on that lower platform and saw them from a new angle.

The other platform is outside of and above the lower platform and its world. This platform, or Vision, is detached from the other, lower platform and can see that it and the world it seems to be in are not real. On that platform you merely observe the lower platform without judgment. When you "see" from that higher platform you experience a true shift, or change. This Vision is what ACIM calls a miracle, the Holy Spirit's Vision, Christ's Vision, or the Real World. (When you are wholly in that Vision I refer to it as a "higher miracle").

So the shift in vision that ACIM talks about is not merely a "nicer" view of the world. It is a shift to a whole other part of your mind that has nothing to do with the body, the thought system of the body (ego/personal thought system), or the world. Sometimes when I tell a client that I can see that something in the world is not real they ask, "But don't you still see (some form)?" Yes, the body's eyes still report forms. But when I see something is not real I am standing on the higher platform. In that Vision I do not just see as unreal what the body's eyes are reporting at the moment. That Vision transcends the *entire* lower platform. In that Vision I see that the image that the body's eyes report, the entire world it seems to be in, the body itself, and the inner vision of the thought system of the body are not real. It is a wholesale shift in vision that transcends the entire experience of the universe of form.

Next week's article will discuss this Vision and the Holy Relationship.

52. The Vision of the Holy Relationship (January 1, 2016)

In the last article I discussed the difference between the two "visions": What the body's eyes report and the meaning (or the awareness of no meaning) that your mind projects or extends. Spiritual Vision is not just a "nicer" way of interpreting the world. It is a wholly different vision that you can invite and welcome, but you cannot make it happen. It comes to you when you are ready and open to It.

When I was a new student of *A Course in Miracles* for a few months I experienced the Vision of the Holy Relationship with another. I saw that we were one and the same, obviously not as bodies and personalities, but in Truth. The inner Vision I had was that the Truth in her was the exact same Truth in me. Even thinking about her brought an experience of deep recognition beyond any human experience. This is the experience that Helen Schucman and Bill Thetford had. I recognized it completely when I read the passages in ACIM about the Holy Relationship. This Vision is what, in ACIM, Helen was reminded to remember in her relationships with others.

I want to be clear that this Vision is not the stoned-out hippy ideal of "Yeah, man, we're all one. Let's all just love one another." It has nothing to do with the level of form. It transcends it completely. It does not result in a desire to change world policies. It reveals that the universe of form is not Reality. It draws you inward, into an awareness of Perfect Formlessness, instead of leading you to change imperfect, unreal forms.

The woman with whom I experienced the Holy Relationship left my life after a few months. But the Vision of the Holy Relationship remained. What this taught me (when I finally chose to accept the lesson) was that this Vision had nothing to do with her or our relationship. The Vision was within my own mind. It was the Vision of the Holy Spirit. That relationship was the mirror in which I saw the Truth within me. The relationship reflected Oneness, or Wholeness. And that Wholeness was within me. It did not come from anywhere outside of me.

My dilemma as a spiritual teacher who uses ACIM as a common language with others is that very few seem to have had this experience. Many experience what I call "higher miracles" in which they have a moment of Spiritual Vision that transcends the universe of form even as they are aware of form. Sometimes they have this experience with others. Sometimes no one else is involved. But the experience of sustained Spiritual Vision that is the Holy Relationship is rare. So what I found was that many students were trying to apply ideas in ACIM in ways that it could not be applied because they were not experiencing the Vision that is the centerpiece of the Holy Relationship. And they were feeling like failures.

So years ago when I first wrote about my experience of the Holy Relationship I discussed it as two experiences: the mystical and the practical Holy Relationship. "Mystical" refers to experiencing the Vision of the Holy relationship. I experienced the mystical in that first Holy Relationship. There wasn't time in that particular relationship for me to really get to the practical application of that awareness. However, years later in my relationship with my wife, Courtney, I was able to apply the practical lessons that came from an awareness that my Wholeness is within me, not in another. This did not involve the Vision of the Holy Relationship but rather what I learned from it. And as a teacher the practical Holy Relationship is what I emphasize since the mystical Holy Relationship seems to be so rarely experienced.

When you read ACIM it helps to understand that when it discusses the relationship between Helen and Bill ("your brother"; originally "each other") it is reminding them that there is a whole other Vision through which they could see each other. That Vision is the Vision of forgiveness because it shifts you to an awareness of Truth. It is not merely a nicer personal view of the other. Even if you have not experienced the Vision of the Holy Relationship but you have had a higher miracle then you do have something to which to refer in your own experience when you read those passages. You can remember that there is a whole other Vision. If you have not yet experienced a higher miracle you can read in those passages a reminder to invite this other Vision into your awareness.

53. Ask: What can I do about my frustration with those who are stuck? (January 8, 2016)

"As my awareness of truth grows, I see aspects of my behavior, attitudes etc. in terms of correctable mistakes rather than crimes against humanity. The boogey man becomes smaller and smaller. This of course is a removal of an obstacle to peace. The problem that arises however, is my frustration with those around me who - out of fear - are so dug in to their stuff - unable and unwilling to budge. This results in a feeling of hopelessness, of helplessness, a "missing piece", a lie that must be tolerated. My options are to reject these friends totally; grin and bear it; knock some sense into them; or what? There's gotta be a better way." – Anonymous

On the surface the fact that you no longer see your mistakes as "sins" would seem like a good thing. However, you still see "sins" or you would not be bothered by others. You still project guilt so you still believe that you are guilty. Your shift from seeing "sins" to seeing mistakes is merely a superficial intellectual shift.

If you do not want to be around people who are not growing then limit or end your relationship with them. They are taking up space in your life that could be filled by healthier people. But doing this may bring only temporary relief. It won't fix your problem of projecting guilt. You are likely to project guilt into new friendships.

The guilt in your mind is taking the form of you thinking that it is "wrong" for people to be stuck in their problems. You must still feel that there is something "wrong" about you that you are seeing in them instead of in yourself. It may be a direct projection where what you specifically see in them is something that you feel in yourself. For example, there may be an area where you feel "dug into" your "stuff". Or each person's specific "stuff" may be something specific that you feel in yourself. Or it may be a general projection of feeling that you are inherently "wrong" and seeing others in their dysfunction merely brings up your general feelings of inherent "wrongness" and guilt. You could also feel helpless and hopeless because you mistakenly feel responsible for their dysfunction or for fixing their dysfunction and this is the source of the guilt that makes it hard for you to be around them. You may feel guilty for choosing to get healthy and "leaving them behind" in the process. In other words, these relationships are long over and you feel guilty for being the one to "leave" by choosing to get healthy. In fact, you could be feeling grief as well as guilt over the end of these relationships. You will have to sort out exactly what form(s) of guilt you are projecting and undo them or you will continue to project guilt.

When you have worked out the guilt in your mind you will no longer be frustrated by others' choices. You may briefly wish that they could see that they are worth a better choice. But this will lead to feelings of compassion, not helplessness and hopelessness. You will see that they have their path to walk and that it is none of your business. Then you will feel free to decide, without judgment or guilt, how much, if at all, you want them in your life.

54. Ask: What is your experience with synchronicity? (January 15, 2016)

"What is your experience with synchronicity? Have you found meaningful synchronicities occur between your outer and inner experiences as your awareness of Truth has deepened? Would you have called meeting E and experiencing a Holy Relationship such a synchronicity because you were ready for that Vision at the time? And do you think that she left your company because you needed that particular trial as well, in order to deepen your understanding?" – OT

This mind has observed that the quieter and slower it has become the more it sees connections, coincidences, patterns, and relationships that are all around at the level of form. Some refer to these connections, coincidences, patterns, and relationships as "synchronicity". This mind does not see any special meaning in them. It is natural to see them given the interconnectedness of things at the level of form. This mind seeing them also has no meaning. Seeing them is simply the natural result of a quieter, slower mind that is more mindfully present.

The self's meeting E (the woman with whom it experienced the Holy Relationship) and the unfolding of that relationship and all that followed is simply the story of this particular "Liz" in the greater story of time. It has no meaning, either. Yes, the self was ready for the experience or it would not have happened. And E did not leave because this self needed a trial. She left and this self chose to see it as a trial until she chose to learn valuable lessons from it. There is nothing making things happen for a reason in the universe of form. What happens in the universe of form is the result of cause and effect at the level of form. Things happen and the mind decides what it will tell itself about what happened, depending on what it wants to learn. So sometimes a self also makes its own synchronicity by deciding to view things as connected whether they really are or not.

55. Ask: Does each animal experience consciousness? (January 22, 2016)

"What I've been wanting to know about is if we can say definitively whether each animal is experiencing consciousness, and does Jesus say definitively or can we say with certainty whether they suffer or do not suffer? And if each animal can experience its reference point in consciousness, does each one need to have enough lifetimes and/or humans praying for them (since it doesn't seem they are able to pray themselves) to receive enough prayers so that their next reboot will be as a human so they can discover The Course?*"* – M

I am not aware of anywhere that Jesus says anything about animals in the context of consciousness. But I'm not too familiar with the Bible so there could be something in there about which I do not know.

The understanding to which I have been led (and have come to see for myself) is that the entire universe of form, including all animals and plants, is the projection of one split mind (the "Son of God" in *A Course in Miracles*). The split mind projects itself only onto one animal, the human animal. So only humans have the kind of consciousness that can choose between Truth and illusion. At the level of form, any animal with a system of pain receptors can experience physical pain and will, when it is extreme, suffer in that sense. But because only humans experience consciousness only humans experience psychological or emotional suffering. Remember, however, that in the human experience pain is inevitable but suffering is optional.

One suffers psychologically or emotionally because of the stories they tell themselves about pain. In any case, both the pain and the suffering are only temporary illusions.

No one needs lifetimes or prayers or *A Course in Miracles* for the Truth to be true. The Truth goes on right now wholly untouched by anything that happens in the universe of form, which is an illusion. Truth and illusion never intersect. No part of the universe of form "goes on" to Truth. What happens in the universe of form is wholly meaningless.

In the story of time (illusion) all stories begin as an expression (effect) of the-idea-of not-Truth. In some stories a dream figure (person) becomes aware of Truth and then their story becomes an expression (effect) of the-undoing-of-the-idea-of-not-Truth. But in either case it is a meaningless effect, not a cause. It does not lead anywhere. So you do not have to worry about anyone or anything finding ACIM or any other spiritual teaching. It does not have any real effect if one does or does not find Truth. The benefits are only temporary. They only matter in the story of time, which is an illusion. And the self which does or does not experience these benefits is only an effect and falls away in the story. Only the Truth is true and eternal.

56. A Happy Personality Does Not Signal Peace (January 29, 2016)

Sometimes I get comments from students of *A Course in Miracles* students along these lines: "I have a friend who is always happy and peaceful even though they aren't spiritual"; "Here I am miserable on this path and I look around at all these people who are content with their lives without working a spiritual path."

Some people just have happy personalities. I used to clean the house of a woman who had such an upbeat disposition that as a child she was given the nickname "Sunny". But I was in her home and saw that she was just like everyone else with her concerns and worries and judgments, etc. Her sunny disposition was genuine for her personality but it was a superficial trait. She was really no happier than anyone else.

A friend of my wife had a large personality that seemed to fill the room when she entered it. She was funny and bubbly and chipper. Her upbeat personality was not a mask; it was genuine. But those close to her also knew of the darkness within her mind. A year ago she killed herself. A happy personality in not an expression of true happiness and lasting peace.

Just as some people have a naturally happy personality others naturally have a more quiet, thoughtful, and rational mind. These traits do not always come from an awareness of Truth. A mind can be quiet, thoughtful, and rational and still be immersed in the world-as-reality.

"Mistake not truce for peace, nor compromise for the escape from conflict. To be released from conflict means that it is over. The door is open; you have left the battleground." (T-23.III.6)

Many people have made a truce with the ego (personal thought system) in their mind: "Don't look within or question me (ego) and I (ego) will leave you alone." They don't experience the ego attacks that students of ACIM do because they are not threatening the ego. In fact, if your goal is to release yourself from guilt and fear, you can look at ego attacks as a sign that you are on the right track.

A bubbly or quiet personality or a truce with the ego does not lead to an end of conflict. The bubbly or quiet personality experiences conflict beneath these superficial traits. And the one who makes a truce with conflict has merely found a way to adapt to it. But none of these personalities have actually transcended the conflict.

I say this often and I'll say it again: When peace came to this mind it did not change the personality of this self. Nor has this mind's awareness of Truth changed the conflict in the ego thought system in this mind. An awareness of Truth has made this mind quieter, more thoughtful, and more rational and this no doubt presents the self differently to others. But the self's personality has not fundamentally changed. It is not an ongoingly happy personality. In fact, this mind gave up the pursuit of personal happiness when peace came to stay. Peace is peace, after all. The fact that peace did not change the ego or the self only made it clear to this mind that those must be released for there to be *only* peace in this mind.

Do you want to change the mind or the ego and personality? Here is the choice for any mind: Being aware of Truth and at peace; or pursuing personal happiness. It can't be both. Yes, the distinction can be very confusing as long as the ego and personality seem to be what mind is. That's why growing your awareness of Truth is so important. Only in an awareness of Truth can you learn that the self, its personality, and the ego are not you so that you can detach from them.

57. On Consciousness (Awareness, Perception) (February 5, 2016)

A couple of week ago I answered a question about whether or not animals have consciousness (#55). My answer provoked several emails of questions and comments. They seemed to be about different aspects of my response but I've come to see that they were all related. So I am going to respond to the ideas in them here in one fell swoop.

First, let me define what I mean by "consciousness" (in other contexts "awareness" or "perception"): A mind that is capable of an awareness of Truth. While one split mind (*what A Course in Miracles* calls the "Son of God") projects the entire universe of form, it projects its split mind onto only one form, the human animal. So while many animals have some degree of intelligence and many experience degrees of emotions, only the human animal suffers the conscious and unconscious psychological conflict of a mind that is split between Truth and not-Truth.

Some indicated that I said or implied that because only humans have consciousness they are somehow special or superior to other animals. I did not say this nor did I imply it. In fact, I implied the opposite with the last paragraph: since nothing at the level of form has any effect on Truth there is no part of it that is special or superior to the rest. It is no different to have consciousness than to not have consciousness. All illusion is illusion and is equally meaningless.

This brings me to another issue that was brought up. Some were disturbed by the idea that it does not matter if they are aware of Truth or not. Of course, I intended this to set them free! The freedom and joy of forgiveness is in the awareness that Truth is not affected by not-Truth (the universe of form). The take away is that you do not have to worry about what you attain or do not attain as a person. You can just enjoy the process and let it take you where it will. There are no bad consequences for not attaining a certain awareness. But "Why bother to become aware of Truth? Why bother with this process?" some asked. In my experience once one has had an awareness of Truth there is no going back. The Truth compels you because It is the Truth. And being aware of Truth does bring relief from the pain of believing in not-Truth (the universe of form). But just as pain is only temporary so is the need for relief from pain only temporary. Either way, it all falls away.

And this leads to the other issue brought up in the emails: Isn't one's awareness of Truth real and eternal? Isn't this what "goes on" after the body is dead?

Remember, awareness (consciousness, perception) is only temporary, whether that awareness is of not-Truth or of Truth. Only Knowledge, which is Truth, is eternal. To be aware of Truth and to know Truth are not the same experience. The highest awareness one can have is of Truth. But that awareness is not Truth Itself. It is not Knowledge. Awareness can fluctuate and vary. Knowledge is static and absolute.

Your mind has diametrically opposed experiences: Truth and not-Truth. The experience of Truth is limitless wholeness. The experience of not-Truth is limitation and lack. Think of them as running parallel in your mind. You can experience both but they never intersect. They never blend. One never enters into or becomes the other. Since Truth is Knowledge (or Being) it is not *aware of* not-Truth. Knowledge transcends all awareness. And at the level of not-Truth you can be aware of Truth but never *know* (be) Truth. This is why if you want the endless Peace of Truth, not-Truth must fall away. It can never *become* Truth.

So in a nutshell: Whether or not something has consciousness or whether or not that which has consciousness is conscious of Truth is unimportant. It all passes. Only the Truth is true and eternal.

58. Ask: Why do I need to make things "right" in the world? (February 12, 2016)

"Last night I watched a riveting documentary on the life and crimes of the notorious millionaire psychopath, Robert Durst. I vaguely remembered hearing about him but actually knew very little. As his Texas murder trial played out in the film, it became clear that he was going to be acquitted. Watching his slick, venal, lawyers manipulate the unsophisticated jury— and then calmly talk about their unscrupulous tactics in later interviews—I felt my stomach tighten with fear and my temples throb with rage. The duplicity of Durst's wealthy family in the cover-up, the unresolved grief of the families of his victims, and of course listening to the vile Durst himself trying to play the world for fools, added to my upset. I tried to detach from the story and contemplate why I felt so threatened for one thing, and how to return to peace (my ultimate goal in all upsets.) The only thing I could come up with is that this case so rocked my sense of how things SHOULD have played out, I felt like I was standing on my head and needed desperately to get "my feet back on the ground". This is a pervasive theme in my life, ie. the need to "SET THE RECORD STRAIGHT"—with the right words, the right truths; How does so and so get away with that? etc. I slept badly and woke up exhausted. What do you think the lesson is here?" – ES

You believe that guilt is real. This is another way of saying that you believe that the world is real. If the world is real then guilt is real. Guilt is the "proof" that the world is real.

The world is the opposite of Truth (God) in every way. It is imperfect, dysfunctional, unfair, unjust, etc. When guilt is real to you, you see this as "wrong" or "sinful" rather than as impossible. You feel an urge to fix it according to what you feel is "right". The world's sin reflects to you the sin that you feel is in you. When you realize that you cannot fix the world you feel powerless and afraid. Really what you are feeling is powerless to do anything about the guilt in you. You are doomed, and this is terrifying.

The lesson here is that you are mistaken. There is no sin; there is no guilt. The world's imperfection does not change the Perfection of Truth in any way. When you get this you will no longer see the world as "sinful" but as nothing. So it won't upset you.

59. It Is All Unfolding Perfectly (February 19, 2016)

This mind used to hear others says that "it is all unfolding perfectly" and couldn't understand their point of view. It understood "the script is written" as "the outcome is inevitable" and yet it still didn't have the full picture. But it does now.

Truth (or God, if you prefer) is Formless Being extending without limit. Being All, Truth must have within It the idea of Its Own opposite. But, being All, Truth cannot have an opposite. The opposite-of-Truth can only ever be an idea, and it is an idea that is undone by Truth's All-encompassing nature the instant that it is thought. It is as though Truth said, "What is my opposite? Oh, yeah, I cannot have an opposite." Poof! It was undone.

(In *A Course in Miracles* the part of the Mind of God where this idea is supposed to have occurred is called the "Son of God").

Since Truth is formless, infinite, eternal, and one, or the same, throughout, the idea of the opposite-of-Truth, or not-Truth, is time-bound, limited, diverse forms. So *within the idea* of not-Truth, or the story of time and space, it seems as though the-opposite-of-Truth began long ago and will be undone in some indefinite future. What you see as the unfolding story of the universe of form is that instant of not-Truth/the undoing of not-Truth playing out in time. (In ACIM all of this is playing out in the mind of the Son of God). Though it was meant to be not-Truth since it was undone instantly it is really the story of the *undoing* of not-Truth. In the story that undoing shows up as figures in the story becoming aware of Truth and seeing that it is just a story.

So a life in the world is not a cause. It is not heading toward some future goal of heaven or hell or purgatory or Truth. It is an *effect*, an expression of the undoing of the idea of not-Truth. Each individual life in the world does not have a purpose in the sense that it will make something happen. It has a purpose in the sense that it is a playing out of an idea. It is an effect of a long-ago cause. At the level of form where it seems to play out, it seems to be the effect of multiple causes at the level of form. But all of those causes were caused long ago.

Because the "script is written", or the outcome is inevitable and not-Truth will be undone, *since it is already over*, the story is unfolding perfectly. And everyone is playing their part perfectly. They cannot do otherwise. If someone becomes aware of Truth then that is their role. However far they take that awareness, that is their role. If someone does not become aware of Truth then that is their role. None of it has any effect on Truth. It is all a meaningless playing out of a meaningless idea.

Within the story you cannot see the larger picture. You cannot see how it is all unfolding perfectly toward an inevitable ending where it is undone. You are distracted along the way by so much that seems to go so wrong. But think of it like a movie. If you don't know the ending then you agonize over every trial that the protagonist goes through. But if you know ahead of time that the movie has a happy ending then you do not suffer over the protagonist's every trial. You relax, watching with curiosity how the happy ending will unfold.

The "protagonist" in this unfolding story is the one split-mind ("Son of God"). It is this mind which is headed toward a happy ending. But an individual story within that "protagonists" greater story may not be happy. However, an individual mind will find happiness and purpose in understanding, if that is its role (and it is yours since you are reading this), that it is part of the

Great Undoing (Atonement). A mind aware of Truth is happy no matter how the self's life unfolds. It knows that only the Truth is true and simply watches the unfolding without judgment.

Within the story you feel autonomous. You feel as if your decisions and choices and lessons are unique and apart from everyone and everything else. But really they are all part of an interconnected whole. Whatever you feel moved to do or to not do is your role. The unfolding story of the universe of form lives through you, though you do not experience it that way. You can learn to live in the flow of the universe by quieting your mind and following your intuition. You can know that you cannot make a wrong choice or wrong move. Whatever you choose or do is part of the unfolding.

The ego (personal thought system) obsesses on the minutiae of everyday life. Every little thought, mood, feeling, decision, etc. is significant to it. But the Holy Spirit takes in the larger, longer view and sees the whole unfolding. That is why in ACIM it says to not judge, not because it is wrong to judge, but because you cannot see the whole picture. Only if you could, could you judge correctly. And that judgment would be that it is all unfolding perfectly.

To summarize: The idea of not-Truth manifests as a universe of form that is the opposite of Truth in every way. In time this idea took form long ago. Simultaneous with this thought was its undoing. So the unfolding of time is the story of the undoing of the idea of not-Truth. Everyone has a part to play in this undoing even if they cannot see it and their part does not look like it is a part of a happy ending. There is relief in coming to a conscious awareness of this. There is relief in not judging it and simply watching it unfold.

How would you approach the self's life in the world differently if you knew that it is an effect rather than a cause? If you really knew, and had not just read, that the outcome is inevitable and that your role, and everyone's, no matter what it is, is an integral part of that outcome? This mind is not sure it is possible to know this until you can really see it. It couldn't see it before even though it had read these ideas. It didn't wholly understand them. And it couldn't see it until it had undone its belief in guilt. Guilt is what made all the minutiae so real and hard to overcome. Guilt is what kept this mind so involved with the self and its story. There is no place for guilt when the outcome is inevitable and where the self is known to be an effect and not a cause.

The irony is that this mind came to see all this clearly only as it saw that it is blissfully meaningless because an idea that is undone has no meaning. Perhaps it couldn't see it clearly *until* it could see that it is meaningless.

(This article is likely to spark some questions. Please hold off as next week I will write more on this topic. Here are other articles I wrote in this last year that touch on this topic and that may answer some questions:

#13 In the Flow of the Universe
#14 One Story
#34 Ask: Any insights on accepting not having the partner and family I want?
#50 The Present and the Process

60. More on It Is All Unfolding Perfectly (February 26, 2016)

Last week I wrote about how this mind has come to an awareness of the self's life in the world as an effect and not a cause. It is an effect whose cause passed the instant it was caused, so therefore it is over. This means, in essence, that what you see unfolding in the universe of form has really passed. This does not mean, strictly speaking, that what you see passing in time is predestined. What you see is done, therefore, it is not to be done. You are really looking back at an idea that is over (and therefore cannot be changed), not living in a predetermined idea unfolding. However, since you think that you are in time, and that the idea began long ago and will be undone in some indefinite future, you experience it as though it is unfolding now.

The reason this mind used to get stuck on this idea that time is over and what it is seeing is past was that, as a self-starter, it felt so self-directed. The piece that this mind was missing (other than the fact that it is a mind and not a self) was that its personal desires and motivations were part of this unfolding. Its personal desires and motivations were the universe living through the self. So this mind experienced it as though the self was autonomous even though it was not. The self is part of a greater story played out through the self's story and the stories of every other self.

One of the ways that the personal thought system (ego) twists this awareness that what is unfolding is done is to de-motivate you. If everything is going to unfold as it will unfold and you cannot affect it why do anything? But that is really an upside-down way to look at it. *Whatever you end up doing (or not doing) is part of the unfolding.* You only have to live naturally, as you have been living. You have all along been a part of the unfolding. The only difference now is that you know it. In the personal thought system you ask, "What do I want? And how do I make it happen?" Instead, you can say, "I want _____ for the self. Is this desire the unfolding universe living through the self or is it just how I'm trying to fill a sense of lack? I will let it unfold naturally. If there is any action to take I will know what to do." You can sit back and let your intuition guide you. To live in the flow of the unfolding universe is a much more harmonious way to live.

If you still need a sense of purpose for the self, here it is: The self's life is part of a greater whole. What is its part? A clue is in what is authentic to the self. What has it always wanted? How and where does it feel it is most itself? Perhaps it has always known its part. In any case, however its life unfolds is the self's purpose. Until you are aware of and living in the flow you will continue to feel self-directed. And that, too, is a part of the unfolding. You do not have to live in a worry that you can do something wrong. You cannot be out of the flow of the universe. You can only be unaware of the flow. Anything that happens is what happened.

So where does free will come into this? The self does not have free will. *The self is an expression of a will that is free.* That will is the will of what I call the "split-mind" and what *A Course in Miracles* calls the "Son of God". In the introduction to ACIM about free will it says, "Free will does not mean that you can establish the curriculum." This means that you do not get to choose that, in your sense that you are not your true Being ("separated from God"), you need to relearn What is your true Being. It goes on to say, "It (free will) means only that you can elect what you want to take at a given time." This means that each individual self will play out the correction to the extent that they can. This is *experienced* as free will, but is in fact not *self*-determined. It is determined by the whole unfolding story of the undoing of the idea of not-Truth. The will that is free is the Son of God's will, which, in an instant thought of the opposite-of-God and in that same instant undid the idea of the opposite-of-God by seeing its impossibility. It was free to do both and that is what is played out in the story of time.

But where does personal responsibility come into this? If you feel moved to take responsibility or to not take responsibility *all of that is part of the unfolding.* If you kill someone and that was meant to be, doesn't it mean that you are not guilty for that murder? Well, yes, but not because it was "meant to be" but because none of this affects Truth in any way and therefore absolute morality is not real. But social morality is part of the human culture at the level of form. In form there are always consequences (for every action there is an equal and opposite reaction). If you kill someone in a way that is not sanctioned by the world (as in war), then there will be consequences. Even if you "get away with it" and are never found to have commit the murder or are never convicted of the murder you will spend your life running and hiding in some way. *All of that is part of the unfolding.* If you are moved to take responsibility and learn and grow, that is your part in the unfolding. If you are not moved to take responsibility and learn and grow, that is your part in the unfolding.

You can see how this sets you free to not judge other selves. Whatever they are doing or not doing is their part in the unfolding story of the undoing of the idea of not-Truth. Your part is to attend to your mind, not to the lives of others. Since you are reading this, your part is an overt expression of the undoing.

61. Sorry, No Incantations Here (March 4, 2016)

Sometimes I sense from my readers or clients that my practical answers to their problems are not what they seek. They want what I call a "woo-woo" answer. They want a transcendent answer that will not involve the tedium of dealing with life in the world on the terms of the world. They want an answer that will not involve the pain of examining their behavior and excavating their motivations. They want the "right thought", the present day's equivalent of a magical incantation, to resolve their problems at the level of form..

For example, let's say a client has been told by her lawyer that she needs to file for bankruptcy. She's upset and wants to know how she "created" this situation in her life. I ask questions about her financial situation, her financial choices, etc. She doesn't want to go there. She just wants to talk about how she can change her mind to transform her situation. What she doesn't realize is that her thoughts do not conjure situations at the level of form out of thin air. Yes, her situation was caused by her thoughts. She had certain thoughts (beliefs) that led to certain choices that led to certain behaviors. Cause and effect at the level of form is usually traceable. There's no mystery here.

Let's say this hypothetical client accumulated overwhelming debt because she spent more money than she had coming in. She made more purchases than she could afford for the endorphin-boost she got from shopping, she lived at a higher standard than she could afford to lift her self-esteem, she did not say no to friends and family who wanted money from her for fear that she would lose their love, etc. In other words, she was looking for wholeness in the wrong places. Her thinking (conscious and/or unconscious) was:

"I don't feel good. I'll go shopping. That always makes me feel better."

"If I look successful everyone will admire me and I will feel good about myself. I have to buy this house, this car, these clothes, etc. so everyone will see how successful I am."

"I'd better give my son money to buy a house or he will be mad and I won't see him anymore."

On a practical, worldly level her belief that she needed things outside of her to feel whole led to the behavior of putting out more money than she had coming in. So the solution to her problem has to be more than a thought that she can chant. She has to look honestly (and hopefully without judgement) at the behavior that led to the debt that resulted in the need for her to file for bankruptcy. Then she has to look at the motivation (her beliefs) for this behavior. When she resolves the problem at the level of her mind (her beliefs) then her behavior in the world will change. This is how she will "create" a more harmonious life in the world.

62. Without Form There Is Wholeness (March 11, 2016)

The experience of Truth is Wholeness. Lack does not exist in Truth even as an idea. But when you are used to identifying with an ego (personal thought system) and you come out of the experience of Truth, Truth strikes you as alarmingly empty because there is no form There. You know you felt whole in Truth but you are frightened because you cannot understand this with the thought system (ego) with which you are used to thinking. How can a thought system that is a form itself and is all about forms understand that Formlessness is an experience of Abundance?

If without form there is Wholeness then the reverse of this must be that with form there is lack. When you see this it is so obvious! Of course when Limitless Mind is reduced to limited forms (thoughts, ideas, feelings, actions, material forms) the experience is lack. No wonder that the pursuit of forms to fill a sense of lack only increases one's sense of lack.

If you just stop and *be*, what is lacking? You may feel an emotional emptiness that prods you to seek forms (thoughts, ideas, other feelings, actions, material forms) to fill the emptiness. But what experiences that emptiness but a form (self)? And that feeling of emotional emptiness is a form, too. To feel emotionally empty is a form that is the experience of form. The resolution to that feeling is not more forms but the dropping of forms.

Sit and just "be". If the experience of emptiness (or other forms) comes over you, tell yourself, "This is just the limited experience of form." and see if you can let it pass. Open your mind to the experience of Abundant Nothingness even if you cannot understand It. The experience will not come from or to a form. It is what Limitless Mind is.

63. ACIM Dissolves Rather Than Absolves Guilt (March 18, 2016)

Despite its use of Christian symbols there are many ideas in *A Course in Miracles* that are radically different from Christianity. In fact, they undo what is traditionally taught in Christianity. It is important for students of ACIM to not only recognize this but to meditate on these differences. Doing so clarifies ACIM and how learning what it teaches can set you free.

"The betrayal of the Son of God lies only in illusions, and all his "sins" are but his own imagining. His reality is forever sinless. He need not be forgiven but awakened." (T-17.I.1)

"A major tenet in the ego's insane religion is that sin is not error but truth, and it is innocence that would deceive. Purity is seen as arrogance, and the acceptance of the self as sinful is perceived as holiness. And it is this doctrine that replaces the reality of the Son of God as his Father created him, and willed that he be forever." (T-19.II.4)

In a nutshell, the fundamental and radical difference between *A Course in Miracles* and Christianity is in their approaches to guilt. Christianity presents a path to absolution from guilt. It validates guilt (sin) as real and then presents you with a way to escape from consequences for it through its god's grace. ACIM teaches that guilt is not real. It is never justified no matter how much you feel that it is. It presents the way to dissolve your *belief in* guilt.

The path of absolution does not free you from guilt, only from punishment for it. The sin occurred but you are just not going to pay for it. So absolution increases your guilt because, in your guilt, you feel unworthy of absolution. Bow down and kiss your god's feet because you who are unworthy have been granted undeserved freedom! How beholden you now should be to that merciful god! (Who, by the way, you feel can turn on you at any moment because, after all, you really are guilty and do deserve to be punished).

The path of dissolving guilt releases you not from actual guilt but from your belief that guilt is real. This is what is meant by "He need not be forgiven but awakened" in the quote at the top. You do not need to perfect or to seek absolution for the self but rather become aware of (awaken to) your Perfection in Truth.

"To sin would be to violate reality, and to succeed." (T-19.II.2)

"The Son of God can be mistaken; he can deceive himself; he can even turn the power of his mind against himself. But he <u>cannot</u> sin. There is nothing he can do that would really change his reality in any way, nor make him really guilty." (T-19.II.3)

This difference between Christianity and ACIM is not small! They are fundamentally opposed. What Christianity says is a real, therefore uncorrectable, sin, ACIM says is a mistaken perception that can be corrected for your peace of mind. Absolution does not offer freedom or peace. But the awareness that there is no guilt but only a *belief in* guilt that can be undone offers true and lasting freedom and peace.

64. Love, Peace, and Joy as Effects (March 25, 2016)

Sometimes students tell me they want to reach a state of bliss or to be joyful all the time. What they do not understand is if they attained these states they would not experience them as bliss or joy because their new state would become the "new normal". Bliss and joy are really only felt in contrast to unhappiness. Peace is only felt in contrast to conflict. Love, or wholeness, is only felt in contrast to lack. They are all personal experiences. And they are only the flipside of the experiences that they are set up to replace.

I could say that Truth is the absence of all feelings and experiences. But really It is not even that. Truth is not defined by an absence of any kind. It cannot be understood in contrast to anything. Truth is beyond all comparisons or contrasts because It is beyond all duality.

That which experiences pain and seeks to be out of pain are the same. So to seek to feel "good" is to seek for only the flip-side of feeling "bad". They are the same coin and nothing real is accomplished by changing feelings. Real change is to be aware of That Which is so beyond all feelings that It is not even the absence of feelings. Feelings were never There.

If you've read my earlier writing you know that for a long time I pursued love and peace and joy. I even defined Truth as the experience of lasting love and peace and joy. Now I see that these experiences are not Truth Itself but only the effects of an awareness of Truth. This is why they can be experienced through other sources. For example, you hear of people who have taken certain drugs or who have had a stroke who have "transcendent" experiences where they feel an expansion of their being and/or boundless love or peace or joy. They have experiences of "light" or they see the illusion of form or the interconnectedness of all things. Those experiences are only *effects* of chemical changes in the brain brought on by drugs or a stroke or an awareness of

Truth. (When the experience is caused by the latter I call it a "higher miracle" because of its source). These experiences are only meaningful in contrast to what had been accepted as reality. But neither the experience one has before and after the "transcendent" experience nor the "transcendent" experience itself is Reality.

This awareness clarifies for me the experience of my last Revelation in September '07. There was the Revelation, Which is beyond description. And, as always, what follows is a higher miracle full of lessons for me. In that case what I experienced on the "way back" from the Revelation was so much joy that I felt that if I felt any more I'd be the joy. Then I swung all the way into the darkest terror of the ego (personal thought system): the fear of not existing. At the time, and for long after, I saw my mind as split between the joy and the terror. Now I see those were in the same place in my mind. The Revelation was the Thing apart. The joy/terror was only the effect of experiencing the Revelation.

65. Acclimating to Peace (April 1, 2016)

This mind thought that all it had to do was stop believing in guilt and it would be at peace and any process would be over. Then it found peace, stopped believing in guilt, but found that it was still in a process. And that process is acclimating to peace. When a mind is used to conflict it does not immediately accept peace.

A couple of weeks ago (#62) I wrote about how a mind used to forms (thoughts, ideas, feelings, material forms) experiences the Formlessness of Truth as emptiness. The contrast between form and Formlessness is jarring at first. Form is boundaries and busyness and contrasts and conflicts. Formlessness is boundlessness and stillness and the same throughout. This is Absolute Peace! What else could be peace but emptiness? It seems so obvious once you experience It.

But Absolute Peace is not the first peace to which you have to acclimatize. The first peace you have to get used to is the peace that occurs when conflict falls away. It begins at the very beginning of the process of growing your awareness of Truth. Very often new students of *A Course in Miracles* who are still in the lessons in the Workbook tell me how disturbed they are when they are no longer bothered by something that used to bother them. Isn't this the peace they sought? Weren't they looking to get off the up-and-down roller-coaster of drama that is the experience of the ego (personal thought system)? Not only do they not trust this new peace, but along with it comes a sense of something missing. It's not necessarily a loss they mourn, but it is an uncomfortable sense of something familiar, even if painful, having fallen away. What fell away was conflict. So right away, even as you have years ahead of you of letting go of the belief in guilt, you begin the process of acclimatizing to peace.

The ego thrives in the discomfort of the split-mind. You (the mind split between ego and Truth) are used to listening to it and you are not used to peace. The ego tells you that something is wrong with you because you are no longer in pain, you no longer join with others in suffering, you feel a detachment from the world, etc. And you will fear that something *is* wrong with you to the extent that you still believe that suffering is normal or right and good and "spiritual". It's a hard belief to overcome because it is central to the ego. The *ego* is conflict and suffering. So it is never in the ego that you come to an awareness of peace. That you can experience peace is how you know you are not the ego.

Since you have to acclimate to the peace that you feel when conflict falls away you can imagine that you also have to acclimate to Absolute Peace. But by the time that It comes into your awareness guilt has fallen away so there is no longer a fear that you are wrong for being detached from the world. You recognize that Absolute Peace is simply not familiar and that now it is time to let It in more and more.

66. This Inner Work is Time Consuming (April 8, 2016)

Often I laugh with my students over how our inner work chews up time without any outward activity to show for it. There is a lot of vigilance and processing required on the path to peace! So we have a sense of being occupied but we can't really explain this to others because the work is going on only in our minds.

Whenever I hear about theoretical physicists and their "thought experiments" I can identify. They spend a lot of time just thinking about how the universe of form works. They may eventually jot down some formulas, but for much of the time they are conceptualizing. It is the same with this inner work for inner peace. We may eventually write what we learn in a journal but for much of the time we are busy with understanding the workings of our own mind. We are occupied observing, analyzing, and processing what we learn.

The deeper you go into this process the more important busy-work for the body becomes to you. Those mundane, repetitive, every-day tasks like washing the dishes, sweeping the floor, pulling weeds, walking the dog, etc. keep the body busy but the mind free to think. Your outer life may look tedious and boring to others but your inner life, the life of the mind where you live, is rich and deeply fulfilling. In the sense of wholeness that results from this inner work you no longer need to seek "fun" or "excitement". In fact, you find them to be unnecessary distractions. You've discovered that finding and then maintaining your inner peace is a much more satisfying and worthwhile way to spend your time.

67. There's No Need to Put the Cart (Behavior) Before the Horse (the Shift) (April 22, 2016)

If I was Queen of All Things Spiritual I would decree that no one could have access to spiritual teachings that were more advanced than they were ready to understand, practice, or accept. I say this because students (and this once included me) do so much harm to themselves reading things that they are not ready to understand or attempting practices that do not come naturally to them. In their guilt they judge themselves as failing because they do not measure up to what they study. And what they study they can only try to understand through the limitations of what they've already experienced and this leads to distortions. I spend a lot of time reassuring readers and clients that they are not failing because they have not yet attained in understanding or practice what someone more advanced has attained. They are in a process and judge against themselves for being in a process. I also spend a lot of time clarifying experiences that they have not yet had but that the ego has distorted or struggles to understand.

It is true that some teachers add to a student's sense of guilt because they seem to forget that they went through a process to reach their level of understanding and of practice. (I try not to do this myself, but it *is* difficult to not teach from where you are). Teachers engage in practices that come naturally to them at their current level of awareness, forgetting that internal shifts led to these practices; the practices did not lead to the shifts. The practices that come naturally to them now are not what came naturally to them two, five, ten years ago.

For example, for years I tried the Buddhist practice of observing the body's breathing as a way to quiet and center my mind. This went nowhere for me. But now when I rest in the Quiet in my mind observing the body's breathing occurs naturally because there is nothing else to do. It is the bare minimum awareness of the universe of form. I do not have to work at this. It just happens. It makes me wonder if others attained this practice naturally and then turned around and taught it to others, forgetting that the practice is an effect that occurs naturally at a certain point. The practice did not lead to the awareness.

Another example is simply observing the personal thought system (ego), which you cannot do until you are able to come from the perspective of the Awareness of Truth (Holy Spirit). You have to observe the personal thought system from somewhere and you are not going to do it when you are in the midst of it. First you have to grow your awareness of Truth. Then observing not-Truth will come naturally.

There can be some benefit in attempting these practices to see if you can do them or if you learn something from the attempt. But you have not failed if you cannot do them. You simply are not yet at a stage where they come naturally. For example, I attempted to live in the present with Truth many times before I was able. What I learned was that I was uncomfortable in the present. I had to accept this. So instead I practiced bringing my mind into the present with Truth several times a day and then I let it wander off again as it would. Only after I had undone my belief in inherent guilt in my mind was I able to live in the present with Truth. The discomfort I had felt before was due to the unconscious guilt that was right below the surface of my conscious awareness when I tried to be present. My mind had to scoot off to the future (mostly), the past (occasionally), or just elsewhere (often). Anywhere but here with the guilt I unconsciously believed was real!

Wherever you are on the path of growing your awareness of Truth useful practices will unfold for you naturally. Any effort that you make should be natural because you are motivated and willing. Any sense of force indicates that you are not yet ready and you are trying to make something happen yourself. I know that it is very difficult in the beginning because you are very undisciplined and you feel that you are going nowhere and that you are not doing enough. You doubt yourself and you fear your commitment is not adequate. But really the only part you have to play is to invite Truth into your awareness. Once you have that experience your part is over. The rest will happen of itself. Being initially undisciplined and unwilling are part of the process. Eventually you will have enough of that and the motivation and willingness for discipline will come naturally.

68. Mindfulness and Being Present to Truth (April 29, 2016)

Once I was in conversation with a client and mentioned something about "being present to Truth". Suddenly he exclaimed, "Ohhhhh. Present *to Truth*." He explained that he had read over and over again in spiritual teachings about the importance of being mindful, or present to what he was doing, whatever it was, as a way to peace. He practiced this for years but he did not experience anything remarkable. It had never been explained to him that he needed to make the conscious effort to be open to Truth in the present. He thought that merely being present was supposed to be enough. And once he did practice being present to Truth his experience was transformed.

This is another example of how cause and effect in spiritual practice are not always adequately explained (see last week's article). Someone has a moment of being present and they experience Truth (a transcendent experience of peace or joy, the awareness of the illusory nature of the world, a sense of the expansive nature of True Being, etc.) They don't realize that this happened only because they were unconsciously open to Truth. They think that merely coming into the present resulted in their experience of Truth. They then teach others in writing or speaking to be mindfully present so that they, too, can experience Truth. But what brought Truth into their awareness was not merely being present. It was their openness to Truth. So when their followers practice mindfulness and do not experience anything remarkable they are left confused about the practice. They do not experience Truth. They wonder, what am I doing wrong?

Mindfulness is actually an *effect* of being present to Truth. It will not lead to an awareness of Truth unless you are unconsciously or consciously open to Truth in that moment. But once you are present to Truth you find that you are mindful simply because the effect is that when you are present to Truth you are present in the world, too.

69. Your Itch to Share is Your Own Desire to Learn (May 6, 2016)

When I began as a student of *A Course in Miracles* over 3 decades ago I was itching to share what I learned with everyone. I didn't, though, because I knew how much I hated it when others proselytized. Even if I didn't mean to convert anyone I knew that's how my sharing would be perceived. I also knew that if I shared what ACIM really teaches others would think I was nuts. I knew how radical it was and I only trusted it myself because I'd experienced Revelation and miracles early on. In fact once in my excitement I took a chance and shared with some acquaintances something I heard from the Holy Spirit and one of them, a nurse, asked, "Was this Voice inside your mind or outside of you?" I reassured her that I was not psychotic; the Voice was in my mind. The experience reinforced for me how it was best to keep my new experiences private. I only discussed some of them with other ACIM students.

I also suspected, correctly, that my itch to share was not from the Holy Spirit. The feeling was too strong. The Holy Spirit is a quiet knowing, not a strong or passionate feeling. So I didn't trust the itch and I didn't want to be led by it. I wrote in my journal when there was no one with whom to share a lesson. If I was ever going to teach ACIM, and I didn't know that I was, I wanted to be led into it by the Holy Spirit. And when it came time to teach, that is how it happened. It wasn't an itch that moved me, but a quiet knowing that this was what I was to do next. And ever since then, when I do share in my writing what I am learning or what I have learned, I am not led by an itch. Instead it just flows out of me.

So what was this itch if it wasn't the Holy Spirit? In time I realized that my own itch to share with others was my own itch to deepen or clarify the particular lesson I wanted to share. The itch still came at times, but the lesson never flowed out of me then. I wasn't ready to share it because the lesson wasn't solid in me yet. I needed to deepen and clarify the lesson in myself before I could share it with others. I've come to see that my writing occurs when I am consolidating a lesson, not when it is new to me. In fact, my writing about something means I'm ready to move past it, on to a deeper level with the same lesson, or on to other lessons.

The vast majority of students of ACIM do not eventually teach others. But of course the itch to share is not limited to those who do end up teaching. The itch is just a sign that you want a lesson to go deeper *in yourself*. If the itch won't pass it can help to write about it in a journal. And if you journalize with the Holy Spirit it can be a practice that helps the lesson deepen in you.

70. The Itch to Share and Learning What You Teach (May 13, 2016)

Apparently my last article was not clear because I received several questions and comments about it. So I will attempt to clarify and answer some questions here.

The point of the article was that one's urgency, or "itch", to share what they learn while studying *A Course in Miracles* is their own desire to "get" what they are studying. You read something in ACIM that you get at a shallow intellectual level and you find yourself with a strong urge for others to get it, too. What occurs is that you, as the split-mind (decision-maker), want the lesson to go deeper for yourself. But the ego (personal though system) in your mind projects this desire outward and sees the lack in others. *They* need this; you already have it. The ego pushes away your desire for the lesson to go deeper by seeing it "out there". It does not want you to get the idea more deeply.

But doesn't ACIM teach "what you give you receive" or "what you teach you learn"? Yes. But both the ego and the Holy Spirit can use the same ideas. So what ACIM means is that you reinforce a thought system in your mind when you share *from it* with others. If you share an idea from the ego you reinforce the ego in your mind. If you share an idea from the Holy Spirit you reinforce your awareness of Truth. So in last week's article I emphasized *from where* the itch to share an idea came from within you. When you feel urgency you can be sure that you feel the ego.

The ego's itch for others to get an idea is not about you teaching to learn the idea more deeply yourself. It is only about projecting guilt (your own imperfection - you do not really fully get the idea yourself yet) onto others. They lack; you don't. So your itch for others to get it is a projection of your own desire to get it. And your teaching from the ego will only reinforce your sense of lack and guilt. You will find yourself emotionally charged up when you teach. [For some the ego is also so insecure that this shows up as wanting to teach others to show that they (the teacher) are superior to them (the student)].

When you are ready to integrate an idea you may be moved by the Holy Spirit to share it to reinforce both the Holy Spirit and the idea within you. Teaching then flows out of you naturally, without the emotional charge that indicates it comes from the ego. For myself, I have never taught from a place of urgency. If I cannot put the ego aside and hear the Holy Spirit I keep my mouth shut. And anyway, if I am not ready to teach an idea from the Holy Spirit, either in speaking or writing, the words just will not flow. I cannot approach the idea with any depth, nor could I answer further questions about it. This does not mean that when I teach an idea I fully get it yet. But it does mean that it is in me enough to teach it from more than a shallow intellectual understanding. The process of teaching deepens my understanding until eventually I see the idea from every angle. That's why you can see my own evolution with concepts over time. What I taught about a concept 2, 5, 10 years ago is not what I teach today.

71. The ACIM Student and Being Different (May 20, 2016)

A reoccurring theme with many serious students of *A Course in Miracles* is how they have felt different all of their lives. Some are okay with this; others still want to be accepted and to fit in. The difference can show up as having been more perceptive than the average person; having a psychological orientation; never accepting what the religion of their family of origin taught; being more sensitive and intuitive; always sensing that there was something more than the world had to offer, etc. The question they often have is, are they different because they were always headed toward a spiritual path (or really already on one)? Or did their being different lead them to seek relief in a spiritual path?

The answer is both. Because you are on a spiritual path you were always headed toward one. But in the unfolding story how you end up on a spiritual path could show up as looking for relief from the pain of being different. In any case, the spiritual path resonates or you would not remain on it.

When I was in life-coach training I once asked a teacher, how large is our market? She said that it is estimated that at any given moment about 1 in 5 (20%) people are on a path of personal growth. (Of course, this is only in the developed world. Where people do not have access to basic education and/or struggle to survive they do not have the luxury.) By a "path of personal growth" she meant anything from reading self-help books to attending 12-step or other self-help programs to psychotherapy to being on a spiritual path. And it is my experience that only a tiny minority (probably less than 1% of the world's population) on a spiritual path are very serious about growing their awareness of Truth. It is no wonder ACIM students often feel they are "different"!

And as your awareness of Truth grows you will only feel more "different" as you detach from the values of the world. The more at peace you are the fewer people to whom you will relate. But the upside is, you are at peace so it does not matter! However, until you experience wholeness in Truth you may have a nagging sense of not fitting in. Humans are social animals. Fitting in is necessary for survival so it is frightening to feel that you don't fit in.

But then again, the whole human condition is one of feeling unique and therefore alone. You may belong to a group but you are a unique member of the group. You can relate to many somewhat but never to any one person wholly. No one ever feels that they wholly fit in anywhere, not even in their families. Until you transcend a human identity you will be afraid of being too "different".

In ACIM it says "'All are called but few choose to listen.'" (T-3.IV.7) This means that the Truth is in every mind but not every mind is moved to find It and to grow their awareness of It. If you need a story for this, ACIM provides one. The story of time is a projection of the idea of the opposite-of-God. This idea was over as soon as it was thought because God cannot have an opposite. In the story of time this undoing shows up as seemingly-individual minds going through a process of becoming aware of Truth.

Some students tell me that they think that the world is in a new era of "awakening". Well, you won't see this if you step back and look at the whole world. They think this because they have surrounded themselves with like-minded people. *Their* world has changed and they project this to the rest of the world. But as their awareness of Truth grows they will stop taking stock of themselves and a world. They will live in the awareness that only the Truth is true.

72. As Though It Should Be Different (May 27, 2016)

"Dreams are perceptual temper tantrums, in which you literally scream, "I want it thus!" And thus it seems to be. And yet the dream cannot escape its origin. Anger and fear pervade it, and in an instant the illusion of satisfaction is invaded by the illusion of terror. For the dream of your ability to control reality by substituting a world that you prefer is terrifying. Your attempts to blot out reality are very fearful, but this you are not willing to accept. And so you substitute the fantasy that reality is fearful, not what you would do to it. And thus is guilt made real." (T-18.II.4)

A Course in Miracles likens the experience of the universe of form to a dream that is a temper tantrum against Reality (Truth/God). The dreamer is the "Son of God" (split-mind) and the self with which you identify is a figure in the dream, one of billions of projections of the Son of God. (To be clear: This dream is only a meaningless idea of the opposite-of-God that has no intention behind it. Only within the dream does the dream seem to have the intention to be in defiance of God).

There are many layers to the way ACIM addresses the idea of "dreams". The section that includes the quote above begins with the dreams you have at night when you sleep. Then it segues into discussing the whole experience of form as a dream. In any case, any dream is an attempt to have another reality, whether that new reality is meant to replace the "reality" of the awake-dream or to replace Reality Itself with the awake-dream. And it is not the dream-to-replace-reality (the universe of form) or Reality that are frightening. Your resistance to them and your attempts to change them frighten you by increasing your guilt. Only if the world is real are you guilty. And you only try to change it because you think it's real.

So in identification with the ego (personal thought system) you resist not only Reality but the reality (universe of form) that is meant to replace It. On a daily basis you struggle against the way things are in the world. A lot of the sense of being a victim that one has in the world comes from an often unconscious belief that the world is supposed to be different from the way that it is. It is an unconscious belief not just that the world is perfectible, but that the perfect world is here and that somehow you are kept from reaching it.

For example, Georgette leaves job after job because in each job she finds that she is in conflict with someone. Well, yeah, the world is a place of conflict between personal identities (egos). She will be in conflict with everyone she knows sometimes. And she will be in conflict with someone in every situation. The process of growth into full adulthood is adjusting to this by taking responsibility for one's own attitudes, beliefs and behaviors to mitigate conflicts. But Georgette's attitude is that there is a job out there where she will get along with absolutely everybody all the time. This may not be a conscious attitude, but unconsciously she goes from job to job seeking for the perfect situation. And when she can't find it she feels that she is being unfairly deprived.

The world is not a perfect place and it never will be. It is not meant to be. It is the idea of the opposite of Perfection (Truth). It is a place of lack and conflict and dysfunction. It is not perfectible because then it wouldn't be what it is. If it was perfectible it would no longer be the opposite of Perfection.

This does not mean that you should never work to change things in the world for what you think would be the better. But it does mean that you have to accept that you will never change the world to be perfect. If you seek to improve (the world as well as the self with which you identify) rather than perfect, you take a lot of pressure off yourself. And you eliminate a sense of victimhood, too. The world is not perfect for anyone.

73. Ask: Is the fear of not existing the "mother of all fears"? (June 3, 2016)

"I just finished reading over your March 23 blog (#64) in which you mentioned having a terrifying experience of the 'fear of not existing'. I was recently thinking about a former friend who had created a persona which expressed itself as an obnoxious role he was compelled to play in all his interactions with others. I thought that he was so invested in this fake identity that if he

was prevented from playing it, he would not know 'who he was' and would be terrified of not existing (not consciously of course). Is this what you were talking about?
I have experienced a horrible foreboding of impending doom a few times when I traced back some fear, through guilt etc. I also experience pre-dawn anxiety every day which always seems to be about various trivial things in my life. Do you think that the 'fear of not existing' is actually the 'mother of all fears'? And most important of all—what to do, especially while it's happening. I always think there's some way to look directly at that fear as a means of dissipating it. I try to apply the 'Rules for Decision' (Chapter 30) to my morning fears but they seem intractable so far." - Anonymous

Reality is formless, boundless Being. So the experience of limited form, or the self, is very uncomfortable. The ego (personal thought system) teaches that your discomfort is guilt for "separating" from your natural state. It tells you that your natural state (Truth) is a power over you and outside of you (a god) that will punish you for attacking it by leaving it. So the "mother of all fears" is the belief that the experience of yourself as a human is real and that it is the result of defying a god that will punish you for it by annihilating you. You will cease to exist. This guilt and fear of annihilation is the core experience of the ego thought system and you experience them as your own when you identify with the ego. What I shared in that article was an experience of being at the very center of the ego experience.

In our identification with a self we fear change because all change brings loss of some kind. We have personas and roles that we cling to and are afraid to release because we fear we will lose more than we gain by doing so. This is what your friend may have experienced. Or he may not have believed that change was possible or that there was a better experience to be had. He also may have found that being obnoxious brought him things he valued and simply didn't want to change.

Your pre-dawn anxiety sounds like something chemical. If you have already traced your thoughts down to the fear and guilt at the center of the ego then continuing to dig around in your mind may only increase your anxiety. Your belief here may only be that "I am this body and its chemically-induced moods are my reality". If this is the case then the best way to deal with it is to accept that this is your experience of that particular body. Remember, acceptance does not mean that you like something. It means that you acknowledge that it is happening without resisting it. Watch the thoughts and remind yourself that it's just the chemicals in that body's brain in the morning. Don't believe in the thoughts, don't embrace them, and don't resist them. Instead, gently correct them with self-talk until they pass. If you're not sure what to say to yourself, think of what you would say to reassure a friend who was sharing these thoughts with you. This practice can line you up with the Holy Spirit's thoughts and pull you out of your morning anxiety faster.

74. Between Me and Me (June 10, 2016)

Each time I read *A Course in Miracles* different concepts stood out for me. Concepts would sink in, I'd move past them, and I was ready to learn new ones. The last time I read ACIM for myself was as I translated it into plain language. Then one lesson was driven home to me over and over again: This whole process to peace was between me and me. My sense of conflict was not between me and a world outside of me. It was not between me and a god outside of me. All of my conflict was occurring only within me. All of the reconciliation I needed was between a part of my mind (the split-mind) that was alienated from the Totality of my mind (Truth). *There was nothing else and no one else involved.* Each time this realization hit me with the force of a thunder clap.

I was already aware that I made my own world by projecting meaning onto a meaningless universe of form. I was used to bringing my conflicts with the world or the concept of a god back to what I was doing in my own mind. But actually experiencing on a deep level that the whole process was between me and me brought a feeling of deep comfort. It always helps to know what is going on in my own mind. But this realization also eliminated fear on the deepest level. Conflict with something outside of me meant I was powerless to resolve it on my own. But knowing the conflict was only within me was empowering.

75. In the Turnaround (June 17, 2016)

When I was a young child sometimes when I played alone I would experience a reassuring, comforting Presence with me. I felt in those experiences that everything would always be okay. These experiences were very rare. I had a happy, secure childhood and I had no conscious need to seek reassurance. But of course I was still having the human experience of everyday lack and insecurity. I was unconsciously open to Truth at those times. These experiences seemed very natural so I didn't question them. Nor did I think of them beyond their occurrences.

As a teenager I would in times of desperate adolescent angst turn to what I thought of as my "inner Therapist". These were very rare occurrences, too. But you can see how a shift had unconsciously occurred for me: The Presence was no longer *with* me; It was *within* me. It was still Other, but I knew It was in my own mind. I thought of It as my "inner adult" the way as adults people speak of their "inner child" left-over from their childhood. It was a future, wise me come to guide and comfort me through hard times. (I pictured It at the time as being all of 25 years old!)

In my late teens I started reading self-help books and eventually psycho-spiritual material. These told me that God was within me. I understood that they were speaking of my Inner Therapist. And then *A Course in Miracles* came along when I was twenty years old and I knew right away that the Voice that dictated it was the Christ in my mind – another name for the Presence that I had experienced as a child and the Inner Therapist I turned to as a teenager. I changed my label for It but the experience was the same.

My study and practice of ACIM led me to grow my awareness of the inner Presence, the Holy Spirit. I learned to call on it as my Guide and Teacher in all things. Later, when it came time for me to teach others, I learned to come from the Holy Spirit within me with others and in my writing.

Recently I have experienced a shift and I now know, not just intellectually but experientially, that that Presence, that Inner Therapist, the Christ Mind and Holy Spirit, is me. I have had surprising experiences of myself as the Teacher to the split-mind (decision-maker) in this mind rather than as the split-mind calling on or coming from the inner Teacher. In these experiences the split-mind is the "other". It wasn't exactly accurate for me as a teenager to think of the Presence as a future me. It was me all along. What was in the future was my *awareness* of this. I have gone from the Presence being *with* me to It being *within* me but Other; to the boundary between me and It slipping and being able to *come from* It as I dealt with the world; to beginning to experience, at least so far within this mind for the self in it, *being* the Presence...

76. The Ego Is Benign (June 24, 2016)

One of the things I help my clients sort out is what is the neutral personality of the self and what is the ego (personal thought system). They are confused because the ego is the thought system in their mind that tells them that the self is their reality and that they need to measure themselves by the self. So it's hard for them to see that the self – the body and personality – is neutral and that it is the ego that is not neutral.

For example, clients will say something like, "I know it's ego but…"

"…I like mountain biking…"
"…I want to study medicine…"
"…I enjoy horror stories…"
"…I prefer to be alone…"

First, you can see by the "but" that what they mean is, "I want this even though I know it's bad." They judge the ego as "bad" so what they see as expressions of ego are therefore "bad". But actually the ego is not wrong or bad. It is nothing. Second, all of those traits that come after the "but" are just neutral expressions of a neutral personality. They have no meaning in themselves. They are not expressions of ego, which is a judgmental, evaluative thought system of lack, guilt and fear. It is the ego that has determined, after you start reading *A Course in Miracles*, that the ego is bad. And it is the ego that judges neutral personality traits as bad.

I used to write about the ego attacking me to hold my attention but I have come to see that the ego is actually benign because it is nothing. It cannot change Truth so the ego has no real effects and I can see that now. When I listened to the ego I projected my belief in guilt, which I learned from it, onto it. I really believed I was guilty, but saw the guilt in the ego, just as I often saw guilt in others. But the ego does not attack. When your attention goes elsewhere it *will* do what it has to do to hold your attention once you turn its way again. It will pursue the thoughts, usually negative, in your mind that it knows work to hold your attention. But if you don't believe in it, this will not work. Just as with others, you are only affected by what the ego says about you if you believe what it says about you.

The ego is really just the thought system of the human animal. And it functions like an animal, doing what it has to do to "survive". In its case, "survival" means seeming to exist for you. Your belief in it is its sustenance. And when you withdraw your attention it seems to "attack" to get you to feed it again. But you won't experience its attention-sustaining measures as an attack when you see that it is nothing.

77. You Don't Have to Go It Alone (July 1, 2016)

When I was a new student of *A Course in Miracles* going through the long and uncomfortable (sometimes downright painful) "period of sorting out" it would have been so nice to speak every now and then with someone who had been through what I was going through and who had actually attained the inner peace I wanted. But there was no one around then who offered a professional relationship like that. So I muddled through in more discomfort and pain than was necessary. And, eventually, when I was ready I became a mentor for others so that they could have an easier time than I did as they made their way to inner peace.

Obviously I do have clients so some people have taken me up on this offer. But it is frustrating for me to hear of others who are still trying to go it alone. Clients tell me of friends who have questions or blocks to peace that they need help working out. They tell them, "Call Liz!" But they rarely do. Sometimes I can tell from comments people write at my blogsite or in emails that they are unhappy or uncomfortable or are ready to work through guilt and would benefit from a session with me. It's not a time-consuming relationship. People get relief from just a half-hour call with me, every now and then or on a regular basis (weekly, every-other week, monthly). I've never had a client tell me that they felt worse at the end of a call. So why don't they call?

Here are some things I've heard:

"I feel I should hear the Holy Spirit on my own." But you read books and listen to tapes and go to a study group or to seminars? Like those the mentoring relationship is just another instrument that the Holy Spirit uses to reach you. And unlike books and tapes and seminars or a public study group, a mentor can answer your specific questions, give specific examples and tools, and clarify points. The give and take of a private conversation brings greater clarity and deeper understanding.

"I don't want to pay for it." But you pay for all sorts of everyday pleasures. Your lattes and booze and massages and ice cream and manicures and cable/satellite TV and books and tickets to movies and sports and plays, etc. There's nothing wrong with that. It's natural to pursue pleasure to offset the pain of the human condition. So why wouldn't you pay for something that brings relief rather than just offsets the pain for a little while? Isn't inner peace a worthwhile investment?

"I'm not worth it." Well, what can be said about this but, "Yes you are and I'm sorry you don't know it." Not feeling worth it is something we can discuss, too!

"I don't want to waste your time." Really, people have said this. (No doubt the feeling was related to the last quote). Well, when I wanted help I felt this way, too. If anyone *was* available to help they were not people who mentored for a living so there was a feeling of taking up their time. But with me it's a professional relationship. I am offering my time, energy, education, and experience in exchange for money so you don't have to feel guilty about using them. A professional relationship puts us on equal footing.

"I don't have anything 'big' enough to talk about." If it's an obstacle to peace size does not matter! And if it's just a burning question it will hold you back, too. Not all of my calls with my clients are about problems or questions. Sometimes clients share what is working and good in their life. They share miracles. A lot of what I do is validate, which helps my clients move past doubts that hold them back.

Sometimes my readers have a vague idea that they would benefit from speaking with me but don't know what to talk about. Anything and everything! Your whole life is your spirituality. We don't have to discuss *A Course in Miracles* directly. As a client once said to me, "You teach spirituality; ACIM is just the language you use." On most of my calls ACIM does not come up directly at all. Just bring to the call whatever is on your mind. I cannot tell you how often clients say, "I don't know what to talk about today" and yet we fill up the time effortlessly.

The point is: You don't have to go through the process to peace alone. You don't have to stew with questions, doubts, or a nasty ego that won't let you move past it. I'm here to help you make it easier on yourself. It is the path to *peace* after all…

78. Ask: What does it mean to tell your brother he is right even when he is wrong? (July 8, 2016)

"The other day was for me one of those high energy days where I found myself engaged in one project after another, mostly home improvement and maintenance type things. I felt no resistance and at the end of the day I experienced what is typically referred to as "the satisfaction of accomplishment" - a type of high that most people regard as oh so healthy. While there is nothing wrong in taking care of business, being creative etc., there can be a negative flip side if, on those languid days when we feel no motivation or energy, we feel guilt as though "We've let someone down". (Who?) Being busy as a way of earning peace is a trap because it is only a facsimile of peace. It is no different than the Buddhist concept of "earning merits" for this or another life or any form of "righteous behavior" called for by other religions, or ideologies. They all perpetuate and reinforce guilt." – ES

Yes, temporary satisfaction, for whatever reason, is not true peace. It is simply the result of accomplishment, as you explained, or the personal thought system (ego) getting its way in something.

However, I think you are confusing two different motivations here. Being busy to attain satisfaction is different from being busy to stave off guilt. There is also another motivation for busy-ness: To avoid looking at something in one's mind. So let's look at each of these:

Busy-ness for satisfaction is actually just a part of being human so there is no guilt involved in this. It is natural as a person to feel satisfied when you have accomplished something. If it wasn't for that sense of satisfaction we wouldn't be motivated to do anything! It's only a problem if one makes an idol of accomplishing things in the hope it would lead to lasting peace. But because this wouldn't work it wouldn't last as an idol for long. As with all idols it would eventually lead to a sense of emptiness and disillusionment rather than peace.

Busy-ness to stave off guilt does come, as you said, from a need to accomplish to appease a power outside and over you – a god. Of course, a person is not usually conscious of trying to appease a god. All they know is if they are not busy they feel guilty or their self-esteem plummets. They don't examine this. They are just driven by the guilt to remain busy. And even if they did examine it they may not be in touch with a belief that there is a god sitting in judgment on them. But, of course, the guilt is the sign that this is exactly what they *do* unconsciously believe!

Busy-ness to avoid examining something in one's own mind is very common. Sometimes people know why they want to keep busy, like when they are openly grieving a loss. However, unacknowledged grief is very often why people don't want to be still. And besides grief, there are a whole host of things in a person's mind that they may not want to look at so they avoid stillness and keep themselves busy.

79. Ask: Can you comment on the satisfaction of accomplishment as a trap? (July 15, 2016)

"I live - by choice - in a very quiet rural area. Every summer the house next to mine is used by a family of brothers from New York City... I can always tell when the youngest brother is around by the level of noise coming from the house - yelling, non-stop talking, and extremely loud music... For four summers now I have experienced an intense emotional charge in reaction to this "barbarian" intrusion...I have essentially demonized these people in my mind, making them bad, wrong etc. My anger knows no bounds when I think about them. Whenever I think about talking to them about the situation however, I dissuade myself... The other day their music was so loud and lasted so long (hours) that I suddenly found myself transported to what I can only describe as The Land of Matter-of-Fact. All anger and fear vanished along with any sense of self-righteous importance...So when I arrived home one afternoon and the music was blasting, I simply parked in front of their house and with my new-found Bearable Lightness of Being, dove in. I found the young man in charge in the midst of his cohorts drinking beer and grilling barbeque and simply stated the facts: "I'm your neighbor next door and I need a favor. Your music is so loud I can hear it in my house even with all my doors and windows closed. I can't sit outside with friends and family on my porch. Could you tone it down?" I could see that even through a mild fog of intoxication, he was getting it. "Too loud? No problem." Since then things have been much quieter.

Do you think Liz, that when one can flatten the effect of a situation and experience it in a matter-of-fact way it is akin to what the Course *calls Innocence?"* – ES

What you experienced was the miracle of guilt dropping away from your mind so that you looked on a situation without an emotional charge. This led to your matter-of-fact experience and presentation, which in turn resulted in the young man that you spoke to being open to you without feeling defensive. This is a great example of how a shift in your perception – a miracle – can have results in your interaction with others. If you had gone in angry it is very likely that the young man would have gotten defensive and angry himself. Then you two would have been in a vicious cycle of anger-attack-defense.

In my experience coming from a place of no-guilt is different from the perception of Innocence. Both are miracles, but the perception of Innocence is what I would call a "higher" miracle. No-guilt is a shift in perception away from not-Truth and toward Truth. It leads to what you described, a charge-neutral (matter-of-fact) experience. This is a more "common" miracle and one toward which you can work by undoing the guilt in your mind.

The perception of Innocence is an extension of the awareness of Truth in your perception. This is impossible to describe, but the best I can say is that the body's eyes see the same forms but they are washed in Innocence. This type of "higher" miracle is often accompanied by an uplifting joy. It is a radically different perception that happens spontaneously when you are, often unconsciously, ready to accept it.

80. Ask: Is a matter-of-fact experience akin to what ACIM calls "Innocence"? (July 22, 2016)

"I live—by choice –in a very quiet rural area. Every summer the house next to mine is used by a family of brothers from New York City... I can always tell when the youngest brother is around by the level of noise coming from the house—yelling, non-stop talking, and extremely

loud music... For four summers now I have experienced an intense emotional charge in reaction to this "barbarian" intrusion...I have essentially demonized these people in my mind, making them bad, wrong etc. My anger knows no bounds when I think about them. Whenever I think about talking to them about the situation however, I dissuade myself... The other day their music was so loud and lasted so long (hours) that I suddenly found myself transported to what I can only describe as The Land of Matter-of-Fact. All anger and fear vanished along with any sense of self-righteous importance...So when I arrived home one afternoon and the music was blasting, I simply parked in front of their house and with my new-found Bearable Lightness of Being, dove in. I found the young man in charge in the midst of his cohorts drinking beer and grilling barbeque and simply stated the facts: "I'm your neighbor next door and I need a favor. Your music is so loud I can hear it in my house even with all my doors and windows closed. I can't sit outside with friends and family on my porch. Could you tone it down?" I could see that even through a mild fog of intoxication, he was getting it. "Too loud? No problem." Since then things have been much quieter.

Do you think Liz, that when one can flatten the effect of a situation and experience it in a matter-of-fact way it is akin to what the Course *calls Innocence?"* – ES

What you experienced was the miracle of guilt dropping away from your mind so that you looked on a situation without an emotional charge. This led to your matter-of-fact experience and presentation, which in turn resulted in the young man that you spoke to being open to you without feeling defensive. This is a great example of how a shift in your perception – a miracle – can have results in your interaction with others. If you had gone in angry it is very likely that the young man would have gotten defensive and angry himself. Then you two would have been in a vicious cycle of anger-attack-defense.

In my experience coming from a place of no-guilt is different from the perception of Innocence. Both are miracles, but the perception of Innocence is what I would call a "higher" miracle. No-guilt is a shift in perception away from not-Truth and toward Truth. It leads to what you described, a charge-neutral (matter-of-fact) experience. This is a more "common" miracle and one toward which you can work by undoing the guilt in your mind.

The perception of Innocence is an extension of the awareness of Truth in your perception. This is impossible to describe, but the best I can say is that the body's eyes see the same forms but they are washed in Innocence. This type of "higher" miracle is often accompanied by an uplifting joy. It is a radically different perception that happens spontaneously when you are, often unconsciously, ready to accept it.

81. Learning Beyond What's In ACIM (July 29, 2016)

Sometimes I write about topics that are not mentioned in *A Course in Miracles* but which come out of my experiences with the Holy Spirit (Awareness of Truth in my mind). Sometimes this prompts emails from readers who want to know where they can read about that topic in ACIM. Some seem to be genuinely interested in reading ACIM's take on the topic. Others seem to imply that because it is not mentioned in ACIM it is not really appropriate for me to write about as part of spiritual practice.

For example, I write a lot about setting boundaries in relationships. I find that boundaries are a very common need among ACIM students. Many seem to feel that being spiritual means taking inappropriate responsibility for others and/or being a doormat. They think that if they just forgive enough another's inappropriate or dysfunctional behavior will change. Or they feel that if they had truly forgiven they would no longer see the other's behavior as inappropriate or dysfunctional. Undoing the beliefs that underlie this form of co-dependency is what I work on with most of my clients.

But there is no discussion about building boundaries in ACIM. For Helen Schucman, co-dependency, the ego's (personal thought system's) universal approach to relationships, showed up not as taking too much responsibility for others but as asking others to take responsibility for her. She was a martyr; a victim full of grievances. Others let her down by not following her "scripts" for them.

ACIM is not a comprehensive teaching that covers everyone's experiences. Yes, most of what it describes about the ego is universal, but some is specific. For example, Helen used illness to make others guilty. Not everyone does this. And not every egoic experience is included in ACIM. For example, some use illness to avoid unpleasant situations, like work or undesired family events. This is not mentioned in ACIM. As with any spiritual teaching, you must discern the spirit of the lesson and not take the letter of the lesson so literally. This is what ACIM means when it says that you will learn to generalize your lessons.

ACIM is not an end in itself. It is the means to becoming aware of the Truth in your mind. And that Awareness (Holy Spirit) will lead you through and past your obstacles to peace, not all of which are described in ACIM. For example, guilt manifested in me, yes, by my projecting it onto others and making myself a victim. But it also showed up as my taking too much responsibility for others. This was a much larger and deeper obstacle for me. I actually felt it was my god-given responsibility to "fix" others and that belief had to be rooted out and undone. This was a long process on which I was led not by ACIM directly, but by the Holy Spirit within me. ACIM led me to the Holy Spirit and the Holy Spirit led me past my obstacles to being aware of Truth, many of which were not specifically mentioned in ACIM.

82. Ask: Any comments on you being an iconoclast? (August 5, 2016)

"The more I read the last blog along with the comments and your responses, the muddier the waters seemed to get (for me) until I read your statement:

'ACIM led me to the Holy Spirit and the Holy Spirit led me past my obstacles to being aware of Truth, many of which were not specifically mentioned in ACIM.'

You have always made the point that studying the Course *was simply a means to an end; that it was even possible to reach an understanding of the* Course *and still not have inner peace. After getting almost nothing from the* Course *per se, the various teachers, authors, books, speakers, and students - I came across* 4HIP, Releasing Guilt, the Mentor Articles *and your personal mentoring. Now that I have established a relationship with my inner Teacher of Truth—which I find to be fairly accessible, simple, quiet and tailor-made, I feel like a phony to consider myself a student of ACIM. Why bother with what seems like a lot of extra baggage. I have enough of my own to sort through, why wrangle with more - especially if the original "brand" comes up short—like the issue of boundaries which other* Course *teachers and students seem to reject outright. Not to mention my own incredulity with the* Course's *origins; the inscrutable, grandiose language; distracting issues with the Jesus connection, and* Course *teachers and students who reject my approach to the* Course *because I'm not loyal to the "brand".*

You Liz, are an iconoclast in the best sense—it's not a role you affect, it's just the place where you come from. Any comments?" – ES

Hmmm. I don't think "iconoclast" would be the word I'd use for myself since my dictionaries all seem to indicate that an iconoclast "seeks to destroy" or at least to "challenge" conventional ideas, icons, etc. Although the result is often that I *do* take apart conventional ideas my goal is to undo guilt and reveal Truth. I chose to be led by my experiences of Truth rather than by my intellect because intellectual understanding is not transformational but the experience of Truth is. And I (eventually) wanted real shifts to know Truth, not just to understand some spiritual teaching.

A client once said to me, "You don't teach ACIM so much as you teach Truth." Truth draws me like nothing else *because It is the truth*. What else could be worthy of my time and effort but the Truth *because It is the truth*? This does mean that, yes, I walk apart from almost all of the rest of the world. I'm not sure what this is called.

I can see why you may not consider yourself a student of *A Course in Miracles* since it has not worked for you. I still think of myself that way, or at least as a former student of ACIM, because it was almost exclusively the tool the Teacher of Truth (Holy Spirit) used to reach me for a very long time. I have left it behind, but it is still the common language and a useful tool that I use with my clients.

83. You Don't Have to Give Up the Loves of Your Life (August 12, 2016)

If you've been reading my stuff for a while please bear with me because I am returning again to an idea that I've visited many times before in many ways. But it is something that comes up often with clients and with people who write to me, even those whom I know have read all my stuff. So here I revisit it:

You do not have to give up the people, things, activities, etc. that you love to have inner peace. You simply want to give them to the Holy Spirit so It can use them as classrooms in which to teach you peace.

So often I hear from students of *A Course in Miracles* who judge against themselves for being too attached to their families, their friends, their animals. They try to force themselves to give up their interests and activities. If they love someone or enjoy or get pleasure from something they are certain that it is "wrong". Somehow they think ACIM asks them to give up these things. But in fact it is the ego with its belief in guilt and punishment that leads them to feel that they must sacrifice. This expectation that they will be asked to sacrifice means they totally miss that ACIM teaches them not to give up but to turn over their "special relationships" to the Holy Spirit. ACIM also warns them to not decide for themselves how to walk the path to peace. Those who are used to listening to the ego have no idea how to find peace.

This self has people and animals that it loves and things and activities that it enjoys and, lo and behold, this mind has inner peace! They are actually separate things. As I have said many times, the ego and the self (body/personality) are not changed by your choice for peace, but the mind changes. The ego continues on with its guilt and fear and you (the mind) simply stop believing it. And as the self goes about its life you (the mind) simply rest in Truth and observe its unfolding story without judging it.

To clarify: You are mind. The self (body/personality) is an idea in your mind with which you identify. It is neutral in that it has no meaning. It is not right or wrong or good or bad. It is actually nothing. The ego is a thought system in your mind about the self as your reality. This is simply a mistake, not a sin. And the Holy Spirit is the thought system in your mind that knows the Truth but also knows that you (mind) identify with a self and have listened to and believe in the ego. So your choice with regard to the self is which thought system you want to direct you in directing the self. You have used the ego and you find it is rather painful. If you want a "better way" then you might want to try the Holy Spirit.

So the self's loves and indifferences and likes and dislikes and preferences are all neutral expressions of its personality. They are not wrong or bad. They are not sins. For the ego they are ways of reinforcing guilt and fear and tying you tighter to the ego. For the Holy Spirit they are classrooms in which It can teach you of Truth. It teaches you of Truth simply by teaching you and you becoming aware of It.

You will not fully understand this until you do it. Just bring the Holy Spirit with you into your work, your relationships, your interests, etc. Start with just one part of your life if that feels safer. If you have questions or problems ask for guidance. The answers are not the point; that you connect with the Holy Spirit is the point. This is how you build trust in It. The result also happens to be that the answers mean the self has a more harmonious, simplified life. This is a nice side-effect, but the result of being aware of the Holy Spirit is inner peace no matter what is happening in the self's life.

So don't give up your loves. This actually blocks your awareness of the Holy Spirit because of your sense of sacrifice. And it also precludes you having classrooms in which to join with the Holy Spirit. Instead share your loves with the Holy Spirit, giving them all the singular purpose of peace.

84. Validation Speeds Up the Process to Peace (August 19, 2016)

In my early years as a student of *A Course in Miracles* (I began in 1984) I didn't really have anyone I trusted to speak to about my experiences. Very early on I experienced a direct Revelation and the higher miracle of the mystical Holy Relationship. No one in the initial study group I attended was discussing ACIM on the level on which I seemed to experience it. And I just didn't know anyone else who was a student. (There was no internet yet!)

So I went off on my own with the Holy Spirit. This was great in that it meant I had to work right away at building my trust in the Holy Spirit. And as ACIM points out, the whole process is the "Development of Trust" (Manual for Teachers) in Truth. But the process would have been smoother and I suspect gone a little faster for me if I had someone in the world to validate some of my experiences. Because I had no one to speak to I had to live with a lot of doubts. And doubts kept me spinning in place and not moving onto the next lesson.

For example, after a couple of years I began to notice a pattern of vacillation between experiences of peace and longer periods of being back in the conflicts of the ego. I noticed that any experience of Truth, no matter how "minor", resulted in a huge backlash from the ego (personal thought system). Even though I saw the pattern it took me a long time to trust what I was seeing and to trust that this was the normal process. Was I really seeing a pattern? Or was my going back to the ego again and again a sign I was failing? The Holy Spirit seemed to reassure me that it *was* a normal pattern and explained that I was swinging between to the two thought systems in my mind to sort them out. But my trust in my ability to discern the Holy Spirit was not strong yet. And my trust in the Holy Spirit was not strong, either. That was another place in which validation would've helped. And because I was not validated in my observations and my discernment I took a very long time to learn to trust them and the Holy Spirit.

Doubts are an inevitable part of the path to peace. But you do not have to stew in them. You can seek validation from others who have more experience on the path, in study groups, online, or one-on-one with a mentor. A lot of what I do as a mentor is validate my clients' experiences. I can hear the relief in their voices when I tell them that what they experience is normal or that yes, they are hearing the Holy Spirit. And I watch them move forward after they are validated.

85. The Choice for Peace is Made Once (August 26, 2016)

For a long time after I became a student of *A Course in Miracles* when things were hard or dark I felt I'd "fallen off the path". I kept thinking I had to choose peace again and again. Why couldn't I just make the choice and mean it? Why did I keep losing my way? What I didn't know was that I *had* meant the choice for peace the first time that I allowed myself to experience Truth. I didn't have to make the choice again. Once I let Truth into my awareness my path to peace was set. I wasn't lost; I was in an unfolding process. The times that I saw as hard or dark or lost were part of that process to attaining peace. But I only saw this in hindsight many, many years later.

What unfolded after the moment that I let Truth into my awareness was that moment manifesting in the story of time. So any choice for peace that I made after that moment was not to choose the whole path all over again. It was a choice for peace *now*. In any given moment if I was not at peace and I wanted peace I needed to choose Truth then and there. The goal of peace had already been chosen and didn't need to be made again. In fact, it was unfolding in that choice for peace in the present moment. Every moment that I chose Truth in the unfolding story of time was an expression of that first choice for peace. Those moments for peace *now* were inevitable.

And it was also inevitable that initially the choices for peace in the present were few and far between. Though I had made the choice for Truth and my path to peace was set what I did not yet have was full acceptance of the Goal. I did not wholly trust It. So in time I had to learn that the Truth *is* true and to learn to trust It. In time trust grew and I chose Truth and peace more often until finally one day I realized peace had some to stay in my awareness. That moment long before when I let Truth into my awareness had manifested in the unfolding story of time.

86. The Two Spiritual Goals (September 2, 2016)

No matter a person's spiritual path there are only two possible goals: To spiritualize the self's life in the world or to transcend the self. The vast majority of people choose to spiritualize the self's life in the world. Even if they've had higher miracles in which they perceive that the Truth is true and that the world is not they do not feel called to transcend the self. Being aware of Truth improves their life in the world and this is enough for them.

But a few feel called to transcend the self usually because they've experienced the reality of Truth in either a direct Revelation (only Truth) or a higher miracle. They feel called to Truth *because It is the Truth* and nothing else will satisfy them. They are willing to be wholly free from guilt.

Even those who feel called to transcend the self will go through a stage of spiritualizing the self's life in the world. It is an inevitable stage when embarking on a spiritual path because when you start out all you know is the self. But whether one is satisfied there or feels called to go beyond only the individual can know.

A Course in Miracles is a useful tool for both those seeking a "better way" and those called to transcend the self. But your goal will determine how you read ACIM and which teachers of it, if any, resonate with you. If what you want is a spiritualized life in the world then you will probably spend your life studying ACIM and perhaps other spiritual teachings. But if you are called to transcend the self then you will understand that you are in a long process. You will recognize that the passages in ACIM that are about spiritualizing the self describe a stage through which you will pass. You will eventually reach a point where ACIM, indeed all study, falls away naturally. So it is helpful to discern which goal calls to you. Is a better life in the world because the Holy Spirit (Awareness of Truth in your mind) is with you enough for you? Or are you drawn to Truth like metal to a magnet?

Obviously, anyone I work with is spiritualizing the self's life. If they were past that point they would not need to work with a mentor. But are they satisfied there or do they feel called to go past the self? This question is always in my mind as I watch their stories unfold. It can help determine how I answer their questions and help them through their blocks. Some know the answer if I ask but unfortunately the majority will say anyway that they want to transcend the self because in their guilt they think that is "superior" to spiritualizing the self. (Of course it is not. Both are temporary and fall away in the end).

Of course one's goal can change. One may begin by thinking they want to transcend the self but find in time that they are quite satisfied with a better life in the world. And someone who thinks that they are happy spiritualizing the self may have an experience of Truth that then calls them to go beyond it.

If you are honest with yourself, putting guilt aside and what you think you "should" answer, which is your goal? If you have clarity on this, even if it turns out to be temporary, you can take a lot of pressure off yourself now. If you want to spiritualize the self you don't have to pursue ideas or study that go beyond this. You do not have to try to understand what does not call to you. And if you do feel called to drop the self you can acknowledge that, for the time being, you are in the stage of spiritualizing the self. You can enjoy it knowing that it will pass naturally. You do not have to force yourself to be beyond it now.

87. More on The Two Spiritual Goals (September 9, 2016)

My last article about the two spiritual goals led to my receiving a few questions. So I will attempt to clarify here.

"Spiritualizing the self" means using one's awareness of Truth to better the self's life in the world. One who does this continues to identify with a self and does not seek to transcend the self. They bring their Awareness of Truth (Holy Spirit) with them into their work, relationships, etc. to help guide them to a more harmonious life. This is the most common choice for people on a spiritual path. It is always the way for those who are religious rather than spiritual. (Some are both).

I wrote that those who are called to go past the self to Truth are willing to wholly let go of the belief in guilt. This implies that, yes, those who do not transcend the self still believe in guilt. You would not continue to identify with the self unless you valued it. And if it is valuable to you then it is real to you so there is still an unconscious belief in your mind that the Truth has been undone and that you are guilty.

Moreover, spiritualizing the self always involves a sense that form (the self) and Formlessness (Truth) are equally real and interrelated. What one does or does not do as a self affects Truth, so there is an absolute "right" and "wrong" way to be a self. This is the way of religions. This belief, again, unconscious, is how guilt is perpetuated. Those who do not feel called to transcend the self usually have a hard time seeing this guilt. And since they are not motivated to transcend the self they are not motivated to find and undo the belief in guilt.

Those who seek to transcend the self must undo their belief in guilt because guilt is what ties one to the self. It takes a long while for them to be ready to see their belief in guilt because, believing guilt is real, they feel that they would be destroyed if they did see it. However, there comes a time when they are aware enough of Truth *as truth* to be ready to see that there is no justification for guilt. (My digital book, "Releasing Guilt for Inner Peace" goes into all of this in depth. You can find it at www.amazon.com or www.lulu.com).

Spiritualizing the self is a little different from a "spiritualized ego". An ego (personal thought system) is spiritualized when one uses spirituality to glorify the self, as in "I'm a good person because I'm spiritual" or "I'm better than others because I am aware of Truth", etc. Those who set themselves up as leaders or teachers with special spiritual knowledge not available to others are a clear example of those who spiritualize the ego. New religions are often based on a spiritualized ego. However, spiritualizing the self does not have to result in spiritualizing the ego. You can spiritualize the self without listening to the ego's pumping up of the self.

As I mentioned in the last week's article, even those who are called to transcend the self will go through a phase of spiritualizing the self. For them their relationship with the Holy Spirit is not so much about getting answers for a more harmonious life for the self. Yes, that happens, but that's a nice side-effect, not the goal. Being aware of the Holy Spirit is the goal. In short:

For one whose goal is to spiritualize life for the self the Holy Spirit is the means to a more harmonious life. For one whose goal is to transcend the self, the self's life in the world is the means to be aware of the Holy Spirit.

Whether one spiritualizes the self or is called to transcend the self is an unconscious choice based on what one truly values. Some simply do not feel called to Truth. The awareness they have that makes life better for the self satisfies them. Therefore, they have no motivation to transcend the self. Once one is aware of Truth the process is going to evolve as far as one is willing. You are always in charge. The Holy Spirit cannot take you further than you are willing to go.

As I said in last week's article neither way is superior to the other. Both are temporary, or time-bound, and fall away. Nothing one does or does not do in the universe of form has any effect on Truth at all. Truth goes on wholly untouched by it. Another way to say this is Eternity (Timelessness) is wholly unaffected by time. So one's choice only affects their own experience in time. No part of what is in time "goes on" to Eternity. The Part of your mind that is Part of Eternity is already There. The part of your mind in time falls away, no matter what it has done in time. So there can be no right or wrong choice about the self. There is just what you want to experience in time. And I've found that some just don't want to bother transcending the self. The pain of life in the world does not offset their enjoyment of it. Finding and undoing their belief in guilt involves more fear than they want to confront in themselves. But there are those of us who, having touched Truth, are called to It *because we know It is the truth.* So how could we be satisfied with what we've seen is an illusion? Growing our awareness of Truth to the furthest extent that we can is the only meaningful way that we can think of spending time.

88. An Example of Misusing the Specificity of ACIM (September 16, 2016)

I know it bothers some of my readers when I teach that *A Course in Miracles* was written specifically to Helen and Bill in their Holy Relationship and that it is helpful to read it through this awareness. I do not mean to take anything away from anyone by pointing this out. Instead my intention is to help readers avoid some of the pitfalls of guilt and misuse of ACIM into which I fell and into which I hear other students fall. ACIM is not diminished as a useful instrument that the Holy Spirit (Awareness of Truth in your mind) can use to teach you because it was written first and foremost to Helen and Bill. Many spiritual teachings are about someone's specific experience and guidance. In fact, it is helpful in deepening your awareness of the Holy Spirit when you have to use discernment to sort out what was meant for another specifically and what lessons you can generalize for yourself. This is how study grows your awareness of the Holy Spirit.

So here I am going to give you an example of how I misused ACIM from my own very, very early experience with ACIM. I tried to apply what was meant specifically for Helen and Bill to my own situation. And I had good reason to think I could because it was regarding the Holy Relationship. I have written about my experience of the Holy Relationship before but not in such detail. The details, I think, may help highlight the point I'm trying to make about applying ACIM too literally to one's own experiences.

First, let me clarify again the two experiences of the Holy Relationship. The first is what I call the "mystical" Holy Relationship. "Mystical" refers to a sustained spiritual Vision of the Holy Relationship in which you see Oneness with another. There are no words that adequately describe this Vision. Of course this is not a Vision of the body's eyes but of the mind. Physically the other looks the same as they always have but you are aware that the two of you share a Oneness that is beyond the body and the world. It is not like "soul mate" because this Oneness is not limited to the two of you. It is as though your relationship is a doorway into an awareness of Something universal that encompasses but also goes beyond the two of you. In the mystical Holy Relationship you and another are in an equal teaching-learning experience. You are ready to learn the Holy Relationship together.

The other experience of the Holy Relationship is what I call the "practical" Holy Relationship. In a practical Holy Relationship you look at the relationship as a classroom where you can grow your awareness of Truth. There is no ongoing spiritual Vision in the practical Holy Relationship. But rather you become aware of your wholeness in Truth and you relate to the other from this awareness. You and the other are at different stages of teaching-learning so you may both be learning lessons but not the same ones or not at the same level when they are the same. You are not sharing an identical experience.

Helen and Bill experienced the mystical Holy Relationship as they took down ACIM. I know this by reading ACIM's descriptions of the Vision of their experience, which I also had. And it was, of course, also an ongoing practical Holy Relationship as they each learned to use the Holy Relationship to learn of their own inherent wholeness in Truth and to come from that with others.

I, too, have experienced both the mystical and practical Holy Relationship but in separate relationships. The mystical Holy Relationship is the story I will share here. I experienced It with a woman I will call E. I wanted to pursue the practical Holy Relationship with E as well but I did not have the opportunity to experience that until I met my wife, Courtney.

As I've written before in my experience as a mentor I have met perhaps only one other person who has experienced the mystical Holy Relationship. While some have shared experiences of spiritual Vision with others what they describe is fleeting, not ongoing. The mystical Holy Relationship is not something I can teach. It comes from the Holy Spirit in one's own mind and they have to be ready for It. I do teach the practical Holy Relationship, however. It is a fantastic tool for growing your awareness of Truth.

You can perhaps see from what I've already written the confusion that must arise when a student who is not experiencing the mystical Holy Relationship tries to apply what is written about it in ACIM to their own relationships. On to my example:

It was 1984 and I was 20 years old for most of that year. I was living in Hawaii, where I grew up. I had been on a psychological journey since I came out to myself as a lesbian when I was 17 and it was fast evolving into a psycho-spiritual journey. I remember reading Terry Cole-Whitaker's "What You Think of Me Is None of My Business" but I don't remember what else except that I was hungry for all of it.

I was also in my first sexual relationship, with M. When I met her M was about 3 months from leaving for law school in San Francisco. We both knew that what we had was not going to evolve into something long-term. It was going to end when she left so it was bittersweet. I used the opportunity to, for the first time in my life, learn to be open and honest in a relationship. This of course meant first being open and honest with myself. I confess that there were a couple of big limits I put on my openness and honesty with M, justifying this to myself because she was leaving and I didn't have to get too deep with her. But it was a start. Life and spiritual lessons were coming at me hard and fast.

As well as many of my other friends M, too, was reading psycho-spiritual material. She told me about some books she'd ordered from the Mainland called *A Course in Miracles*. She lent me her copy of Jerry Jampolski's "Love is Letting Go of Fear" to introduce it to me. And she took me to an ACIM study group a couple of times.

I knew M's best friend and some others but she had a couple of close friends she spoke of often that I was going to meet at her farewell dinner. She had shown me pictures of them and told me their names. But when they walked in to the restaurant I saw only one. A still, quiet Voice in my mind said, "There's E." I knew her name from M pointing her out in a picture but it was as though the still, quiet Voice was pointing her out to me. However, I only noted this later. At the time I was caught up only in M. I did really like E. She had the kind of sense of humor that I adored. I wished I'd met her sooner.

Before she left, M received the massive *A Course in Miracles* and I looked through the 3 books. I was intrigued. I decided that when she left I'd order my own, though they were expensive for me and I was going to be on my own for the first time. (I took over M's basement apartment. I was to move 3 more times in the next year and a half). I also committed to go back to the ACIM study group. ACIM called to me.

M left and I grieved as one does over a first love. I was determined to learn every lesson I could from the experience. I received ACIM and started reading it and recognized in it my whole way. I was so hungry for it that I read the Text and Manual for Teachers as I did the Workbook. I couldn't get enough of it, though my resistance was so strong at first I often fell asleep after reading a single paragraph. Somehow I pushed through that. I carried all 3 hardbound books in a backpack with me wherever I went so I could read them whenever I had a spare moment.

And I saw E again, I think at the ACIM study group. We connected quickly and became friends.

We were very much attuned spiritually. I quickly fell in love with her. And at some point the spiritual Vision thing happened. I have no recollection of how it began. But I do remember a day we spent playing board games. After she left when I thought back on the day all I could remember was Light sitting across from me. All I had to do was think of E and I would be transported to Oneness. What uplifting Joy came with this Vision! And what terror over It when I wasn't experiencing It. I recognized the ego's resistance for what it was right away. It was my first experience of seeing the split in my mind that ACIM reveals: The joy of Spirit and the terror of ego.

It was also at this time that I experienced my first direct Revelation. It took me weeks, if not longer, to acknowledge to myself it happened. I was learning right away that everything ACIM says is true. If it wasn't for the Joy my experiences engendered in me I would not have been able to cope with the anxiety they engendered in me, too.

I don't know if E experienced the same thing. But one day she told me that she had never felt attracted to anyone as she was to me. She felt connected to me emotionally, intellectually, physically, and spiritually. This clinched the relationship for me. And I thought she might be trying to express the Vision I was experiencing but didn't have the words. I must've gotten deep enough into the Text to have read about the Holy Relationship because I recognized that it was what I was experiencing. I was determined to go with her through the initial anxiety and resistance as laid out in ACIM. I don't remember if I ever expressed to E my experience of the Vision or the fear. I suspect I hinted around the edges because I was too terrified to speak of it directly. I was afraid of chasing her away.

As we made our New Year's Eve plans that December we discussed what each of us had done the year before. It turned out we had actually been at the same notorious New Year's Eve party. And I remembered her! She had been the woman in line for the bathroom who was cracking jokes. The one whose sense of humor I had adored...

By Christmas we were closer than ever. Everything was warm and fuzzy. Not being Christian, Christmas was always a cultural family holiday for me. But that was the first Christmas that I experienced as a spiritual occasion. The Vision of the Holy Relationship, after all, is the Vision of Christ. Did we go to a New Year's Eve party? I think we may've gone to the same notorious party we'd both gone to the year before.

And then something changed. Slowly, I think. Well, people don't stay uniformly close. The closeness would come around again. Only it didn't. One week a couple of months later I noticed E hadn't called for a week. I hadn't called her because I didn't want to seem desperate (which I wasn't *quite* yet). I was living in Honolulu. She lived on the west side of Oahu. I called her home and found out she was staying with a friend in Honolulu. So I called her there. She said, "Oh, you know how it is, sometimes you just have to get away..." Oh, poor, naïve young Liz! She took this to mean "get away from one's routine for a while". But of course E meant "Get away from *you*." I didn't understand this until much, much later. But at the time I began to sense she was not interested in being close again.

I fell into numbing shock. How could we be so close and then...? How could she have said...? Who would walk away from someone they connected to in every way? And, moreover, who would walk away from a *Holy Relationship*??? I couldn't believe it. I was devastated. And frankly embarrassed. Obviously I had felt much more than she had...I talked to no one about it. How could I explain the Vision and losing the Holy Relationship? It would just seem like ordinary heartbreak to them. And it was a much bigger loss to me than that. I just pretended to others that all was okay. We were just friends who had drifted apart naturally...

We did not speak for a long while. And then the final blow came. Did E call me or had I called her? Anyway, she said she had some friends coming into town she'd like me to meet. Hope! Why would she want me to meet her friends if she wasn't coming back into my life? There was an event at the Unity Church where our ACIM group met. (I still attended the study group but E had dropped out). They would be there and so would I. I go and see her and she brings her friends over to me and…introduced me as "her good friend, Liz." That's it? "Good friend"? Okay, it was 1984 and we were all at least partly in the closet and I didn't know if she was out to her friends. What was she to call me anyway when we had never characterized our relationship? But it was not her words so much as her manner. *She treated me as only an acquaintance.* I knew then she was not coming back into my life.

Well, let's roll forward over the shock, grief, and confusion that you can imagine followed for months afterward. Eventually E went to Japan and joined a group that, if it was not actually a cult, it was pretty close. They seemed to specialize in "purifying". That was a clue to me that there was something dark going on with E. Even with my dim understanding at that point of what ACIM taught about guilt I saw guilt in her joining a group that was about "purifying". I began to be honest with myself about many things I had deliberately pushed aside; things that were inconvenient to my fantasy of E and I dwelling blissfully in a Holy Relationship. She had said at the outset that she wasn't ready to settle down, etc. So many little things that I didn't want to see. But I let them be overridden by some things she said and the Vision of the Holy Relationship. I had in many ways tossed out the self-honesty I had begun to learn with M. Well, lesson fully learned this time! As painfully as one possibly could

I was angry for years. I raged at E for saying lovely things and then leaving. I raged at God for giving me the gift of the Holy Relationship and then taking it away. Of course I knew God did neither. I finally raged at me for letting the Holy Relationship into my awareness in the first place. What kept me going, why it took so long to get over, were two things that gave me hope that she would come back: One was what she had said about how she felt connected to me in every way. Who would give that up? I was too young and inexperienced to understand that people flee in fear from things of value all the time. The other was everything I read in ACIM about the Holy Relationship. *I recognized it all as my own experience.* I read Chapter 17 more than any other part of ACIM, especially *The Healed Relationship*, because when I read it I would have the Vision again. Just as when I thought of E. The Joy! And I clung to what it said:

"The temptation of the ego becomes extremely intense with this shift in goals…"

Surely, this is what happened with E? She fled because she was afraid of the Holy Relationship. I was terrified, too. How I longed to go through it with her! How wonderful it would be to come out the other side together. Certainly she was meant to come back. Why else would I have experienced the Holy Relationship? Therefore:

"…Have faith in your brother in what but seems to be a trying time. The goal is set…"

And:

"Now the ego counsels thus; substitute for this another relationship…Hear not this now! Have faith in Him Who answered you…Abandon Him not now, nor your brother…"

Oh, my, you can imagine how I clung to these words! If I just have faith she will return. How could I move on? How could I abandon her? Though she was thousands of miles away and could receive but not send letters (a rule of her group)…I threw away common sense, which is the same as saying I refused to listen to the Holy Spirit.

I have had students quote lines like these to justify staying in relationships that they have clearly outgrown or are downright abusive. So you can imagine how it was for me who not only read these lines but *was actually experiencing everything described about the mystical Holy Relationship*. How could it not all be meant for me, too? What if I gave up too soon? As well as clinging to these words for hope I was terrified I'd "sin" (I wouldn't have used this word but that was what I felt) by giving up on E.

Well, obviously these words were not specific to my situation. E was never to return. Which, by the way, I knew, though I fought this for years. I have shared before about my sensing sometimes when I was pushing against the flow of the universe (#13). This was one of my earliest lessons with this. I knew intuitively that she would not return, but, dammit, *this was not how I wanted it to be*. So I insisted on clinging to what ACIM said *to Helen and Bill* as though it was for me despite my knowing it was not for me. I had invited the Holy Spirit into the relationship. But I did not do so with E. I chose to ignore all those passages about *two choosing together* to let the Holy Spirit shift the goal of their relationship.

There are many examples of specificity in ACIM that are not wholly transferrable to one's own situation. What students can take away from Helen and Bill's situation is that there is another Vision that is not the view from the ego. It does not have to be sustained for you to learn from It. You can invite the Holy Spirit into your relationships and they will be transformed as you are, with or without the other joining with you. Basically, there is another way. But that does not mean it will look exactly like Helen and Bill's way.

Just to wrap up: All of this took place in 8 or 9 months. It was my "period of undoing". I did learn from the Holy Relationship. I continued to have the Vision just thinking of E. But I would push It away because It was not on my terms , which was that E had to come back to me. I pushed Joy away because it was not on my terms! What insanity!

For a long while a major lesson in this experience pushed at me. I finally relented after a few years and learned it: If I could have the Vision without E present clearly she was not the source of It. The Source had to be with me. And that was the Holy Spirit. In the end I learned that the Holy Relationship is really with the Holy Spirit. My relationship with E was simply the doorway to that.

I did see E again. Along the way a hypnotherapist said what I described with E was a push-pull relationship. When I got too close E pushed me away. When I got too far away E reeled me in. To make a long story short (finally!) I saw E again just before I moved to Las Vegas in 1992. She was still part of that cult-like group but back in Hawaii. And I felt her do it again – she tried to reel me in. But this time I said no. I got my power back doing this, though it was not my conscious intention. I can say I was done with her. But really I was done with the part of me that still held on to her. I had the Holy Spirit, Which was all that I really needed from that relationship.

Eighteen months later I met my wife, Courtney, and entered into a practical Holy Relationship with my (our) wholeness in the Holy Spirit at its center.

89) The Seemingly-Parallel Goals for the Self (September 23, 2016)

A few weeks ago I wrote about the two spiritual paths, spiritualizing the self and transcending the self, and then a week later a follow up. Since those articles some have spoken to me about their confusion over which path is theirs. Part of the confusion is because, as I wrote, even those on a transcending path will go through a long period of spiritualizing the self. The greater arc of their path will lead to transcending but while they are in the stage where they spiritualize the self they can't really see beyond it.

Another reason for some confusion is that they expect that if they had truly made the choice for Truth, Truth would be all that they wanted. And it just doesn't work that way. The choice for Truth *is* made in an instant but in time that choice unfolds as a process. For a long time, even if your goal is to transcend the self, you have what seems to be two parallel goals for everything.

As an example, last week I wrote about my experience of the mystical Holy Relationship. I experienced the Holy Relationship in the midst of an ongoing (for me) special relationship. My desire for the special relationship did not fall away because I experienced the Holy Relationship

"It is no dream to love your brother as yourself. Nor is your holy relationship a dream. All that remains of dreams within it is that it is still a special relationship. Yet it is very useful to the Holy Spirit, Who has a special function here." – T-18.V.5

All relationships in the world are special in that they are each unique. Just as each self is unique. But, as always, the Holy Spirit can transform "special" for its own purposes. Where the ego (personal thought system) uses "special" to reinforce the unique self, and therefore your sense of separation from Truth, the Holy Spirit gives the special relationship a purpose that leads you back to Truth. This is what makes the special relationship a Holy Relationship.

The self is what desired a special relationship. Specifically, in my identification with a self I wanted a lifelong relationship. That desire was neutral. It had no meaning in itself. It was not good or bad or right or wrong. It was not a harmful or harmless desire because it was neutral. Whether it was helpful or not for this mind was determined by this mind's goal (wholeness) and the teacher (thought system) it chose to reach that goal.

The ego is a thought system of lack, guilt, and fear. Through it I came to believe that a special someone would fill the lack it told me was there in me. All my fantasies were of meeting the "right" woman and being "saved" from the pain of lack, guilt, and fear. This is the kind of "special" that *A Course in Miracles* points out is not helpful. It does not undo lack; it reinforces the belief that lack is real. It does not undo guilt and fear; it reinforced the belief that guilt and fear are real. This is why special relationships are so conflicted and painful. I couldn't see this then because the only way to wholeness that I could think of was the way that the ego showed me. But given that my goal was wholeness the ego was not the helpful teacher.

The Holy Spirit, however, saw this same desire for a special relationship as a classroom where I could learn that I am already whole in Truth. On some unconscious level I was willing to learn this. So I experienced the mystical Holy Relationship in which I experienced an ongoing higher miracle. In that higher miracle I experienced the Oneness, or Wholeness, that was in my mind beyond the self and the ego. The Holy Spirit *was* the helpful Teacher.

My desire for the special relationship did not fall away with the Holy Relationship. I was presented with the choice of to which thought system I wanted to attend, so which would grow in my awareness. As I shared, for a long time I was angry and chose the special relationship. But eventually I accepted the lesson of the Holy Relationship. And when I met my wife years later I was ready to express those lessons in a practical Holy Relationship with her. Our relationship is still special in that it is unique, as is all form in the world. But in content it is Holy because I choose to use it to learn that I am whole in Truth. The ego's "special" fell away because I no longer needed to look to anyone else for wholeness.

This is how the path works: You have two thought systems in your mind, ego and Holy Spirit, each with their diametrically opposed goals for the neutral world of form in your mind. When you become aware of them you can decide which you want to follow. For a long time, as you sort them out, you will choose both. They will seem to run parallel in your mind; they will seem to be simultaneous. But really you cannot be in both at the same time. However, you will vacillate between them so quickly sometimes it will seem like you are in both at the same time.

As long as not-Truth (the universe of form) is in your mind the self and the ego will be in your mind. The self's neutral desires and preferences will be there and the ego will tell you how to use them to be whole. But as you grow aware of the Truth in you and become aware that you are already whole you won't feel a need to follow the ego. You will hear to it tell you how to use the universe of form to be whole but you will disregard it. You will rest in wholeness and watch without judgment the story of the self unfold.

90. Ask: Why does the ego always speak first and how do I counter it? (September 30, 2016)

"A Course in Miracles says that the ego speaks first, is always wrong, and the Holy Spirit is the Answer (see T-6.IV.1:1-2) Why does it speak first? How to counter it? Rule no. 7 for me is the last & easiest of the Rules for Decision and seems like a good antidote for the ego speaking first." – ES

The ego (personal thought system) always speaks first because it wants you to listen only to it. It is defensive, so it is reactionary and emotional, and this grabs and holds your attention, pushing out all reason and any other Voice.

You don't need to counter the ego. In fact, trying to do so will only give it more power over you. Instead, you want to allow its response to come up and go past. Then you can turn to the Holy Spirit (Awareness of Truth in your mind). Sometimes you can do this quickly; other times, when you are more emotionally charged, you may have to take some time to let the charge pass.

The Rules for Decision (Chapter 30, Part I) provide an excellent process for getting past the ego when you are locked in its response. Rule #7 is:

"Perhaps there is another way to look at this. What can I lose by asking?" (T-30.I.12)

Sometimes you may be able to go to just this rule. But the rules before this one can be helpful because they get to motivation when you are really stuck: You don't like how you *feel*. This is what motivates you to open your mind to another way of looking at a situation.

91. The Whole "Awakening" Thing Falls Away (October 7, 2016)

This may be one of those things no one can understand until they experience it, but I'll try.

I used to focus on "awakening". I wrote about it a lot. (Sometimes I called it "enlightenment"). The concept behind this word is attaining a state of awareness that the Truth is true and that illusion is not true. I call this state the Awareness of Truth (also, Holy Spirit or Christ Consciousness). But my experience has led me to see that attaining this state never happens. Oh, yes, the Awareness of Truth is real and can be a mind's experience. But It is never *attained.*

This split-mind is always aware of Truth to some degree now. That the Truth is true has become a quiet knowing that suffuses its experience. This split-mind is also still aware of an ego (personal thought system) and its world but they are less and less significant to it. But would this split-mind say it has "awakened"? It would feel inaccurate to say so. *What* would have awakened? This split-mind is aware of the Awareness of Truth in it. Would it be *awake* if this split-mind was not just *aware* of the Awareness of Truth but *was* the Awareness of Truth? But then there wouldn't be a split-mind. The split-mind can be *aware* of the Awareness of Truth. But it cannot *be* the Awareness of Truth because then there is no split.

A split-mind (also called "decision-maker" or "learner") is split between the Awareness of Truth and the ego. When it releases the belief in an ego What is left is the Awareness of Truth. So at that point there is no split-mind. There is nothing that has attained something. There is nothing that has "awakened" or "become enlightened". There is no decision-maker or learner because there is no decision to make and nothing to learn. The concept of awakening or becoming enlightened implies that something attains this. But Truth just is and It is All that is. There is nothing to attain It. This concept, this goal of "awakening", has fallen away from this mind because it sees that the Awareness of Truth is always here and there is no need to "attain" It.

92. Are they "awake"? (October 14, 2016)

Often students will ask me if I think a certain spiritual teacher is awake. I tell them that I don't even know what that means. A self cannot be "awake". THE Awareness of Truth (Holy Spirit, Christ Consciousness), Which is all that could be called "awake", is in every mind. Seemingly-individual split-minds are aware of the Awareness of Truth to varying degrees but I would not call any of them "awake". As I wrote last week, a split-mind never attains the Awareness of Truth. It falls away and the Awareness of Truth is what is left. But only the one experiencing this would know that this has occurred. And they would feel no need to bring it up unless they were asked.

A split-mind can never see past itself. It only ever sees its projections onto others. Sometimes those projections mirror itself; sometimes they are what the split-mind hopes to see. Clients will share with me their disappointment in someone they thought was "awake" but then who did something human that they have determined no one awake would do. They are looking to a self (body/personality) for what will never be awake. You will never see an awakened *person.* But you may become aware of the Awake mind - in yourself. And when you do you will be aware of It in others, too. Then you may be able to sense a mind that has transcended the self but you could never be sure unless you asked.

Back in the 90s or the aughts there was a movement among Christians, especially the young, where they asked themselves, "What would Jesus do (WWJD)?" The idea was to ask oneself this in any given situation to model appropriate Christian behavior. But of course the story of Jesus is an allegory about the transformation of mind. To focus on behavior is to spiritualize the self. To look to another for a model of an awake mind is to make the same mistake. The Awake mind is found within, not in the behavior of any self.

93. Trust Builds From Everyday, Ordinary Miracles (October 17, 2016)

Occasionally I hear from students or readers their discouragement that they have not experienced direct Revelation or "higher" miracles. Sometimes they think that without those experiences they will never attain peace. But it was not those experiences that helped me to build trust in Truth. What was helpful in building trust was the simple practice of being open, or willing, for Truth to come into my awareness in whatever form I needed. The simple, everyday miracles that were the result of this practice led to my trusting Truth and finding peace.

A Revelation, as *A Course in Miracles* uses the term, refers to a direct experience of Truth. It is beyond perception and is Knowledge Itself. In this experience there is no world; the world is not even a thought There. A Revelation reveals the end goal of a spiritual path. If a revelatory state was sustained the world would be over for you. So it is rare to find a spiritual seeker who has experienced Revelation and even for those of us who have they occur very rarely.

I coined the term "higher" miracle to refer to those more dramatic miracles where you have a shift in awareness where you know Truth to be true and the universe of form to be not-True. Sometimes the focus of a higher miracle is on the Truth as true and sometimes it is on the universe of form being not-True. A higher miracle is at the level of perception, thus it is what ACIM calls a "miracle" rather than a Revelation. It is just this side of Knowledge; just this side of Revelation. It is the highest level of perception, or consciousness, that one can attain. It is the consciousness of the Holy Spirit or Christ. These are a fairly common experience among spiritual seekers and you will experience them more often as you undo your obstacles to Truth. It can eventually be your state of mind, but the world would not last long in your mind once it was.

Both of these experiences fall under what ACIM calls a "Holy Instant". Revelation would be the ultimate Holy Instant. But as ACIM points out, time can close over an instant. So while these experiences show you that the Truth *is* true, their effect on your conscious mind does fade.

What I call an "everyday, ordinary" miracle would be getting an answer from the Holy Spirit, a new way of looking at something that shifts you toward peace, a needed insight, peace that seems to descend on you out of nowhere, etc. These, too, are Holy Instants, but they are much more mundane and therefore more easily accepted into your day-to-day life.

The path to peace is a cumulative process so all miracles, whether "higher" or ordinary, everyday miracles, build on each other in your subconscious until one day you reach a tipping point and find that you trust Truth. This is when peace comes to stay in your awareness. But the ordinary, everyday miracles are far more consciously transformative than the more dramatic Revelation or higher miracle. They come from the simple practice of communing with Truth everyday with the only goal being to open to Truth. (This is the first habit in my book *4 Habits for Inner Peace*). Nothing much may happen when you meditate and open to Truth. But later, throughout the day, the ordinary miracles will occur. It is as though you open a door while communing and Truth walks into your awareness in whatever form you need throughout the day. Allowing and recognizing these everyday miracles are how trust in Truth grows.

So don't lament the experiences that you have not yet had. Instead, be willing for Truth to be in your awareness here and now in whatever form you need.

94. Trust Takes Time, With People and With Truth (October 28, 2016)

I've always preferred to be in love than to fall in love. Oh, sure, falling in love is exciting. But it's also terrifying. (There's a fine line between exciting and terrifying). It takes time and exposure to a person to know if you can trust them. And in the beginning your feelings for this stranger far outstrip your knowledge of them. If you feel early on that you *can* trust them it is an illusion based on your trust for someone of whom they unconsciously remind you. In other words, when you fall in love you risk getting hurt. And this makes it stressful.

It is the same when one first becomes aware of Truth. Can this wonderful experience be trusted? Of course it is stressful when you begin a spiritual path. Oh, sure, it's exciting at the beginning, too. You are so hungry for the experience. You are so hungry for books and teachers and anything that will bring the experience to mind. But don't underestimate your distrust. This is why when you step away from those moments and books and teachers you are in doubt. You swing back to the uncomfortable, but familiar, personal thought system (ego) and its world. It seems safer to return to familiar pain than to risk an unfamiliar pain if the Truth turns out to be untrustworthy.

As trust is learned to be justified in a relationship, love deepens, and stress falls away. It is the same with your relationship with the Awareness of Truth (Holy Spirit). But here's the difference: With people there is always a limit to trust. What we really learn with others is where we can and cannot trust them. For example, you may learn that your partner can be trusted to be there for you emotionally. But he or she cannot be trusted to handle the finances. Is that a deal breaker for the relationship? It depends on you and your values. We all prioritize our values. In all of our relationships with people we unconsciously and consciously weigh our values against what the other has to offer in the relationship. No one is perfect. No one is going to fill all of our needs or meet all of our values. We let in those who meet the needs and values we hold highest.

But with the Awareness of Truth in your mind there is no need to limit trust. It is wholly trustworthy. However, coming from human relationships and their relative trustworthiness, it takes a long time to accept this. It seems too good to be true that there is Something wholly trustworthy. And in the world of relativity anything that seems too good to be true is not true. Students so often ask me why this process to peace takes so long. Well, because it all comes down to trust. That's why in the Teacher's Manual *A Course in Miracles* lays out the process as the "Development of Trust".

I found it helpful along the way, when I saw that I was not willing to let in the Awareness of Truth, to acknowledge that I just didn't trust It enough yet. It did not matter that I wanted to trust. Trust isn't something that can be forced. It cannot be faked. I either trusted or I did not trust. There's no middle ground. No matter how much I wanted to trust the proof that I did not trust was in my unwillingness to let in the Awareness of Truth. Accepting this unwillingness reminded me that I was not at the mercy of some outside power. The block was in me; nothing outside of me was withholding peace from me. Accepting this, at least, empowered me.

Trust grows through exposure to the trustworthiness of that which you want to trust. That's why the path to peace is a two-pronged approach: Let in the Awareness of Truth. And if you cannot, find and undo your blocks to letting in the Awareness of Truth. This takes time.

I found it helpful to not only acknowledge my lack of trust to myself but also to the Awareness of Truth. "I know You're here. But I just don't trust you. Here's why…" This way I at least kept the lines of communication to It open.

95. Technique: Come Into the Room (November 4, 2016)

Back in the day my thing was not dwelling on the past. It was living in the future. Some of this was goals and plans. But most of it was just fantasy, even fantasizing about one day being at peace. But either way it was not being here, now, the only time in which it is possible to be at peace.

The personal thought system is always about the past or future or just elsewhere. The "elsewhere" thinking can be dwelling on something that is not in front of you, like a completely made up time, place, or story; or something going on in the world or someone else's life. This was common for me, too. So when I found I was in the future or elsewhere and I wanted to be present I'd bring myself back into the room. I'd remind myself that this is where I am now. All I have to do is deal with what is right in front of me right now. And any lessons I have to learn are right here.

To do this I'd say to myself, "Come into the room" and then I'd make a point of looking at what was in the room with me. It did not matter where I was, at home or in public. If I was outside I'd say, "Come here, now" and I'd look at those things nearest me. This would ground me in the present. I'd remind myself that this is where I am. I am not with myself when my mind is in another time or place. And if I am not with myself I am not with the Awareness of Truth (Holy Spirit) or peace.

Sometimes students tell me that they can't stop dwelling on the plight of others in the world. So I share with them this technique. Be with what is right in front of you. This is where you are. You cannot live anyone else's life. You cannot solve problems that are not in front of you. If you are to act in some way to help someone else, near you or a world away, you will know in the present what actions to take.

Other students are concerned with lessons they've read or heard of but that they have not yet learned for themselves. I tell them to forget what they do not yet know or do not yet understand. The way you get to more advanced lessons is to learn the lessons in front of you now. What are you going through in your life now? What is there to learn? Just as in school, what you learn now prepares you for what you will learn later.

What I learned from this was how much of my experience, my "life", was a fantasy of ideas. I saw how my "world" was a world of thoughts. There is a lot that can go on in my mind. But there is very little actually going on right in front of me. How much simpler and more peaceful it is to live with only what is right in front of me!

96. Dealing With World Convulsion (November 11, 2016)

This was not the article I intended to send today. But I know that many of my readers, all over the world, are upset about the results of Tuesday night's election in the US. And those results did not happen in a vacuum. Sure, there are always political swings one way or another and wars and financial crises, etc. But right now those things are happening on a global scale and affecting far more people than usual. The world goes through this kind of global upheaval now and then and it is intensely uncomfortable when it reaches your part of the world. Some of my readers, I know, live in parts of the world that have been convulsing for a while. Maybe you have never known much but chaos. But most of my readers are in the West and are used to stability. Paradigm shifts are rare in the modern history of their countries. It is much nicer to be past it and reading about it in history!

But here we are. And what are you to do to deal with the stress? Of course the size of the stress does not really change the approach you need to take to be at peace. It also does not matter if you are stressed about something going on personally or globally. I recommend my *4 Habits for Inner Peace*. If you have the book you may want to re-read the habits. I will discuss them in this context here. You can do them in any order. And if you find only one or two work for now, just do those. Use what works!

Habit #1: Commune with Truth Daily

This is the most transformative of all of the habits. And it leads to the other habits. It means turning your mind inward, stepping out of time, and resting in Truth for a while every day. When you go to do this you will probably initially find your mind processing. (See Habit #3). Let that happen and let it wind down. Then remind yourself that this is your time to be with Truth. You can return to the world afterward.

This practice is necessary to help you to detach from the world.

Habit #2: Turn Within to Truth Throughout the Day

This is a mini-version of communing with Truth. Simply take moments throughout the day to turn your mind inward and remember that only the Truth is true. You can do this at any time, no matter what you are doing or where you are because it occurs only in your mind. It's just a moment. If you have more time, then you may want to close your eyes for a minute or two. This practice, too, will help you to detach from the world.

Habit #3: Call on the Teacher of Truth for Guidance

If your thoughts are churning then have a discussion with the Teacher of Truth (Holy Spirit) in your mind. It may help to do this in writing, which can take you into your deeper thoughts and feelings. Just lay it all out to the Teacher of Truth: Your thoughts, your fears, your hopes, your anger, your guilt, etc. Doing this can help you to quiet your mind so that you can commune with Truth afterward. It can also help you to see how your beliefs, not the situation, cause your feelings of upset.

Habit #4: Allow Love to Extend Through Your Mind to Remember That You Are Love

When you look on something that upsets you, turn your mind inward to Truth. When you touch Truth, It automatically extends to what you see. How this shows up for you will be unique to each situation. But each time you will feel liberation from guilt and fear. This is not something that you make happen; it is the result of willingness to have Truth in your awareness.

You will only find detachment from the convulsions of the world when the Truth is true for you. These habits are how you use your experience in the world to grow your awareness of Truth. At first they take conscious effort. But in time they become, well, habits. They will be your automatic response to stresses in your life or in the world. Detachment will come easier.

97. What Do I Want This Mind to Be About? (November 18, 2016)

"He must learn to lay all judgment aside, and ask only what he really wants in every circumstance." (M-4.I.A.7)

The above quote is from the Development of Trust in the Manual for Teachers of *A Course in Miracles* where it lays out the stages through which a student will go. This refers to the fifth stage, the "period of unsettling". But I've always found that sentence to be vague. In my translation of ACIM into plain, everyday language I translated it as:

"Now, to attain Complete Peace, you must learn to lay aside the personal mind and forgive in every circumstance." (M-4.I.A.5)

This was to make clear that "what he really wants" means *peace*; that laying judgment aside means laying the personal thought system aside because it is always evaluative (judgmental); and exactly how this is done (forgiveness).

Peace is always here. So "asking for Peace" really means being willing to let go of that which is not Peace. When not-Peace is released (forgiven) Peace remains.

In practice, when my mind is churning on upsetting thoughts, I ask myself "What do I want this mind to be about?" This reminds me that I am not the victim of my thoughts. I am in charge of this mind. And it reminds me that I have a choice. There are only two thought systems from which to choose: The personal thought system (ego) or the Awareness of Truth (Holy Spirit). The personal thought system churns. If I am willing, the Awareness of Truth will offer me another way to look at the situation on which my thoughts churn which will quiet my mind. Those are my choices.

98. Questioning Does Not Necessarily Mean Tossing Out (November 25, 2016)

When I was very young I realized that I didn't feel love when others loved me but rather when I loved. This is why I was a nurturer. I had learned, though not in these words, that what I give I receive.

When I was twenty I became a student of *A Course in Miracles* and read that lesson in those words. But I made the mistake of thinking that ACIM could not be talking about a lesson I had already learned. Helen Schucman was in her fifties when she scribed ACIM. Certainly she had to have already learned this lesson? Maybe this meant something else? So I took the lesson deeper and learned that it was saying, as it says elsewhere more plainly, that I can only give to myself.

My mistake was thinking that I could not know something at twenty that someone at fifty had yet to learn. Of course we do not all learn the same lessons in life. And even when we do we do not learn them in the same order. A twenty year old *can* know something that someone at fifty has yet to learn. I was young and inexperienced and insecure and didn't trust my own learning. I also felt ACIM was so radical that it couldn't also contain mundane lessons. Another mistake. Yes, in its ultimate teaching that the universe of form is not Reality it *is* radical. But it is also meant to be used in a mundane world. It was answering Helen and Bill's call for a "better way" to be in the world.

This is only one example of the mistake of thinking I couldn't already have learned some of ACIM's lessons before I picked up the books. Many ideas in ACIM *were* wholly new to me. But those that were not, those lessons that I had already learned, I questioned. And I questioned every other lesson I'd learned and continued to learn in life. This should've been a good thing because it could've opened my mind. Questioning means one considers the validity of what they have already learned. If the lesson is valid then questioning it strengthens it. If the lesson isn't valid then it is tossed out. But questioning does not mean that one inevitably tosses out what they have learned. And this is what I did for a long time. I tossed out, or at least distrusted, all that I had learned and continued to learn about the world and my experience in it. My mind was closed, not open.

What ACIM actually teaches is that I should bring lessons to the Holy Spirit to determine what is useful and what is not. But since I didn't do that for a very long time I drifted through the world unmoored. I think I thought that this was spiritual! But in fact I was just lost because I didn't trust my own observations and experiences. When I finally did allow the Holy Spirit to guide me through the world I found my experiences and observations in the world were validated by the Holy Spirit. Most of it was useful. I found common sense prevailed. I found my footing again and felt grounded in the world. It turned out that being grounded in the world is not un-spiritual; it is the result of spiritual awareness. I was not going to transcend the world by denying my observations and experiences of it. I had to first accept those before I could begin to transcend the world.

The funny thing is, these mistakes led me to look deeper into ACIM's teachings. I kept thinking that it couldn't mean just what it said on the surface. And I found that deeper meaning every time I sought it with the Holy Spirit. I found a singular, profound, cohesive message that I eventually expressed in my translation of ACIM into plain, everyday language. Oh, well. Even our mistakes have their uses if they are given to the Holy Spirit!

99. From Projecting Fear to Extending Compassion (December 2, 2016)

Let's say you have a bully in your life. Or maybe you just know of a bully. This person may be always on the attack. Or perhaps they only bully when they feel threatened. In any case, when you even so much as think of them you are feel fear.

This fear does not come from them. This fear is because of beliefs in your own mind. This person is a symbol of the guilt and fear in your own mind. Unconsciously you recognize the motivation for their behavior is guilt and fear. And you can understand this because you are like them. You understand being defensive when you are afraid. So what you see in them is a projection of your own guilt and fear. They are a mirror of your mind and this is the actual source of your fear.

So how do you move past projecting fear and increasing it in yourself? You bring your unconscious beliefs to conscious awareness. You do this by asking yourself, "Why do they behave this way?" You can answer this because you, too, are human and you understand human behavior. You are also defensive at times even if not in the ways that you see as bullying. You may be passive-aggressive. Or you may take out your anger by yelling at others without hitting below the belt emotionally. Perhaps you've learned to deal with your guilt and fear in other ways. Maybe you turn them inward rather than outward and you are depressed or you self-medicate. However you show up as defensive, now that you understand the other's motivation you can shift from fear to compassion.

Compassion extends both ways. To feel compassion for another you must be willing to be compassionate about the same traits in yourself. If you cannot find compassion for another it is because you are not willing to be compassionate toward yourself. But when you are compassionate toward yourself you will find it extends automatically to others.

It does not follow that being compassionate means you do not set boundaries with others' dysfunctional behavior. In fact, it is guilt and fear that makes you remain around a bully because unconsciously or consciously you believe that you deserve to be bullied. Since you must be willing to accept compassion for yourself before you can extend it to other, understanding and compassion come from a place of self-respect in you. And self-respect automatically results in boundaries with others' dysfunctions.

When you come from a place of understanding and compassion you no longer take the other's behavior personally. You realize that they are acting out their own guilt and fear. And because you do not respond with your own defenses one of two things occur: The other falls away from your life because they are not getting the reaction from you that they want. Or they change toward you and treat you with the respect that your new attitude toward yourself demands.

100. Ask: When we attack aren't we projecting guilt? (December 9, 2016)

"We often hear that when we attack another in thought or action we are attacking ourselves. I wonder. Aren't we simply projecting our guilt and in so doing we are avoiding looking at that guilt which in turn reinforces it, thus delaying its release? Or is that the equivalent of self-attack?" – ES

You attack when you feel you need to defend yourself. And you feel that you need to defend yourself when you feel vulnerable. So you must be identifying with a self in a body in a world. This mistake is described in *A Course in Miracles* as an "attack" on yourself. So in any situation where you perceive that attack is real, whether you are the attacked or the one doing the attacking, the first attack you make is the one yourself. All other attacks then proceed from this first error.

Part of the error of perceiving yourself as a self in a body in a world is to believe that guilt is real. Yes, you are projecting guilt when you attack others. You really believe the guilt is in you but you try to get rid of it by seeing it in others and seeing yourself as an "innocent" victim. This is the ego's (personal thought system's) "solution" for the discomfort you feel in guilt. Yes, this is a way to avoid acknowledging that you really believe the guilt is in you. And, yes again, this reinforces guilt in your mind and delays your undoing your belief in guilt. You can only undo guilt where you really believe it is. So delay, too, could be seen as a further "attack" on yourself.

101. You Are Not A Victim; You Are Making A Choice (December 16, 2016)

Often I hear from clients who are in painful situations that they are not ready to leave. They feel powerless but they are not. And this is what I show them. They are in the situation because something they value in the situation outweighs the pain of the situation. When I point this out they find what it is that they value and they feel empowered. They realize that nothing is being done to them; they are at choice.

Here are some examples. (These are generic and not from any client's specific story):

Bob's boss, Teri, finds reasons to blame Bob for things that go wrong even when Bob is not responsible. Bob has examined his own behavior in each situation and taken responsibility where it is appropriate. But he's also learned from other employees who have worked for Teri longer than Bob has that Teri always finds a scapegoat. And now it is Bob. Bob is unhappy and feels powerless. But he doesn't leave because he needs the income and he has no other job prospects. When it is pointed out to him that he chooses to stay because his desire for the income outweighs the pain of staying Bob feels better. Whenever he is tempted to feel like a victim he reminds himself that he is making a choice and why he is making that choice. This make him feel empowered and he finds he is able to push back in a charge-neutral way when Teri blames him for mistakes that are not his. This has made his job less stressful.

Janelle's Aunt Betty is a bitter, complaining woman who is never satisfied and never grateful. Betty is elderly and needs a lot of assistance around the home and with errand-running and doctor visits. Janelle is the one in the family who has the time to take care of Betty but she resents this. Betty is very hard to be around. When asked why she takes care of Betty, Janelle thinks about it and says it is because family is important to her. She also does not want to have any regrets when Betty is gone. She wants to be able to look at herself as a "good niece". It is pointed out to Janelle that she takes care of Betty for herself. After recognizing this, when she is tempted to feel like a victim, Janelle is able to remind herself, "I am doing this for myself. I am doing this because family, no matter how obnoxious, is important to me. I am doing this so that I don't have regrets later." She has shifted to feeling empowered about taking care of Betty. Feeling empowered she has also found compassion for Betty, who Janelle now realizes is just a frightened old lady. She still does not enjoy taking care of Betty but she no longer feels powerless.

Krista is unhappy in her marriage to Mark. He is selfish and distant and has no interest in learning and growing to make their marriage better. When asked why she stays she says that if she leaves him her income will be enough to live on but her lifestyle will be greatly reduced. Wavering between staying and leaving has been a very close thing. Until now maintaining her lifestyle only just outweighed the pain of staying in the relationship. When she sees that staying is her choice based on her values she realizes she is not a victim. She comes to the realization that her fear of a lifestyle change is really not greater than the pain of staying in a dead-end relationship. She feels empowered to make the choice to leave.

In any situation in which you are unhappy you are always at choice. The power is yours. You stay because the pain (fear and/or practical considerations) of leaving outweighs the pain of staying. Be honest with yourself. Find what it is that you value more than what you would gain by leaving. Then you will understand your choice, accept it, and feel empowered. Or you will find that what you thought you valued is not really worth more than what you expect to gain by leaving the situation and you will be empowered to act.

(By the way, you can apply this to the question, "Why do I keep going back to ego?" You go back because you think it has something of value for you. You are not a victim of the ego; you are the one making the choice. When you learn that Truth is more valuable you will stop choosing ego.)

102. The Holy Spirit Works In You (December 23, 2016)

A Course in Miracles teaches that God (Truth) did not make the universe of form and does not come into it. Yet some students make comments to me about how the Holy Spirit made certain things happen in their lives in the world. Well, actually It didn't. The Holy Spirit is in your mind. It affects your perception of the world and your interaction with the world but It does not leave you (or anyone else) and go out into the universe of form and make things happen. If you attribute "good" things in the world as coming from the Holy Spirit, wouldn't you have to attribute "bad" things to the Holy Spirit as well? Or, perhaps, just that It is indifferent to the things that you deem as "bad" and so doesn't intervene?

The universe of form works on cause and effect at the level of form. These causes and effects are a very complex, interwoven tapestry. What you think of as "you" in the world – the self (body/personality) – is part of the universe of form. The self is the product (effect) of various causes in the world as well as of your mind. And it causes effects at the level of form. Its attitudes, behaviors, choices, and energy all interconnect with the universe of form. When you allow the Holy Spirit into your awareness It changes your mind, and therefore the attitudes, behaviors, choices, and energy of the self. These changes ripple out into the universe of form and cause different effects than if you were still almost wholly ego (personal thought system) identified. And the universe of form in turn responds to the changes in the self.

Here are some examples:

Attitude:

Nancy has spent many years growing her awareness of the Holy Spirit. It has become her Constant Companion. Her trust in It to always bring her the answers she needs has resulted in her having the confidence to handle anything that she encounters in the world. Her confidence shows and she is looked to as a leader by her family, employer, and co-workers. This has led to new responsibilities and positions in the family and at work.

Behavior:

Jorge comes from a large family that gathers often for birthdays and holidays. But he has social anxiety and used to drink heavily in social situations to deal with it. When he was drunk he was a bully and verbally abusive and no one wanted him around. The family asked him to stay away if he couldn't remain sober. He eventually turned to spirituality and as he became aware of the Holy Spirit within he took responsibility for his social anxiety. He got into therapy and was prescribed a low dose of an anti-anxiety medicine to take while he and his therapist worked on techniques to lessen his anxiety in social situations. His family and friends are happy to see the changes in his behavior and he has found his social life with his family resuming.

Choices:

Cassandra has met a nice guy who treats her with respect and that she likes a lot. She doesn't realize it but her self-respect and self-confidence were what attracted him. Soon after she met him an old boyfriend came back into her life. He was the "bad boy" type that she always found hot and sexy. But actually it was more complicated than that. She used to feel bad about herself and she was unconsciously attracted to him, and he to her, because of her lack of self-respect. He saw someone he could selfishly neglect and verbally abuse and she saw someone who treated her the way that she felt she deserved. However, when he re-entered her life, Cassandra had been on a spiritual path for a while and had become aware of the Holy Spirit within herself. She now has self-respect. She has quickly found the physical attraction to the old boyfriend empty and has no desire to get involved with him again. She chooses the new guy whose behavior toward her mirrors her self-respect.

Energy:

Carl was a very angry person. He didn't realize it but for years his angry energy was taking an unseen toll on the cells in his body. After embarking on a spiritual path he found with the Holy Spirit the sources of his anger and worked them out. He didn't know it but the positive changes in his energy had a positive, healthy effect on the cells in his body. If he had continued on as angry he would've experienced a grave illness when he was older. But his new attitude changed his energy in a positive way and halted the damage to the cells in his body. What he did see, however, was that his change in energy had an effect on those around him. His relationships became more harmonious and positive opportunities showed up at work and in his personal life.

Sometimes there is confusion about the cause for what shows up in the world because you may have a spiritual break-through at the same time something you need shows up. For example, you may hit bottom in a situation and be finally open for help. You may call out to the Holy Spirit, consciously or unconsciously. Then the help you need shows up in form. It can seem that the Holy Spirit supplied the help but what shows up in form is caused at the level of form. Where the Holy Spirit comes into it is in your recognition of the answer for your call for help. For example:

Hernanda was a compulsive over-eater and was grossly overweight. She had been on and off diets and food plans all of her adult life but she could not manage her eating. For years those around her have suggested she get help and she tried different things but she was not yet willing. When she reached middle-age she was diagnosed with diabetes. This terrified her and she hit bottom. She cried out to the Holy Spirit for help and this time she meant it. She remembered a therapist/life-coach/personal trainer she had worked with briefly years before. She recognized that this was the help she needed to get back her health. She got off to a rocky start but she stuck with it and in time lost the weight to reverse the diabetes and has been able to maintain a healthy diet with rare slips.

Help at the level of form was always there for Hernanda, but when she was truly willing the Holy Spirit was able to guide her to the form of help that would work for her at that time.

103. What If You Knew That The Ending Was Happy? (December 30, 2016)

A Course in Miracles teaches, not in one place but by cobbling ideas introduced throughout, that the unfolding story of the universe of form in time is the expression of the moment in the Mind of God (Truth) of the-idea-of-not-God/the-undoing-of-the idea-of-not-God. The idea of the opposite of God arose and was undone instantly by God's All-encompassing nature. But what was undone immediately in Truth seems in time to have begun long ago and as if it will be undone in some indefinite future. However, the outcome is inevitable; the "script is written". The idea of Not-Truth will be undone in time because it is already undone in the Mind of Truth. Looking at your life today or at the world today you cannot see this. But step out of time (Holy Instant) and you can see that everything in the story of time is perfectly a part of that undoing.

Looking at the story of the universe of form unfold is a lot like when you watch a movie. What you see on the screen already happened months ago when the action was filmed. You are looking at the past when you watch a movie. And so it is as you watch the story of the universe of form unfold. The idea behind what you see arose and was undone in an instant. It is past because it is already over and only your belief in the projection of that moment as time does it seem as though it is still happening.

You only ever see a teeny, tiny part of the story of the universe of form. To stay with the movie analogy, it is as though you dropped in on the middle of a film and you don't know how the tiny bit you see is related to what's gone before and what will come later. But what if you knew the ending? How would that color your view of the little bit you see? If you watch a movie with harrowing scenes and you don't know the ending it can be harrowing to watch. But if you know ahead of time that, no matter what happens in the middle of the movie the ending is happy, then the harrowing scenes are not so bad because you know they lead to a happy ending. You can apply this to the story of the universe of form. You can trust that, no matter what seems to happen in the little bit you will see over a single short lifetime, the greater story ends in peace. And each part is an essential part of that peace unfolding.

When something does not go your way, in your personal life or in the world at large, your personal disappointment will always flare first. But as this passes, if you invite the Awareness of Truth into your mind, It will help you to step back and look at the larger picture. You will realize, "I don't know why this happened this way. But it is all part of a larger unfolding toward a perfect ending."

"All things work together for good. There are no exceptions except in the ego's judgment." – (T-4.V.1)

"The aim of our curriculum, unlike the goal of the world's learning, is the recognition that judgment in the usual sense is impossible. This is not an opinion but a fact. In order to judge

anything rightly, one would have to be fully aware of an inconceivably wide range of things; past, present and to come." (W-10.3)

104. Free Will (January 6, 2017)

Whenever I write about the story of the universe of form unfolding as an expression of an idea that is already over, as I did last week, it brings up questions from readers about free will.

"Free will" means the ability to make choices and act independently of any other power. Immediately you can see that a "person", or "figure in the dream" as *A Course in Miracles* would call one, does not have a will that is independent from the split-mind (dreamer of the dream; Son of God). Every person's story is part of an intricate, complex unfolding of the universe of form. What feels like one's independent desires and choices is really the story of the universe of form being expressed through their seeming-individuality.

Even knowing this, your desires and choices and the actions to which you direct the self *feel* as though they are your own. You *feel* independent when you are identified with the dream figure. But knowing that the self's story is part of a greater whole you can learn to find the flow of the universe to live more harmoniously with it rather than to try to force to happen what simply is not going to happen. (I wrote about this in articles #13 and #14). You can find the purpose for the self in the flow, knowing that its unfolding story, whatever it is, is an essential part of a larger unfolding story.

In Truth there is only Truth so there is no need for a "will". (In ACIM, "God's Will" refers to God's Extension of God in God, not to God's desires in the world). Truth is whole, so there is nothing to desire, nothing to choose, nothing to make happen. But within the idea-of-not-Truth, not-Truth seems to have a "will" that is separate from Truth. The split-mind projects, or "wills", a universe of form in which to play out the idea-of-not-Truth. It is free to do this, but this freedom comes from the nature of Truth, Which does not oppose. Not-Truth is undone instantly in the Mind of Truth not through opposition but simply by Truth's All-encompassing nature. Not-Truth arising in Truth is like fire trying to start in water. It is impossible so it is over before it can start. Not-Truth is never more than an idea just as fire starting in water can be imagined but can never actually occur.

A Course in Miracles introduces the idea of free will right in its introduction:

"...Free will does not mean that you can establish the curriculum. It means only that you can elect what you want to take at a given time…"

If you read this as a seemingly-individual split-mind it refers to your *experience*, which certainly seems, to a new student, to be independently chosen. It *feels as though* you independently make the choice to learn what ACIM (or some other form of the universal curriculum) teaches. The personal experience is the narrowest reading of that passage. But if you read this as speaking of the one split-mind that projects the universe of form then it refers to how the undoing of not-Truth in time occurs independently of Truth. The outcome is inevitable but how that outcome is reached is time's, not Eternity's, story.

So your seemingly-individual will is not independent from the will of the one split-mind. It is an expression of the free will of the one split-mind.

105. "I Need Do Nothing" Discussed (January 13, 2016)

I've written a few times about how the heading in *A Course in Miracles*, "I Need Do Nothing" (T-18.VII), is universally misused by ACIM students. They read this line and their ego (personal thought system) panics because they think that they are not supposed to direct the self to do anything at all ever again so their life in the world will fall to pieces. And then their mind shuts. They are then unable to take in anything that follows that heading and they miss the point of that section entirely.

(A study hint: If you read something in ACIM that inspires fear you are misreading it with the ego. Truth inspires liberation, not fear. Put it aside for a while, then invite the Holy Spirit into your mind and read it again with Love. If you are still too afraid to let the Holy Spirit through then you may benefit from studying with someone who has more experience – like a mentor!)

The section headed by "I Need Do Nothing" is really about the release from guilt that you find in the Holy Instant. In the Holy Instant you realize that you are Home in God, not separate from God, so you are not guilty. Therefore, you "need do nothing" – you don't have to perfect the self or make it "right" or "good" - to be released from guilt. This section has nothing to do with ceasing all activity of the body. It is solely about the mind. In fact, it acknowledges the "busy doing" of the body in the world.

Since this section is almost never read as it was meant, I thought I'd take you through it paragraph by paragraph to ease the anxiety that the heading seems to evoke in students' minds.

(The italicized parts are from ACIM and from my translation of the Text into plain language, *The Message of A Course in Miracles* (MACIM). I use both here so you can choose which you prefer. My comments then follow and are not italicized).

(T-18.VII);(MACIM-18.7) I Need Do Nothing

(ACIM)
1. You still have too much faith in the body as a source of strength. What plans do you make that do not involve its comfort or protection or enjoyment in some way? This makes the body an end and not a means in your interpretation, and this always means you still find sin attractive. No one accepts Atonement for himself who still accepts sin as his goal. You have thus not met your one responsibility. Atonement is not welcomed by those who prefer pain and destruction.

(MACIM)
1. You still have too much faith in the body as a source of strength. All your plans involve the body's comfort, protection, or enjoyment in some way. This means that you interpret the body as an end in itself and not as a means for correction and that you still find separation from God attractive. You have not accepted correction if you still have separation as your goal and therefore you have not met your one responsibility – accepting correction of your perception that you are separate from God. You will not welcome correction while you prefer pain and Self-destruction.

You have too much faith in the body <u>as a source of strength</u>. [The "body" in ACIM includes the physical body, the personality of the self, and the thought system of the self (ego)]. That's why you are so concerned with it. You see it as an end in itself, so you are attracted to it.

This means you are unconsciously attracted to guilt (the belief that sin, or separation from God, is real). Remember, elsewhere in ACIM it says that your "sole responsibility" is to accept the Atonement (correction of your belief that you are guilty for being separate from God) for yourself. Your attraction to the body, therefore your belief in guilt, makes you believe that correction is impossible. So you do not meet your one responsibility of accepting correction. You won't welcome correction while guilt (pain and destruction) seems meaningful to you.

(ACIM)
2. There is one thing that you have never done; you have not utterly forgotten the body. It has perhaps faded at times from your sight, but it has not yet completely disappeared. You are not asked to let this happen for more than an instant, yet it is in this instant that the miracle of Atonement happens. Afterwards you will see the body again, but never quite the same. And every instant that you spend without awareness of it gives you a different view of it when you return.

(MACIM)
2. There is one thing you that have never done: completely forgotten the body. Perhaps it has sometimes faded from your awareness but it has never completely disappeared from your awareness. You are asked to do this for only an Instant but in that Instant the miracle of correction happens. After that Instant you will be aware of the body again but never in quite the same way. Every Instant that you spend without an awareness of the body will give you a different view of it when you return to an awareness of it.

Helen is being told that she has not yet allowed a Holy Instant, Which is described here as completely forgetting the body for an instant. (As you read this you may or may not have allowed a Holy Instant). An instant is all that is needed. In that instant you realize that the body and the story for time are not real. You are not separate from God so you are not guilty. Even though it is only an instant, it is enough to change how you view the body. You begin to realize that the body has nothing to offer; it is just a temporary experience as you learn to remember God. The body is no longer an end in itself; it is a means to remember God. The more you experience the Holy Instant the less you value the body.

(ACIM)
3. At no single instant does the body exist at all. It is always remembered or anticipated, but never experienced just <u>now</u>. Only its past and future make it seem real. Time controls it entirely, for sin is never wholly in the present. In any single instant the attraction of guilt would be experienced as pain and nothing else, and would be avoided. It has no attraction <u>now</u>. Its whole attraction is imaginary, and therefore must be thought of in the past or in the future.

(MACIM)
3. There is no instant in which the body exists at all. You always remember it or anticipate it but you never experience it now. Only the personal self's seeming past and projected future make the body seem real to you. Time controls your perception of the body entirely because your perception of separation from God is never wholly in the present. In any single instant you experience the attraction of separation from God as pain and nothing else and if you recognized

this you would avoid it. Guilt has no attraction to you now. Its whole attraction to you is imaginary and therefore you must think of in the past or in the future.

Time is the illusion on which all other illusions rest. This includes the body. You have a story for the body's (self's) past and you imagine its future and this is what makes it seem real to you. Your attraction to the self's story means that, unconsciously, you are attracted to guilt. The story for the body, which is the story of your guilt for being separate from God, contains stories of guilt from the body's imagined past and you expect punishment for your guilt in the body's future. You have a hard time being present because guilt arises in your mind and you experience how painful guilt is. So your mind avoids guilt in the present in an imagined past and an anticipated future in which you do not consciously see the guilt.

(ACIM)
4. It is impossible to accept the holy instant without reservation unless, just for an instant, you are willing to see no past or future. You cannot prepare for it without placing it in the future. Release is given you the instant you desire it. Many have spent a lifetime in preparation, and have indeed achieved their instants of success. This course does not attempt to teach more than they learned in time, but it does aim at saving time. You may be attempting to follow a very long road to the goal you have accepted. It is extremely difficult to reach Atonement by fighting against sin. Enormous effort is expended in the attempt to make holy what is hated and despised. Nor is a lifetime of contemplation and long periods of meditation aimed at detachment from the body necessary. All such attempts will ultimately succeed because of their purpose. Yet the means are tedious and very time consuming, for all of them look to the future for release from a state of present unworthiness and inadequacy.

(MACIM)
4. Until you are willing to see no past and no future for just an Instant you will have reservations about the Holy Instant. You cannot prepare for the Holy Instant without placing It in the future. The instant that you desire the Holy Instant you will be released in It. In the world that you perceive one way to God is to spend your time preparing for the Holy Instant and this does have its moments of success. This course does not attempt to teach more than that path teaches in time but it does aim at saving time. You may be trying to follow a very long road to the Goal of God that you have accepted. It is extremely difficult for you to reach total correction of your perception that you are separate from God by fighting against perceived "sin". You will have to expend enormous effort trying to make Holy the body that the personal mind despises. It is also not necessary for you to spend a lifetime in contemplation and long periods of meditation aimed at detachment from the body. All these attempts would ultimately succeed because of their Purpose but these means are tedious and very time consuming and they all look to the future for release from a present state of unworthiness and inadequacy.

You must be willing to let go of time, the body, and therefore guilt, just for an instant, to experience the Holy Instant. That is all. If you think you need to prepare for the Holy Instant you are putting release from guilt off into the future. The belief that it takes time to be released from guilt puts distance between you and the Holy Instant. You don't have to perfect the body (fight against sin), which is so difficult because the ego despises it. You don't have to take yourself off to a cave or a monastery and spend a lifetime struggling to detach from the body. These would ultimately work, but they are the long way to peace because they make sin (guilt) real to you and put peace off to the future. Instead, you can use the Holy Instant right now and save time.

(ACIM)
5. Your way will be different, not in purpose but in means. A holy relationship is a means of saving time. One instant spent together with your brother restores the universe to both of you. You are prepared. Now you need but to remember you need do nothing. It would be far more profitable now merely to concentrate on this than to consider what you should do. When peace comes at last to those who wrestle with temptation and fight against the giving in to sin; when the light comes at last into the mind given to contemplation; or when the goal is finally achieved by anyone, it always comes with just one happy realization; "I need do nothing."

(MACIM)
5. Your way is different from these paths, not in Purpose, but in means. A Holy relationship is a means of saving time. One instant of Holiness that you extend to your relationship with another restores Reality to your mind. You are prepared for the Holy Instant and all that you now need to remember is that you need do nothing. It is far more useful now for you to concentrate on this than to consider what you should do. When Peace comes at last after wrestling with temptation and fighting against "sin", when enlightenment comes after a lifetime of contemplation, or when the Goal is achieved in any way it will come with the happy realization: "I need do nothing".

Helen and Bill are being told that they are given a different means, the Holy Relationship, to save time. But what can you, who may not have a Holy Relationship, do to save time? Remember from earlier in ACIM that the Holy Relationship is the expression in time of the Holy Instant. But whether you have this expression available or not the Holy Instant is still available to you and to everyone. No one needs to prepare for it. All you need is willingness to put aside guilt and experience God. The realization, *"I need do nothing"* to make yourself not guilty comes when you are willing to recognize that you are already not guilty.

(ACIM)
6. Here is the ultimate release which everyone will one day find in his own way, at his own time. You do not need this time. Time has been saved for you because you and your brother are together. This is the special means this course is using to save you time. You are not making use of the course if you insist on using means which have served others well, neglecting what was made for you. Save time for me by only this one preparation, and practice doing nothing else. "I need do nothing" is a statement of allegiance, a truly undivided loyalty. Believe it for just one instant, and you will accomplish more than is given to a century of contemplation, or of struggle against temptation.

(MACIM)
6. Here is the ultimate release that you will eventually find. You do not need time for this because time has been saved for you since you extended your Self to your perception of another. This is the special means that this course uses to save you time. You are not making use of this course if you insist on neglecting the means that was made for you in favor of other means. Save time for your Christ Mind with this one preparation and practice doing nothing else: "I need do nothing." This is a statement of undivided allegiance to your Christ Mind. Believe it for just one

instant and you will accomplish more than you would accomplish in a century of contemplation or of struggle against temptation.

The Holy Instant is the moment of release, or forgiveness, from guilt. It is the special means offered by ACIM as a short-cut for those who are willing to use it. You only have to be willing to realize that you "need do nothing" to make yourself guiltless because you have never left God and so are not guilty. Your willingness to use the Holy Instant attests to your commitment to peace. If you just accept for one instant the awareness that you are Home in God you accomplish in that instant what others have taken a century to accomplish through contemplation and attempts to make the self perfect.

(ACIM)

7. To do anything involves the body. And if you recognize you need do nothing, you have withdrawn the body's value from your mind. Here is the quick and open door through which you slip past centuries of effort, and escape from time. This is the way in which sin loses all attraction <u>right now</u>. For here is time denied, and past and future gone. Who needs do nothing has no need for time. To do nothing is to rest, and make a place within you where the activity of the body ceases to demand attention. Into this place the Holy Spirit comes, and there abides. He will remain when you forget, and the body's activities return to occupy your conscious mind.

(MACIM)

7. To "do" involves the body. When you recognize that you need do nothing you will withdraw the body's value from your mind. This is the door through which you quickly slip past centuries of effort to escape from time. This is the way that the separation loses all of its attraction for you now because you deny time and the past and the future are gone for you. When you need do nothing you have no need for time. For you to do nothing is for you to rest and to make a place within your mind where the activity of the body ceases to demand your attention. The Holy Spirit then comes into and abides in this place of rest within you. And the Holy Spirit will remain with you when you forget again and the body's activities return to occupy your conscious mind.

When you recognize from the Holy Instant that you don't need to perfect the body to be with God and be released from guilt you release yourself from valuing the body. It, and therefore guilt, cease to attract you *right now*. You don't need time to do this. You just need to rest in the Holy Instant with the Holy Spirit. And the Holy Spirit will remain in your mind when you return your mind to the body's activities.

(ACIM)

8. Yet there will always be this place of rest to which you can return. And you will be more aware of this quiet center of the storm than all its raging activity. This quiet center, in which you do nothing, will remain with you, giving you rest in the midst of every busy doing on which you are sent. For from this center will you be directed how to use the body sinlessly. It is this center, from which the body is absent, that will keep it so in your awareness of it.

(MACIM)

8. There is always this place of rest within you. Within it you are more aware of the Quiet Center than of the storming personal mind raging around it. This Quiet Center in Which you do nothing remains with you and gives you rest in the midst of all the busy doing to which the Holy Spirit sends you. From this Center you will be directed in how to use the body for correction of your perception of separation from God. It is this Center, from Which the body is absent, that will keep you aware that the body cannot separate you from God.

The Holy Instant is always with you, a Quiet Place within to Which you can return to rest. The more you practice it the more aware you will be of a Quiet Center as you go about the body's busy-ness. From the Quiet Center you will be directed how to use the body in a way that will not increase your guilt because it is from this Center that you know that you are not guilty.

As you can see, there is nothing in this section about ceasing all of the self's activities. On the contrary, it makes statements in the last two paragraphs that acknowledge the activities and busy-ness of the self. Moreover, this section emphasizes the ongoing message of ACIM: You don't have to prepare yourself for God by perfecting the self. All you need is willingness, which is of the mind, to be released from guilt and to experience God. So why would it then tell you that you have to live a certain way? This would contradict its central message of forgiveness, which is that nothing you do or do not do as a person has any effect on God at all. This is hard to accept because needing only to have a willing mind completely cuts out the body and ego from the process. This is what this section is explaining.

You bring the Holy Instant with you into the midst of a normal life in the world. You don't have to stay in a Holy Instant. You only have to be willing to practice it a few times a day. And it becomes the means through which you grow your awareness of God. This releases you from the value that you have put on the self, and therefore from valuing separation from God and guilt.

106. Correcting "this is not real" Mistakes (January 20, 2017)

A Course in Miracles reminds us that only the Truth is true (only God is real). Truth (formless Being) is Reality. The universe of form is not-Truth or is not reality. You come to understand this not through your intellect but through what I call a "higher" miracle. These are shifts in your perception where you actually experience the Truth as true and you see that the universe of form is not real. Sometimes the focus of the higher miracle is more on one or the other of these but what's essential to understand is this is an *experience* not just an intellectual acceptance of an idea, or belief.

Here are three mistakes students make applying the idea "this is not real" to the world:

First, students try to apply this idea without having experienced it. This leads to feeling depressed and de-motivated: "Why should I bother doing anything when it isn't real?" Until you have experiences that show you that the universe of form is not real just forget about applying this idea. You cannot apply it without misusing it unless you have experienced it. What you can do is be open to having experiences that show you that the world is not real. Instead of focusing on "this is not real" focus instead on growing your awareness of Truth in your everyday life. Your trust in Truth will grow and this will prepare you to have experiences that show you What is real and what is not real.

The actual shift that occurs from the experience of a higher miracle is release from guilt and fear. It is a joyful, uplifting experience. When you realize that you cannot affect Truth with anything that you do or do not do in the world you feel set free to allow the self to do what is authentic to it without judgment. It takes many higher miracles for this awareness to sink in, however. Right after a higher miracle you may experience the ego's (personal thought system's) resistance and feel de-motivated and depressed for a while. But you can always counter these by remembering the liberation that you experienced at the time of the miracle. Once you have experienced a higher miracle you have a basis to start applying "this is not real" by remembering the higher miracle.

Another mistake that students commonly make is to try to apply "this is not real" to singular events or circumstances. "How can I see this horrible event is not real?" What you imply to your mind is that only this "bad" event is not real but everything else is real. It is impossible for your mind to accept this division. And it is also not an appropriate application. When you have an experience of "this is not real" it encompasses the whole universe of form, not just certain aspects of it. You must be willing to turn away from *all* illusion, not just those aspects that you judge as "bad".

The third mistake is closely related to this last one. Students try to see that an event or circumstance, or even the entire universe of form, is not real while looking right at it. I don't mean looking at it with the body's eyes, because what the eyes report is neutral and has no meaning in itself. Students look right at their interpretation of the event or circumstance and at the same time try to see it is not real. But looking at it and interpreting it is exactly how you make it real to you! You cannot give illusion meaning and at the same time see it is not real. You cannot detach from illusion with the thought system that is part of it. You cannot be in the midst of illusion and see it is an illusion. You must step into the Awareness of Truth (Holy Spirit) to see that illusion is illusion.

In practice this means you have to be willing to turn your mind away from illusion and inward to Truth. Instead of focusing on what is not real, you must look toward What *is* Real. The body's eyes may continue to report the same forms but your mind will shift toward Truth. The personal thought system's interpretation will fall away and you will see the forms that the body's eyes report as insignificant.

In fact, it is always best for you to allow the awareness "this is not real" to arise spontaneously. It will do so as you grow your awareness of Truth. If you have had experiences of seeing the universe of form is not real you can try to invite the experience again by applying "this is not real", but if you do not experience a shift then stop trying. Instead, turn to Truth and the awareness will come.

107. The "Evidence" for Truth (January 27, 2017)

My wife and her friends play role-playing games, online and in person. They create elaborate fantasy worlds and if you overhear them you hear how real their characters (avatars) and fantasy worlds are to them. Years ago I had huge judgments against this. There was one friend of hers in particular that I judged as immature and unable to deal with life. He "hid out" in these fantasy worlds. I couldn't just release these judgments so I realized I must be projecting. I was willing to look at my own thoughts and beliefs with the Holy Spirit (Awareness of Truth in my mind) and what came up out of the depths of my subconscious mind was, "How is this any different from what you do with *A Course in Miracles*?"

*Whoa…*what??

Here was the ego's (personal thought system's) total unawareness of Truth. Of course Truth is not real to it because it is the opposite of Truth and cannot understand Truth. But my projections of judgment meant I held its lack of awareness of Truth as my own doubts about

Truth. In dark periods of severe doubt I'd listen to the ego explain away my spiritual experiences and fear it was right. For example, it would say that my Revelations and higher miracles were just the result of random chemical or electrical changes in the brain. It would mock me for thinking that certain "convenient" thoughts were the "Holy Spirit". It would tell me that I was just an anxious person who could not cope with life so I had to "hide out" in a fantasy of another reality that I called "Truth", etc. It could be quite vicious and frankly convincing.

"Faith" is not a word I've ever liked because for me it has the connotation of "blind faith", which means believing in something without evidence. And "belief" is just an intellectual acceptance of ideas anyway. Faith and belief were never enough for me. But *trust* is different. Trust comes naturally through experience. Trust is not something that one can fake. You either trust or you don't so pretending to trust (blind faith) is extraordinarily stressful. And I felt I deserved more than just "faith" or "belief". I didn't want mere ideas or the stress of pretending. What I wanted was evidence so I could *trust*. If Truth is true, I reasoned, there has to be evidence of It somewhere in my experience so I could learn to trust It.

Agonizing episodes of doubt eventually resolved when in time a quiet knowing returned. But when I found I feared that the ego was right about Truth being a fantasy I realized I needed more. I needed irrefutable evidence. But where? I went through my experiences of Truth and found that the ego was right that everything *could* be explained away...Except for one thing: The transformations that had occurred in me since I began the path to Truth and inner peace. Putting aside the experiences of Revelation, higher miracles, and everyday miracles, which the ego could explain away, there were huge shifts within me that could not be explained. I had peace, confidence, detachment, and a deep sense of security in always having the Answer with me. But there was no one working on me. So there *was* Something working *in* me. And it wasn't what I had always thought of as "me" because certainly I had never worked hard at the process. I had done a lousy job with the Workbook. I was a terrible meditator. I never reached a quiet mind or a transcendental state. I was inconsistent and rather lax with any practice. I spent most of my time, in meditation and throughout the day, in ego. Where I did work hard on myself is not where transformation ever came because I was always focused on the wrong things: the ego and the self. When peace came to me it came apart from them, which was so unexpected to me. So *much* of the path unfolded in ways I never expected or imagined or even knew was possible. I had no idea *what* in my mind needed to be done and *where* in my mind it needed to be done to be at peace. So I could not possibly have caused the transformations I'd experienced with what I had always thought of as "myself". My only contribution to these transformations was willingness for them to occur. And this willingness was not my submitting my will to someone with a stronger will to transform me. Not only was there no such person but how would they do this anyway since the transformations were *within* me? It had to be that there was Something within my mind beyond the body and the ego that is untouched by them but transforms my experience of them and myself when I am willing. This was the "evidence" of Truth that I could trust.

108. "I am not a body, I am free..." (February 3, 2017)

Sometimes when I share with my clients that I used to take certain ideas and phrases in *A Course in Miracles* and meditate on them to take them deeper they want an example. So here is an example of what I mean by meditating on a concept:

"I am not a body. I am free.

For I am still as God created me." (W-Review VI-intro.3)

Notice how this phrase begins with a negative but quickly fills in the blank: "I am not a body. I am free." It is never a good practice to stay in a negative or "not" phrase. It would leave me in emptiness. The obvious question that arises in my mind with the negative "I am not a body" is "Then what am I?" So the answer is immediately given: "I am *free.*"

What is fascinating is that what I am is not described as something abstract like "I am Spirit" or "I am Mind". Instead ACIM gets to the *experience* of what I am: Limitless. It also reveals with the word "free" that my identification with a body is the reason that I feel limited. So instead of trying to conceptualize what I am in Truth, I should pay attention to my *experience*. I recognize that I am aware of Truth by the experience of freedom or liberation or limitlessness.

Then: "For I am still as God created me." "For" meaning "because" and "still" meaning "nothing has changed". I am still Limitless because God's Creation is not changed by my temporary experience of the limited body. Elsewhere in ACIM it redefines "creation" as "extension". The limitless Extension of God's Being is God's "Creation". I am Limitless because God's Limitless Being extends into me. This is just another way of saying that, in Truth, God and I are one and the same.

In my translation of the Workbook of ACIM into plain, everyday language (*Practicing A Course in Miracles*) I bring all of this forward:

"I am not a body. I am Limitless, because I am Eternally One with God." (P-Review 6-intro.3)

109. Ask: Can you clarify "God created love"? (February 10, 2017)

"... I don't recall precisely where in ACIM, but I remember reading the sentence "God Created Love." This sentence struck me as, in my thought process, it implied at one point Love did not exist in God's Awareness or at least was not as Complete in His Awareness as it is now. (Trying not to include "time" in this concept.) I also believe the statement was made "God IS Love" (emphasis I believe is mine).

After some attention on this (and I realize the disadvantage of trying to understand God from my particular viewpoint), I came to the conclusion that Awareness by Nature is expansive and seeks to increase. As such, it would explain a God that increases in Awareness— that is "Expansive" in Nature.

If this is True, it is logical to consider that God started at a point of Awareness and increased His Awareness from that point. It is also logical to conclude that any sane and logical expansion of Awareness would ultimately reach the Awareness of the concept of Love and would realize that Love is the Ideal Scene i.e., any solution or thought or action etc. based in Perfect Love is invariably the optimum solution/action.

At that point of Awareness, the most optimum action would be to "become love." This "becoming of Love" would also suggest certain logical subsequent (time again) action(s) such as sharing and the "Creation of a Son," because love desires or foments the desire to share of itself...Do you have any thoughts on this subject? Can you clarify?" – MM

A Course in Miracles redefines many words in new ways so that, as you figure them out, you come to see how very different is your limited experience of a self from Truth (God).

"Creation" is one word that it is vital as a student of ACIM that you understand is used in a new way:

"If creation is extension, the Creator must have extended Himself, and it is impossible that what is part of Him is totally unlike the rest." (T-19.III.6)

In the world we use the word "creation" to mean "to bring something into being". As you see in this quote in ACIM "Creation" is the extension of God's Being. And God's Being is one and the same throughout. Therefore, any part of God's Extension is God and what is not like God cannot be of God. It is an illusion.

God is whole and complete so God has no need to bring something into being, to expand, or to become something. "Love" is another word in ACIM that is used differently. As people what we call "love" is attachment based on like, familiarity, family connection, etc. In ACIM, when Love refers to God, It means "wholeness". The experience of God is True Love, or wholeness.

Those passages in ACIM about God increasing are from our point of view, not God's. The idea of "extension" is also from our point of view, not from God's. In God there is only God. There are no boundaries or limitations in God so God does not need to "increase" or "extend". Into what would God do so? God? Then we are back to: In God there is only God. The idea of "extension" only arises because, from our point of view, God seems to be blocked. So ACIM uses the term "extension" to explain that God is still in your mind ("extends" into your mind) even when you are not aware of God. God seems to "increase" as more seemingly-separate minds experience God.

God is also beyond "awareness" ("perception" or "consciousness" in ACIM). God is Knowledge and what God knows is God. Again, in God there is only God. This is the meaning of "Oneness".

So "God is Love" and "God 'created' Love" simply mean God is Whole and God's Wholeness extends everywhere, always. God is All-that-is.

The experience of a self is always lack and limitation of some kind. You get fulfilled in one area temporarily and it only makes you aware of how you are not whole in another area. And then eventually you may find that are not fulfilled where you once were. You are always busy *doing*. From this perspective it is hard to understand pure Being (God), in Which you do not have to do anything to be whole. But that Wholeness is within you and it is to just this experience that ACIM leads you to open.

110. Emotional Satisfaction or Freedom (February 17, 2017)

A few months ago I wrote a couple of articles about the two possible spiritual approaches (#86 and #87). The most common approach, the one of religions and most everyone else on a spiritual path, is to spiritualize the self and its life in the world. The other approach is to transcend the self.

A while later I was having a discussion with my wife, Courtney. Her path is to spiritualize where mine is to transcend. I have never put it in those words to her because from past experience I know that she doesn't understand my desire for liberation from the limitations of the self. In this discussion she said, again, that she finds my spirituality to be cold and cerebral. She wants warmth; she wants emotional satisfaction. I understood, but did not explain to her, that she finds my path lacking because for her it is only an idea. She has not experienced what I have. I find it joyful because for me I seek the experience of liberation that is beyond considerations of emotional coldness or warmth. Liberation transcends the human experience.

This is when I realized that another way to characterize the two possible goals is that often those who spiritualize the self are seeking for emotional connection with others and/or a Supreme Being. They seek for emotional satisfaction that is characterized as emotional "warmth". Those who seek to transcend the self seek for liberation from all limitation, including emotional satisfaction. It is easy to see how, to those who seek to spiritualize life in the world, "liberation" may seem emotionally "cold". But I can assure you that there is no lack in liberation.

I don't remember the first time I learned of the idea of transcending the self. I believe I was a teenager and read something about Buddhism. I do know that I immediately recognized the Truth in the idea of transcending the self and experienced a delightful taste of the liberation that was possible. Of course this was immediately followed by stark terror at the idea of dropping the self. So I shut down any thought about it but it was too late. Once tasted, liberation cannot be forgotten. It is like being a prisoner and suddenly discovering that there are no guards and the door to the outside world is open. How could you stay? I was destined to end up on some path toward liberation after that taste of it.

Emotional satisfaction has a powerful pull and it continued to attract me along the way, too. But over time I also experienced liberation more fully than just that initial taste. And there was no comparison between the two experiences. Emotional satisfaction is a puny experience compared to the power and joy of liberation from limitations. I can only think that those who do not seek liberation have simply not tasted liberation yet. Once experienced, even if only faintly, liberation draws you like metal to a magnet. Nothing else will satisfy.

111. More on Emotional Satisfaction or Freedom (February 24, 2017)

Last week's about the two possible approaches to spirituality and how one way to characterize them is the pursuit of emotional satisfaction for the self or transcending the self led to a lot of comments and questions that I will try to clear up here.

(The article was a follow-up to two other articles I had written on the same topic. Some of the questions readers had could be answered in those earlier articles and links were provided in last week's article. If you still have questions I suggest reading those as well as last week's article for a fuller look at the topic).

The emotional satisfaction I wrote about in the last article was not referring to what one seeks in relation to others. It was referring to the desire for an emotional connection with Truth (God) that one would characterize as "warm". I was highlighting how which goal we pursue in spirituality can often be revealed by the experience we seek. Many who seek to spiritualize the self and its life in the world seek an emotionally warm experience. I brought up how my wife finds my spiritual path to be cold and cerebral because she seeks emotional warmth from her spirituality. She does not find *me* cold and cerebral. And she finds our relationship emotionally satisfying. But she is also aware that our relationship is not what would make her whole. She expresses her opinion on my spiritual path as her own perception given her own goal, not as a judgment on it or as an attack on me. So I do not take her comments personally or find them offensive. As I wrote, I know her opinion arises because she has not experienced liberation so she really does not know what it is I want. Our relationship is fulfilling and harmonious to both of us because neither of us asks the other to make us whole and we both respect the other's spiritual path. Even though our spiritual goals and paths are very different what we do share is a relationship with the Holy Spirit (or what she calls her Higher Power or God). And it is to the Holy Spirit we both turn, instead of to each other, when we seek wholeness.

So as you can see emotionally warm relationships are not only possible when seeking liberation but are the result of growing spiritual awareness. It's just that for those of us who have tasted liberation from the self a warm emotional relationship with Truth for the self does not make sense. In the last article I was not saying that you cannot have both emotional warmth in the self's life and to seek liberation from the self. I was saying that as *spiritual goals* they are mutually exclusive. If you want from Truth an emotionally satisfying relationship for the self you cannot at the same time want liberation from the self. Neither path is better or worse or right or wrong. It's just what you want and it can be helpful to know which you want as you read something like *A Course in Miracles* and its teachers. Your goal for yourself will determine how you read ACIM and which teachers make sense to you.

As I mentioned in one of the earlier articles, even those who seek liberation go through a stage of spiritualizing the self. It's unavoidable at the start because the self is all you know even if you have had instants of liberation. The mind seeks to integrate the two experiences and it takes a long time to accept that a unified mind is not the result of blending the experience of the self with the experience of liberation from the self. A unified mind is what is left when the self is dropped from the mind (liberation).

Both paths are about avoiding pain. Those who seek to spiritualize the self seek a less painful life in the world. And they will be satisfied with that. Those who have tasted liberation know that it is possible to transcend pain by transcending the self. They are not just pushed toward liberation in the hopes of transcending pain. They are pulled toward liberation knowing it is possible.

Here's something I wrote that was going to be part of another article but that fits well here:

The contrast between the experiences of Truth (liberation) and not-Truth (the self) is always wondrous to me. I am always struck by how completely unlike the other is each experience. And this contrast makes it so clear to me why not-Truth can never satisfy. It is like craving steak and having only apples available. The apples may be good as far as apples go, but no matter how many you eat they will not satisfy you when you crave a steak. The texture, taste, and nutrients are all wrong. And so it is with life in the world. No matter how good it gets it is never wholly satisfying. There is always a craving for the limitlessness and wholeness that only Truth can offer.

112. Ask: How can I lead my study group out of comparisons to peace within? (March 3, 2017)

"In my ACIM study group, I notice that when we get to a passage with convoluted syntax or a concept that pushes us out of our comfort zone, we'll quickly engage in an off-topic discussion, for example, about 'the media', 'religion' or 'churches'. This is usually prompted by a participant's remark about how the world of illusions doesn't understand or live by the Course we so much appreciate. Like the rest of the group, I want to think there is something outside of me that can make me feel 'good' about the Course. I'm curious how I can find a way to let go of feeling either 'good' or 'bad' and help the group locate the source of peace within the Course text." – GB

What you describe is very typical for new students. The ego's (personal thought system's) thinking is always evaluative: right/wrong, good/bad, better/worse, etc. It's simply the way it works. But although this thinking is from the ego I suspect its source is actually the speaker's way of expressing gratitude for having found the way to peace that works for them. And what they see in the outside world is their own past—the way it used to be for them. So you could simply point this out, perhaps by stating it as your own experience: That you, too, look out at the world and see how you used to be and how grateful you are to have found your way to peace.

113. To Deny the Body is "Unworthy" of Your Mind (March 10, 2017)

All students come to *A Course in Miracles* identified with the ego (personal thought system), which is another way of saying that they come with their mind steeped in guilt. So when they read that the body is not real they think that they are guilty for identifying with it. Actually, they do *feel*, unconsciously or consciously, guilty for identifying with it, but that does not mean that they *are* guilty for identifying with it. However, reading that the body is not real only increases their guilt at first and they attempt to deal with this guilt by pretending that they do not identify with it ("I know I'm not a body, but…") or by denying or repressing their body's feelings or desires.

Denial is never the way to deal with guilt. It suppresses the source of guilt (the belief that the body is real) instead of undoing it. And denying your experience also denigrates the power of your mind, which leads to feeling powerless.

"The body is merely part of your experience in the physical world. Its abilities can be and frequently are overevaluated. However, it is almost impossible to deny its existence in this world. Those who do so are engaging in a particularly unworthy form of denial. The term "unworthy" here implies only that it is not necessary to protect the mind by denying the unmindful. If one denies this unfortunate aspect of the mind's power, one is also denying the power itself." (T-2.IV.3)

This is one of the most important quotes in ACIM because it means to prevent the very common mistake of dealing with guilt through denial. As it says, the body is only a part of your experience of the physical world. It is not wrong. You over-evaluate the body's ability to make you feel whole, which is a mistake, not a "sin". If you deny the experience of the body you deny the power of your mind, the source of your experience of it. And then you cannot move past the experience.

To move past your identification with a body you need to first acknowledge that you are the source of this identification. If you don't you will feel some other power is the source of your identification and that you are powerless to change your mind. But once you acknowledge the power of your mind and the power of its choice to identify with the body you can use this identification to grow your awareness of Truth. Invite the Holy Spirit (the Awareness of Truth in your mind) to be your partner in everything to do with the body: Its health, its diet, its relationships, its work, its interests—everything. In time, as the Holy Spirit becomes real to you and you learn to trust It, It will lead you past your identification with the body and into the Awareness of Truth. This, not denial, is what ACIM teaches you to do with the body.

114. Why Don't I Just Kill Myself and Go To Heaven? (March 17, 2017)

The usual way of thinking about getting into Heaven is to wait until the self dies. And often Heaven is something to be won through righteous living in the world. In this view there is a direct correlation between the self's life in the world and Truth (Heaven). Even if one does not have to earn Heaven it is implied that It can only be experienced when the body falls away. The body is one's obstacle to being aware of Truth and experiencing Heaven.

A Course in Miracles, however, teaches that Heaven is here within you now and all you have to do is choose to be aware of It. There is no intersection of the self's life in the world and Truth. You can experience both, but never at the same time, because they are diametrically opposed. Each cancels out the other. So the body is not an obstacle to Truth. But your *belief in* the body as your reality is. Heaven, then, is what is left when you let go of the belief in the body as your reality. This is an action of the mind and it has nothing to do with the body.

Despite this I still get this question from students of *A Course in Miracles*: "Since I don't have to earn Heaven through this life in the world why don't I just kill myself right now to go to Heaven?" The person asking this always reassures me that this is an intellectual inquiry and that they are not feeling suicidal. I explain how killing the body does not lead to Heaven because doing so also kills of that which seeks Heaven. That which is in pain in its identification with a self (body/personality) is also that which seeks relief (Heaven) from that identification. If you have never tasted ice cream but want to do so do you taste ice cream or kill yourself? Which would bring you the satisfaction you seek? Killing yourself would eliminate your desire for ice cream but it would not satisfy your desire to taste ice cream. It would also eliminate the "you" that you think wants to try ice cream.

Imagine a line stretching infinitely into the distance. It has no beginning and no ending. This line represents Truth, or Heaven, in your mind. Imagine that along part of the Infinite line a faint, wispy, finite line runs parallel to it. This finite line is the illusion of time. The finite line's beginning represents the beginning of time and its ending represents the end of time. At no point do these lines intersect.

The space between the Infinite and the finite is the split-mind (Son of God in *A Course in Miracles*). The Infinite is the Reality within it; the finite is what it imagines. It, too, begins and ends with the wispy finite.

What you think of as your individual split-mind is a tiny part of the space between the Infinite and the imagined finite. It lasts for only a tiny part of the wispy finite. Again, at no point do the Infinite and the finite intersect. The end, or "death", of a part of the finite or of the finite as a whole, does not make a bridge between the finite and the Infinite. The end, or death, of any part of the finite is part of the finite. It does not affect the Infinite at all.

Death is not a bridge between Truth and illusion. It is part of the illusion. When an illusion ends no part of it "goes on" or "crosses" over to Truth. No part of illusion becomes Truth. Truth continues on, as it did for the duration of the illusion, completely untouched by the passing of the illusion.

The split-mind only has to be willing to put aside its belief in the story of time (finite) to be aware of Heaven. Death ends belief but it does not correct it. Death defeats the object of a changed perception because perception ends with death. Suicide would end, but not satisfy, one's desire to perceive Heaven because it ends the desirer, too. A split-mind is no longer split when one part of it has fallen away.

Perception (awareness, consciousness), desire, lack—these are all temporary (time-bound) experiences. They can be satisfied in time through an awareness (perception, consciousness) of Truth. But they, and the awareness of Truth, end in time. Only Truth Itself has nothing to do with time.

115. Ask: Can you explain perception ending in time? (March 24, 2017)

(This question refers to the last article)

"...I had to draw a picture of this to begin to understand. It helped! The last paragraph I do not understand though. Could you start with that on your next newsletter and explain it a little more..." - HW

Here is the last paragraph from the last article:

"Perception (awareness, consciousness), desire, lack— these are all temporary (time-bound) experiences. They can be satisfied in time through an awareness (perception, consciousness) of Truth. But they, and the awareness of Truth, end in time. Only Truth Itself has nothing to do with time."

Using the language of *A Course in Miracles*, "Knowledge" refers to God or Truth. In God there is only God and what God knows is God. "Perception" (also "consciousness" or "awareness") refers to our split-mind's experience apart from Knowledge/God. Unlike Knowledge, where all is One, or the same throughout, perception has degrees, gradations, etc. There is the perceived and the perceiver and what is perceived varies and is variegated. The highest perception one can attain is Awareness of Truth (Holy Spirit; Christ Consciousness). This perception prepares one for Knowledge. At the highest level of perception one is still aware of the universe of form but knows it is not real. But Knowledge is beyond the universe of form. The universe of form and perception are not part of Knowledge and do not enter It at all.

Knowledge is Timeless and perception is always temporary – in time. All perception, even the perception of Truth, ends with time.

The point I was making in the article was that someone who asks the question "Why don't I just kill myself to go to Heaven?" is asking from a lower level of perception. Otherwise they would not ask the question! They are not looking to transcend desire but to satisfy their desire for Heaven. And desire can only be satisfied at the level of perception. Desire can be satisfied now, in time, not through death, when perception ends.

116. Ask: Can you clarify the ego's use of time as hell? (March 31, 2017)

"I just read in ACIM that the ego teaches that 'Heaven is here and now because the future is hell.' Then in the next chapter it says 'the Holy Spirit teaches thus: There is no hell. Hell is only what the ego has made of the present.' It seems to contradict; maybe you could talk about this in one of your future posts..." – AS

Actually, those quotes are in the same chapter and subsection (*The Two Uses of Time*) of the Text of *A Course in Miracles*, just a couple of paragraphs apart. Here is the first quote in context (my underlining):

"The ego teaches that Heaven is here and now because the future is hell. Even when it attacks so savagely that it tries to take the life of someone who thinks its is the only voice, it speaks of hell even to him. For it tells him hell is here as well, and bids him leap from hell into oblivion. The only time the ego allows anyone to look upon with equanimity is the past. And even there, its only value is that it is no more." (T-15.I.5)

Notice that this paragraph says that the ego teaches that both the present and the future are hell. So there is no contradiction to what it says two paragraphs later:

"The Holy Spirit teaches thus: There is no hell. Hell is only what the ego has made of the present." (T-15.I.7)

It also says that the ego will "allow" you to look on the past with equanimity. This does not mean, though, that when it is convenient for its purposes it will not also teach you to look on the past as hell. The ego makes hell of time, period. As it says further in that same paragraph:

"There is no escape from fear in the ego's use of time. For time, according to its teaching, is nothing but a teaching device for compounding guilt until it becomes all-encompassing, demanding vengeance forever." (T-15.I.7)

But the Holy Spirit uses the Holy Instant to release you from time:

"The Holy Spirit would undo all of this now. Fear is not of the present, but only of the past and future, which do not exist. There is no fear in the present when each instant stands clear and separated from the past, without its shadow reaching out into the future. Each instant is a clean, untarnished birth, in which the Son of God emerges from the past into the present. And the present extends forever. It is so beautiful and so clean and free of guilt that nothing but happiness is there. No darkness is remembered, and immortality and joy are now. (T-15.I.8)

117. Ask: Is the fear of death behind all upsets? (April 7, 2017)

"Like the other 7 billion people on the planet, every day I am offered opportunities to play out and examine my guilt in a myriad of ways. In the past I would ride the emotional runaway train into bad moods, depression, inertia, despair, rage against self, others and the world. After studying the Course *for a number of years however, I handle all this differently. After processing the details of the upset up to a point (which may include acting out, feeling lousy etc.), I ask the question: 'What is REALLY going on here?' The answer is always the same: There is a fear - make that terror - that if I don't find that missing sock, undo that faux pas I made that day, clear up that medical issue, put that person in his place etc. etc. - I will be cast aside and obliterated. (I know it sounds insane, even insanely funny, but think about it the next time you experience an upset.) So I ask: 'Is the fear of death behind all upsets?'"* – ES

Actually, you had it at the beginning of your question: Guilt is behind all upsets. If you believe that you are guilty you expect, and may even feel that you deserve, punishment. This is the source of your fear. It just so happens that for you the punishment that you fear for your guilt is to be "cast aside and obliterated", which is I guess how you define "death". For others, the punishment they fear may be something else. For example, fear that they will lose a loved one, or go broke, or reincarnate and go through another life, etc. Sometimes it is just a nebulous fear that "something bad will happen".

Your practice of allowing your emotions to process and then asking yourself what is really going on is a good one. It is not comfortable but it is a positive step to be in touch with the guilt and fear as they really are. This must come before you can begin to undo the guilt and therefore the fear of punishment.

118. The Self-concept Fell Away (April 14, 2017)

When this mind entered the "period of settling" (*A Course in Miracles*, M-4.I.A) the way that "he has not yet come as far as he thinks" showed up for it was to realize that the period of settling and the three periods before were only preparation for letting go of self-identification. The real shift was yet to come.

About two-and-a-half years ago this mind realized its self-concept had fallen away. It wasn't *falling* away; it *had fallen* away. This mind had entered the fifth period, the "period of unsettling". Self-identification was beginning to fall away. This mind became aware of this speaking with clients who would ask it questions about how this mind saw itself as a self. This mind would have to tell its clients it had no way to answer. Their questions left this mind disoriented because when it tried to find the answer nothing was there. Many times on the path this mind has had periods of disorientation as its self-concept shifted. But now it was unable to find even a shifting self-concept.

First, how this mind defines "self", "self-identification", and "self-concept": For this mind "self" refers to a body and personality. They are neutral forms with no meaning in themselves. When a mind's locality and perspective is through a body and personality that is its "self-identification". This includes the personal thought system (ego). A mind's "self-concept" is when a mind defines as a self, including the self's traits, experiences, story, etc. For example, the self in this mind is a teacher. That is just an aspect of her personality. She would teach in some capacity no matter what career path she took. But if this mind felt that being a teacher is what it is that would be a self-concept.

The self and the self's thought system, past, experiences, opinions, or preferences are still in this mind. But this mind does not feel a need to defend them. Defining and defending a self occur when a mind has a self-concept. This mind cannot say it does not identify with a self. But the falling away of the self-concept seems to be the beginning of the process of letting go of identifying with a self. The process of the self-concept falling away was also a gradual process though the recognition that it had occurred was sudden. Many years ago this mind realized that it had been working at being a "spiritual person". It realized that this had become an obstacle to peace and had to be released. This mind also long ago stopped having goals. In the past few years its belief in guilt fell away. At one point it occurred to it that it never, ever, under any circumstances had to listen to the thought system of the self (ego). These, and probably many other things, were part of the process of the self-concept falling away.

But what, exactly, did it mean to no longer have a self-concept? And how does a mind direct the self's life without a self-concept? There was no way to answer these questions just by thinking about them. The only thing this mind could do was continue on and let the answers unfold.

Now this mind can answer these questions:

What does it mean to no longer have a self-concept? For one thing, whenever this mind attempts to get involved in the world in some way it has an overwhelming feeling of, "I don't have to be doing this anymore. I'm past this." This mind has no desire to build or express a self-concept.

This mind finds it is no longer concerned with personal happiness and peace. Peace has come to this mind, but not to the personal thought system. The self is never happy or at peace for long, but Peace is always in this mind apart from the thought system about the self. It finds being focused on the self empty and meaningless. It does not matter one iota to it what the self experiences. Only the Truth is true so only the Truth matters.

Have you ever seen a movie where a character is dead but does not know it? They continue to interact with the world but you can tell something is always "off" in the interactions. This mind experiences the world like that. It is aware of the world but not a part of it. It is like a ghost in the world, not a part of it, no longer belonging, but watching it unfold.

How does a mind direct a self's life without a self-concept? This mind no longer thinks in terms of motivation or "why" for the self. The self is moved as the self is moved and it is all equally meaningless. This mind merely observes. So most of the time this mind does not direct the self. There is no longer a sense of deliberate doing but of the self being in the flow. The self goes through the motions; it passes time. Then it is in the flow of the universe. But when it does require directing, direction flows effortlessly from the Awareness of Truth (Holy Spirit). The boundary between this mind and the Awareness of Truth is all but gone. In fact, this mind often comes from the perspective of the Awareness of Truth as it interacts with the split-mind, or the "decision-maker", as it deals with the personal thought system.

This mind is still unlearning the habits and reflexes of maintaining a self-concept. It still automatically turns to the personal thought system for its point of view. It has to remind itself, "I don't have to think this way anymore" or "I don't have to think about this anymore." Perhaps this is what is described in ACIM about the "period of unsettling" when it says that *He must learn to lay all judgment aside…"*

It seems what has unfolded with the self-concept falling away and what continues to unfold is the self-identity falling away altogether. This mind now finds that questions like "What observes all of this unfolding?" or "What is 'this mind?'" are meaningless and any answer would be, too. The resistance of the personal thought system is no longer relevant to this mind. It just observes it. It no longer matters to this mind what happens to the self going forward because the self is unreal. It does not matter to this mind what happens to this mind because whether this mind is aware of Truth or not has no effect on Truth. Nothing at the level of perception is real. None of it matters. All that is real, all that matters, is Truth.

119. Manifesting the Undoing of Not-Truth (April 21, 2017)

After it wrote last week's article, "The Self-concept Fell Away", this mind had the sense it wasn't accurate to say that the self-concept falling away was only the beginning of self-identification falling away. What it saw was that indeed self-id had fallen away but it had not yet fully caught up to this fact.

This split awareness is not new to this mind. For many years now it has seen that life in the world is over for it. It knows this with certainty but then it is back in the story of an unfolding process of undoing. This is because it vacillates between the two diametrically opposed parts of it. In one part it is not so much that it is past the world as that it has never entered it. In the other it is in a process of leaving. It is this experience that led this mind to truly understand how the universe of form is the unfolding in time of an idea (not-Truth) that was over as soon as it was thought. This split-mind is the manifestation of this.

For one part of this mind there has never been a self. For another it is in a process of self-id falling away. This experience of diametrically opposed views of the same subject is beginning to extend into other experiences as well. One moment this mind is immersed in something in the world and the next it has a 180-degree change in view and sees that it is nothing. This, too, is not new to this mind. What is new is how often, how quickly, and how starkly the shift occurs and comes into focus. What was once theory and then rare and vague experience is becoming a more frequent, more immediate experience. And all this mind has to do is watch it unfold. That is all this mind has ever had to do, but it took a lot of learning to know this.

120. Keep An Open Mind As the Undoing Unfolds Through You (April 28, 2017)

Back in 2014 when this mind described to a client its then-recent inability to answer some questions about the self within it he recommended the book, *"The Experience of No-Self"* by Bernadette Roberts. Ms. Roberts was a contemplative nun for 8 years but left the convent and returned to the world (or, as she calls it, "the marketplace"). However, she continued to live a contemplative life as she became a wife and mother, among other things. One day, after over 30 years on the journey, while meditating she discovered that she could not locate her self. And, even more disturbing for her, she could not find God because she was used to being in union with God and now there was no longer a self and an "Other" with which to be in union. She had not been seeking this and she had no idea it would happen.

At the time of reading this, this mind was uncertain exactly what it was experiencing or was about to experience so it was unsure if our journeys were arriving at the same place (both yes and no). But this mind was struck by how Ms. Roberts' expectations determined what, in the end, had to be undone in her mind to grow more fully aware of Truth. This mind realized it was in for the same undoing of expectations, though this mind's expectations were different from Ms. Roberts' expectations. For example, Ms. Roberts had read and experienced what is found in traditional Christian contemplative thought and this shaped her expectations. She had sought and found the union of God-within, or a "higher self", with God-without only to have that blown out of the water that day. She did not know that the self would fall away. This mind had not sought "union" of any kind because it saw the inherent separation in that idea. It sought to be aware of the Oneness (Unity or Wholeness) that is already within but of Which it was not consciously aware. This mind *did* expect that would lead to a "self" falling away. But it also, sometimes overtly, sometimes rather subtly, expected it to be replaced by a "Higher Self" experience of some kind. Instead this mind found that all self, in fact all "identity", falls away.

Your mind's manifestation of the undoing of not-Truth is very specific to the way your seemingly-individual mind works. You cannot help but form expectations of how this will be. You hear and read things and you automatically form concepts. But these can eventually become obstacles, too. Sometimes you will be constrained by the shape they take; sometimes you won't see beyond them to what else could occur; sometimes, you will miss miracles and shifts because they did not take a form you expected; sometimes you will be looking for shifts in the wrong place [as I did for so long waiting for the ego (personal thought system) to change]. The lesson is not to fight your expectations. Let them arise but also keep an open mind. You will find, as Ms. Roberts did, and as I have so often, that your path will not unfold how you thought it would because your expectations were based on what you thought you already knew. But remember, Where you are headed is completely unlike what you already think you know. So could you really know how to get There?

121. Ask: Guilt always seems to triumph so why bother? (May 5, 2017)

"In a recent mentoring session I spoke with you about a situation involving a woman I had been seeing who turned out to be a disappointment. Upon reflection I saw that she was a poor choice in the first place… I took what I considered to be a mountain of evidence to support my conclusion and thought I could call the whole thing a mistake on my part and simply walk away. While my feet did the walking, my mind continued to be haunted by the details with a vague sense that somehow this was my fault. I could see that this could be explained by the concept of "generalized guilt" that you often talk about, but the guilt remained.

I had a chance to talk about this with a woman I met recently whom I would describe simply as a peer – someone with life experience, intelligence, insight, and credibility. She responded unequivocally that this woman was not for me and that I could do much better. I immediately felt a calming resolution from this interaction. (Whether it lasts time will tell.) I wondered about what chemistry between me and this "peer" led to this resolution when nothing else I tried seemed to get the job done.

In any case, here I am attempting to practice the Course, *fully accepting the truth of its guilt model. I've also trimmed down my expectations for I can achieve realistically at this time. I also simplified my practice to examining the facts when encountering obstacles and fostering a relationship with the HS. But when all is said and done what stands out is that for me GUILT WILL ALWAYS TRUMP THE FACTS. So what the f*** am I doing this for? I feel like a fraud and a chump for bothering.*

So Liz, can you give me a good reason to continue along this path, including mentoring with you?" – Anonymous

First, the guilt you described seems to have been about something specific rather than generalized guilt. Generalized guilt is when you feel guilty for no reason. "Generalized guilt" is really just the description of what it feels like to identify with the ego (personal thought system). But guilt over something specific can be relieved by undoing it somehow. For example, by bringing to conscious awareness a false belief and undoing it with the Holy Spirit. Or, as seemed to happen for you, by an unconscious belief being undone by something happening in your conscious world.

You were relieved of guilt when your peer validated you. The guilt was for something specific – perhaps a sense of personal failing that your friend erased by validating your perceptions and actions. The "chemistry" between you and your friend is simply that she is someone you respect and whose judgment you trust. You also must have been willing to be relieved of guilt. This is a good example of "the Holy Spirit always answers". Sometimes you hear It directly in your mind; sometimes Its answer comes through a book or a person or something you hear on TV or in a song. You were willing to be relieved of guilt, you felt moved to share your story with someone you trust, and she said what you needed to hear to release the guilt.

You seem to have missed the miracle! Guilt did not triumph; you let it go. Perhaps if you can see this you will find reason to continue on the path, which, as you are guided, may or may not include further mentoring with me.

122. What if I (or they) run out of time? (May 12, 2017)

A concern of many who work with or contact me is that they will "run out of time", meaning, that they will die before they reach what they consider "enlightenment" or "awakening". Some also are concerned about loved ones who have no interest in being enlightened. What about them?

[Spiritual *awakening* or *enlightenment* can mean different things to different people. But I find in general that what spiritual students mean by these terms is a *sustained* awareness that *only* the Truth is true. This would be the highest level of awareness (consciousness, perception) one could attain. It is also known as Christ or Buddha Consciousness.]

The question of running out of time is a personal one of course. There is fear behind it that one must attain enlightenment before they die or they will end up in purgatory or have to come back in another life. But both views represent a mistaken view of what life in the world is about. It is not a cause for a future effect, as in, if you do it right you will go to Heaven. It is an effect, or expression, of an idea long past (discussed below). So you cannot "run out of time" with regard to your role to play because how your life unfolds, whatever degree of awareness you attain, is the perfect expression of that idea through you

Now, let's get into the idea that is the universe of form:

True Being ("God" in *A Course in Miracles*) is formless, infinite, eternal (timeless) and the same throughout (one). Mind is the aspect of Being through which Being knows Itself. (Mind, Being, Truth – these terms are all interchangeable). Being All, the Mind of Truth must contain the idea of Its Own opposite. But being All, Truth cannot have an opposite. It is as though Truth thought, "What is my opposite? Oh, yeah: I'm All; I cannot have an opposite." So the idea of not-Truth was over as soon as it was thought. It was cancelled out by Truth's All-encompassing nature.

Since Truth is formless, infinite, eternal, and the same throughout, the idea of not-Truth is time-bound, limited, diverse form. So *within the idea of not-Truth* it seems as though the idea of not-Truth began long ago as a universe of form and will be undone in some indefinite future. The experience of time is the idea of not-Truth/the undoing of the idea of not-Truth unfolding. The outcome of this unfolding is inevitable because the idea of not-Truth is already undone. In other words, everything in time is heading toward the inevitable conclusion of undoing.

So, let's get back to you and your part (and everyone else's). What are you? The part of the Mind of Truth where the idea of not-Truth seems to occur is called the split-mind because it is still a part of Truth but it seems to also contain not-Truth. It seems to be split off from Truth and it seems to be split between Truth and not-Truth. (In ACIM this part of the Mind of God is called the "Son of God"). This split-mind is where the universe of form and its story seems to occur. And the split-mind is projected into the universe of form as billions of versions of itself in forms, or bodies. Each mind seems to be split between Truth (the Awareness of Truth or "Holy

Spirit" in ACIM) and not-Truth (personal thought system or "ego" in ACIM). But each mind is at first only aware of not-Truth, or the personal thought systems in it, and identifies with a body.

Because the outcome of the story of time is inevitable, everyone's life is a part of the Undoing (the "Atonement" in ACIM). However, only some minds manifest overtly the Undoing. This is expressed as a mind becoming aware of the Truth within it to whatever degree. Some may have only glimpses of Truth and really know for only a moment or moments that the Truth is true. Others may attain a full awareness that only the Truth is true. But whether one is aware of Truth at all, and if one is aware to whatever degree they attain, it is really all the same because every life is an expression of the Undoing. So no one can fail to do their part. No one can "run out of time" in that sense.

I realize this is small consolation when your focus is on your own personal experience. You may not care about the bigger picture. You may only want to know what you are going to get out of it. But if you are drawn to grow your awareness of Truth that is your part to play and you will play it out as far as you can. You won't be able to help yourself because that is your part to play. And in time you will come to see the larger picture and it will mean more to you than your personal attainment.

What about those you love who have no conscious awareness of Truth and no desire for it? They, too, are playing their part perfectly. If nothing else, they are your teachers in forgiveness and in that way they lead you to further manifesting the Undoing.

No matter what you feel motivated to do or motivated to not do that is the story of the universe of form, the Undoing, unfolding through you. This is true of the spiritual and what does not seem spiritual. You cannot see this "down on the ground" in the midst of the story. And knowing this is not necessarily helpful in the day-to-day of life. But it is helpful to remember this when you do not like what is unfolding for you personally or in the world at large. You can step back and remember that no matter how it looks now it is the Undoing unfolding. As you quiet your mind to be aware of Truth you will find that you also become more aware of your part in the flow of the universe. And you can be reassured that, as far as your part goes, you cannot fail; you cannot "run out of time".

123. Ask: Is there anything this separate sense of self is responsible for? (May 19, 2017)

"Liz, thank you for your recent post on what if I run out of time. It's helped me to stop struggling and let things play out. My question is: Is there anything this separate sense of self is responsible for?..." – AS

Yes:

"The sole responsibility of God's teacher is to accept the Atonement for himself. Atonement means correction, or the undoing of errors." (M-18.4)

Now that you are aware of the Undoing of the idea-of-not-Truth (the "Atonement" in *A Course in Miracles*) you are responsible for accepting the Undoing for yourself. This may seem to contradict what I wrote last week about the Undoing's unfolding being inevitable. But "down here on the ground", as it were, the Undoing unfolds *through* your taking responsibility for correcting in your own mind the error of believing in not-Truth. This shows up in your day to day life as whatever study and practice you feel moved to do. And also what you feel not moved to do, as well. From now on, however you feel moved, it is the manifest expression of the Undoing.

I realize that this is something that you probably cannot see. I can only see it for myself in hindsight. Once I had an experience of Truth my path was set. Often I felt I'd wandered off or that I was failing. But all of that was really a part of the path. My part with regard to making a choice was really over. I accepted Truth into my awareness and I was taken along from there. All of my efforts to force it to happen were not necessary. I just needed to check in everyday with the Awareness of Truth (Holy Spirit) in my mind and trust that what efforts were needed by me would arise organically.

I wish I could've trusted this. It would have made it a lot easier. But the path is called the "Development of Trust" (Manual for Teachers) for a reason. If I had trusted I would've been much further along than I was! And it is the lack of trust that makes it so very uncomfortable for so long. But just know this: Once you've invited Truth into your awareness your path is set. The Undoing will now unfold through you whether or not you are consciously aware of it. It may mitigate any discomfort to step back and remind yourself of this whenever you feel that you are lost or failing.

124. The Effects of Real Perception Become the New Normal (May 26, 2017)

When this mind entered the "period of undoing", or the first period in the Development of Trust discussed in *A Course in Miracles* (M-4.I.A), I experienced spiritual Vision through the Holy Relationship. This Vision is what is called, among other things, the "real world" in *A Course in Miracles*. In my translation of ACIM into plain language (*The Message of A Course in Miracles*) I called this Vision "Real Perception" because "real world" confused some students. They expected to see a different material world or for the material world to change. But Vision is a perception not of the eyes but of the mind. I can understand why It is called another "world" in that you perceive a different "reality". But it is not concrete like what the eyes show you. It is, well, a *perception*. The best I can do is to describe It like a smile beyond the concrete world. But of course there is no smiling mouth seen! It simply cannot be adequately described. (To myself I just call It "the Vision thing"). But the experience of It is happy lightheartedness.

The body's eyes are therefore not the means by which the real world can be seen, for the illusions that they look upon must lead to more illusions of reality. And so they do. For everything they see not only will not last, but lends itself to thoughts of sin and guilt. While everything that God created is forever without sin and therefore is forever without guilt. (C-4.2)

At the time, Real Perception presented quite a stark contrast to what this mind was used to. It was wonderful and joyful, but it was also quite frightening because it was a perception that revealed Reality was not this world. And while I must've been ready to see This, I was not ready to stay in an awareness of It. Real Perception eventually faded to infrequent experiences. I didn't understand it at the time, but my belief in guilt drew me back into the personal thought system (ego). I had only begun the process to lasting peace, which required I undo my belief in guilt. But my experiences of Real Perception altered the way that I perceived and experienced the universe of form as well, often in ways that I didn't see. The effects of Real Perception on my perception of the world seeped in slowly and unconsciously without me realizing it. In time I just became aware that I didn't see the world as others did, which was how I once saw it. And this difference only grew more stark as I grew my awareness of Truth and undid my belief in guilt.

For example, a few years ago a close friend of mine was going through a crisis. As she shared her experience with me I tried to step into her mindset to understand her point of view. But it made absolutely no sense to me. This was not an intellectual perception. In fact, intellectually I understood that she was looking at the situation through the filter of her low self-esteem and fear of abandonment, she was taking someone else's attitudes personally, etc. I could remember having similar responses myself earlier in my life. But when I tried to step into the personal thought system (ego) I became disoriented; I felt like I'd fallen down the rabbit hole. At the time I didn't understand why this occurred. I didn't realize I'd advanced past the point where the personal thought system (ego) made experiential sense to me. All I knew was that I could no longer understand at all a point of view that I once shared. I supported my friend with sympathy but not with empathy.

The process begun so long ago with those first experiences of Real Perception has come full circle. Real Perception is now *right here*, just below my conscious awareness all the time, and easily accessible. Now I watch Real Perception transform my perception of the universe of form.

For example, a few weeks ago I attended a relative's Confirmation in the Catholic Church. While the priests referred occasionally to how we are all "sinners" I did not hear this term in the "hell and damnation" sense. I heard it with a gentle shrug: "We are all imperfect as humans. So what?" I found the priests to be quite innocent and gentle and loving.

Toward the end of the service the parishioners prepared to take communion. I observed how solemn were the faces of those who lined up for the sacrament. And then I observed a different expression on their faces as they returned from the sacrament. I would not have been surprised to see humility on their faces. But I was surprised instead to see something else. At first I only distantly noticed something was "off". I wasn't giving it any thought. But when I turned to look down my pew I saw a man a few seats away looking in my direction. He had just returned from taking the sacrament and what I saw on his face was torment. In wonderment I looked back at the others returning from the sacrament and realized what I had been seeing on so many faces: Guilt.

"This world of light, this circle of brightness is the real world, where guilt meets with forgiveness. Here the world outside is seen anew, without the shadow of guilt upon it." (T-18.IX.9)

Because I no longer believe in guilt Real Perception "bleeds through" and "washes" the world of form with Innocence for me. Subtly and quietly these effects of Real Perception have become my new normal.

125. Ask: Why not empathy as well as sympathy in your last article? (June 2, 2017)

"Re: Your last article…I am wondering 'WHY Not EMPATHY as well as SYMPATHY' in the last sentence of your paragraph #4 in this edition?" – MA

"Empathy" means the ability to enter into what another is feeling because you feel or have felt that way, too. "Sympathy" can mean this or compassion or pity where you feel sorry for another without entering into their feelings. Because I was using them comparatively I meant sympathy as "compassion" rather than "empathy". I was making the point that a shift had occurred for me. I could no longer step into the personal thought system (ego) without feeling disoriented. My awareness that the personal thought system does not make sense was no longer just intellectual but experiential. So instead of trying to empathize with my friend, or enter into her feelings as I once would have done, I could offer her only sympathy.

126. Listening for the Holy Spirit (June 9, 2017)

One of the common things I hear from clients and readers is, "I *do* trust the Holy Spirit. I just don't trust myself *to hear* the Holy Spirit."

"Trust not your good intentions. They are not enough. But trust implicitly your willingness, whatever else may enter. Concentrate only on this, and be not disturbed that shadows surround it. That is why you came. If you could come without them you would not need the holy instant." (T-19.IV.2)

You have only two thought systems in your mind: The ego (personal thought system) and the Holy Spirit (Awareness of Truth). At any given moment you give your attention to one or the other. And that will be whichever one you trust at the moment. (For a long while you will trust both and vacillate between them). When you put your attention on your ability to hear you are thinking with the ego. It is what tells you to focus on your own abilities. It is what tells you to doubt your own abilities. But the Holy Spirit knows that you can hear It because It is the Truth in you. It knows that you just need to *listen for* It and you will hear It. So focusing on your ability to hear, rather than on just listening for the Holy Spirit, actually blocks your ability to hear the Holy Spirit!

Willingness, or openness, to hear the Holy Spirit is demonstrated by simply *listening for* the Holy Spirit. Your willingness does not need to be perfect. You do not have to be doubt free. You just need to sit back, relax, and listen for the Holy Spirit in your mind, whatever else is going on in your mind. You may not hear the Holy Spirit at that moment but with this practice you open your mind for It to enter your awareness when you are ready to hear It.

When you want to listen to music you do not consider your own ability to hear it. You just turn on the music and listen. It is the same with the Holy Spirit. It is "on" all the time. The difference, though, may be that you know that when you turn the music on you will hear it but you may doubt that the Holy Spirit is here. But what would you lose by listening for It? If It does not exist you lose nothing because everything will be the same as it is. But if It is here you have Everything to gain. Why not give it a try?

Another obstacle may be your belief that you are not worthy to hear the Holy Spirit. But remember, the Holy Spirit represents your True Being. Does a tree have to be worthy of being a tree? Of course not. No more do you have to be worthy of What you are. Only the ego thinks in terms of worth. You must question what the ego tells you because it does not stand up to Truth. The Holy Spirit thinks only of bringing into your awareness What you are. Remember this if you find yourself resistant to listening for the Holy Spirit: You are listening for your Reality.

127. Ask: What does listening to the Holy Spirit entail? (June 16, 2017)

*"I hope this isn't a silly question but listening to the Holy Spirit entails what?
Are we listening to an audible voice, or a deep knowing of what is right, our intuition etc. How
does it actually manifest when we've heard the Holy Spirit?..."* – AS

This is most definitely not a silly question. It is an essential question.

We speak of "hearing" the Holy Spirit (the part of your mind that is aware of Truth) but It does not always come into your awareness as a Voice. (If you do hear a Voice It is, of course, *within* your mind. If It seems to come from outside of your mind and no one is actually speaking to you, you are hallucinating!). Often the Holy Spirit's answers and guidance come in unformed thoughts, or, as you said, a deep knowing or intuition.

The Holy Spirit is in every mind and people hear or feel It all the time without identifying It as the Holy Spirit. The ego (personal thought system) in your mind has many voices and causes many feelings so once you make the conscious decision to hear and feel the Holy Spirit it can take a while to discern It from the ego. Also, once you do hear the Holy Spirit the ego will try to mimic It with words and ideas that it thinks would come from the Holy Spirit. This is why it takes a while to be certain that you do hear the Holy Spirit.

The hallmark of hearing the Holy Spirit is a feeling of liberation from guilt or fear or a dropping of boundaries. You feel a lifting up and out. You feel "lighter", both in the sense of gaining clarity (less dark) and in feeling less weighed down. This is at the moment that you hear or feel the answer or guidance. Later, when you return your attention to the ego, you may feel guilt and fear that you heard the Holy Spirit or over what you heard. And this characteristic of hearing the ego. When it is the ego guilt and fear either do not change or they increase, even when the ego says something that you find emotionally satisfying.

When you do hear a Voice It may sometimes seem to come from the depths of your mind. Other times It will seem *right here* within you. It is "still and quiet"; It has no emotional charge. If *you* feel any emotional charge upon hearing It, it is uplifting joy.

If you ask for guidance and are uncertain if you have heard the Holy Spirit or the ego let it go. I find that if the guidance is from the ego the idea will just fall away from me. If it is from the Holy Spirit it will quietly persist in the back of my mind. Sometimes I will just later have a quiet knowing of the answer, often when I wake up in the morning.

128. Overcoming Resistance to Meditation (June 23, 2017)

Meditation is the core practice of a spiritual path. (By "meditation" I mean sitting quietly and simply being with Mind, not reaching for an altered state). Why and how you meditate evolves over time, but its centrality to gaining inner peace cannot be overemphasized. Unfortunately, it is also the most difficult practice because your mind's resistance to it is strong. You are mind and meditation should be natural. And it will become so as you become more aware that you are mind. But in your unnatural state of identification with a self (body/personality) you (a mind) find unnatural what is natural. The driver of your identification with a self, the personal thought system (ego), is threatened by anything that turns you inward to the mind. This is the source of your resistance (and why so many give up on meditation).

When my clients complain about their resistance to meditation I suggest that they pay attention to the feelings and thoughts that come up when they try to meditate. Feelings and thoughts reveal unconscious and conscious beliefs. The beliefs that emerge when you are resistant are the obstacles that need to be revealed, examined, and undone. This is not only so that you can meditate but also so that you can ultimately find lasting peace.

It is also helpful to know *why* you meditate. Reminding yourself of this can help motivate you:

I am mind and meditation gets me in touch with mind. It helps me get in touch with what I am.

Through meditation I learn what is in my mind. My beliefs are the source of my attitudes, behaviors, and choices. Knowing my beliefs helps me to understand what motivates my attitudes, behaviors and choices.

In meditation I can process out thoughts and feelings so my mind will quiet. This will help me not just throughout the day but also to unwind and to sleep.

The Truth is in my mind and the awareness of Truth is the only way to lasting peace.

As I grow aware of Truth, the Quiet Center of my mind, through formal meditation, I will take this Quiet with me as I go about my day.

As my mind quiets and slows through meditation I gain time to respond to my thoughts before I react from them.

The quieter, slower mind I gain through meditation helps me intuit the flow of the universe. I find and live in the flow rather than force my way through life. This is a much more harmonious way to be in the world.

You have to be willing to face incredible discomfort when you first learn to meditate. In time resistance ebbs—but then it will flow back again. You just have to ride out each wave of resistance and recognize that it helps you to get in touch with the false beliefs in your mind. But the quiet, slower mind and the peace that come from the awareness of Truth are well worth the effort to meditate. And after a long while meditation will require less effort as you desire its results.

There is no one right way to meditate. Some need quiet; some like to be guided. Others like music or chanting. It may work better to have your eyes open rather than closed. You need to be flexible as what works for you for a while may need to be dropped for a new approach. Don't seek immediate results. Results may or may not show up when you meditate, but they will show up as you go about your life. At first these results may be a dramatic contrast to what you are used to. But as you integrate meditation into your life the results will be more subtle. They will become your new normal. Then you may only recognize what meditation brings to you when you *do not* meditate. But your peace of mind is worth both persistence and consistency.

129. Ask: What's with "remembered not" to laugh? (June 30, 2017)

"...How curious that the text says 'remembered not to laugh' instead of 'forgot to laugh' (because it is impossible to be separate from God). Since it was such a mistake, what's with 'remembered'???" – KA

Actually, it is "remembered *not*". The "not" is what makes it mean "forgot". Here is the phrase you referenced:

"Into eternity, where all is one, there crept a tiny, mad idea, at which the Son of God remembered not to laugh. In his forgetting did the thought become a serious idea, and possible of both accomplishment and real effects." (T-27.VIII.6)

Well, you want to remember to laugh? It is all because Helen Schucman had a love for iambic pentameter, the meter in which Shakespeare wrote. *A Course in Miracles* was dictated to her in this beat so that she would be more open to and comfortable with it. She would find it beautiful. Unfortunately, this led to some awkward passages, just as you shared. Instead of "forgot" we get "remembered not". However, the next line clarifies with "in his forgetting". The tyranny of this meter is why there are also many confusing double negatives sprinkled throughout ACIM.

I took care of all of that when I translated ACIM into plain language [*The Message of A Course in Miracles* (Text) and *Practicing A Course in Miracles/The Way of A Course in Miracles* (Workbook/Manual for Teachers)]. I removed unclear, awkward phrasing and double negatives, among other things.

Here is that phrase in *The Message of A Course in Miracles*:

"Into Eternity, Where All is One, there crept a tiny, mad idea of separation at which you who are One with God forgot to laugh. In your forgetting, the thought became serious to you, its accomplishment seemed possible, and its effects seemed real." (MACIM-27.8.6)

It's not as beautiful to read but I hope it is clearer!

130) On Life-After-Death and Level Confusion (July 7, 2017)

A topic has come up recently with clients and readers that has illuminated for me why my explanations of what happens to the ego or the split-mind when a self seems to die often leads to further questions that I have not been able to satisfy for others. It is because of what is called in *A Course in Miracles* "level confusion". This means confusing what happens on one level of the mind with what happens on another.

To explain, I hope more clearly than I have in the past, I am going to use the language that I feel is more directly descriptive than the language of ACIM. Here's a key:

Truth = God
Macro split-mind = Son of God
Micro split-minds = Sons of God
Not-Truth = macro ego

Personal thought system = micro ego

(ACIM does not distinguish between "macro" and "micro" ego just as it often does not distinguish between "macro" and "micro" Son of God. This distinction is implied in ACIM by the context of each particular passage.)

Awareness of Truth = Holy Spirit
Undoing = Atonement
Manifest undoers = Teachers of God

The questions I have received have to do with whether individual perception or awareness and/or personal thought systems exist before a self (body/personality) is born and after a self dies. The answer is no, but I always receive push back on this answer, often with quotes or links to other teachers. I have finally seen more clearly that this is because students confuse levels of the mind, or the macro split-mind and the micro split-mind. Micro split-minds begin and end with the body with which they were identified. But the macro split-mind continues on until it is undone.

Here's why this answer:

Truth, being All, must think of Its Own opposite. But being All, Truth cannot have an opposite. So Truth's opposite, or not-Truth, can only ever be an idea. And it is an idea that is over as soon as it is thought.

Since Truth is one (the same throughout), formless, boundless, and timeless, the idea of not-Truth is time-bound, limited, diverse form – the universe of form. The part of the Mind of Truth where this idea occurs is the macro split-mind. It seems to be split off from the Mind of Truth, but it cannot actually be apart from Truth. So Truth is still in the macro split-mind even as it projects not-Truth, or the universe of form. It is split between Truth and not-Truth.

Time is the illusion on which all of this illusion of not-Truth rests. In time it seems that not-Truth, or the universe of form, began long ago and will be undone in some indefinite future. The unfolding story of the universe of form is the instant of the idea-of-not-Truth/the-undoing-of-the-idea-of-not-Truth playing out in time. So the universe of form seems to be the idea of not-Truth but its unfolding story is actually the *undoing* of the idea-of-not-Truth. It is the effect, or expression, of the undoing of the idea-of-not-Truth.

The macro split-mind projects itself into the universe of form as billions of seemingly-individual versions of itself, or micro split-minds. Micro split-minds are also split between Truth and not-Truth, or the thought system of the Awareness of Truth and the personal thought system. Each micro split-mind is projected onto a unique body. And the personal thought system in each mind is what teaches that micro split-mind that it is a self, or a body and personality with a unique story. Each split-mind seems to be born into a world of this consciousness which is reinforced by other split-minds that believe the universe of form to be reality. But since the Truth is in each micro split-mind, each micro split-mind has the potential to become aware of Truth. Those that do, to whatever degree, are the overt manifestation of the Undoing. They are the manifest undoers. Those that do not become aware of Truth are also part of the Undoing because the undoing of not-Truth is inevitable. Not-Truth will be undone because it is already undone. But their parts are not overt manifestations of undoing. They contribute in other ways, for example, as indirect teachers of those that do become aware of Truth. Or perhaps their lives cause a future situation in which a manifest undoer will learn. In any case, everyone is doing their part perfectly because their part is not to *cause* the Undoing. Their part is the *effect* of the Undoing that has already occurred. The story of the Undoing unfolds through their seemingly-individual story.

So, in time, micro split-minds are "born" and "die" with the body with which they are identified. Their story in time has a beginning and an ending. But the story of the universe of form continues on until the macro split-mind's Undoing is complete. These are the two levels of mind that students often confuse. Micro split-minds do not have to attain complete undoing. They do not have to be "perfected" or completely "healed". They do not fail or go on and repeat another "life" if they do not. Each has its own unique part to play and will play it perfectly. It is the macro split-mind that goes on until it is undone, its Undoing playing out in time through billions of stories of micro split-minds.

What does this mean for you, who seem to be a micro split-mind? The Truth in your mind is Timeless. It does not come into time. It goes on now outside of the story of time. This is your Eternal Being. The self (body and personality) and the personal thought system with which you identify will fall away in time. The benefit for you in getting in touch with Truth, Eternal Being, the Constant and Unchanging, is the peace that your awareness of It will bring to you *in time*. And if you come to fully see that the universe of form is not real and you attain full awareness of Truth, your mind will put the self and its body and its thought system aside, not through "death", but through transcendence. You are a manifest undoer and to whatever degree you grow your awareness of Truth is your part to play in the Undoing. You cannot mess this up and you will not have to repeat it!

131. Ask: What remains of the specific "me" after death? (July 14, 2017)

"Thanks for this article, On Life After Death and Level Confusion; *a very complex subject, but you've provided some clarity. It opens up questions concerning 'reincarnation'. If the micro split-mind (body and personality) dissolves at 'death' then what (if anything) remains of the specific 'me' (soul?) that 'rolls over' into another worldly experience? Much of what we read on this subject implies that the spiritual 'progress' (Undoing/ Healing) we make in this life will lighten the burden in our 'future' lifetimes. On the other hand I've come to understand that there is no 'specific me', there is no 'world'...only the Macro split-mind projecting itself as billions of micro-minds. So, when this particular 'Parenthesis in Eternity' (J. Goldsmith) closes do we say that only Awareness remains, and it is no longer identified with a specific entity?*

I've always been curious about the difference between the ego saying that if we return to the Mind we will be 'obliterated', and the Course *saying we 'disappear into the Heart of God'. My personal analogy is a drop of water on a dock that someone wipes up with a towel and discards versus someone lifting the drop (individual 'self') and returning it to the Ocean. The Awareness that was the essence of the drop experiences Itself as the All. Does that sound roughly correct? (I'm trying to keep it simple as this could go on and on as an academic exercise)!"* – RB

The point I was trying to make with that article was that one reason that beliefs like reincarnation persist is because of level confusion. A micro split-mind's experience of individuality is confused with the macro split-mind's projection of billions of individual forms of itself. A seeming-individual ends in the story but the story continues on without it. No part of that seeming-individual "goes on". It has only one "lifetime". But the macro split-mind has billions of lifetimes. In other words, there is no *re*-incarnation just billions of incarnations of the macro split-mind. Some micro split-minds are able to tap into those other micro stories and they feel that they lived them themselves individually but really they just tapped into the macro split-mind. (This is why so many people claim to be the reincarnation of the same famous person).

There is nothing specific about your experience as an individual that goes on after death, in time or into Eternity (Timelessness). That experience is the false that falls away. So there is no "soul" or individual spirit. But there is Something Universal in your mind That is Eternal. The Truth in your mind is completely apart from time and It is universal because the Truth in your mind is the same Truth in every seemingly-individual split-mind. And you don't have to wait for the death of the self to experience It. You can practice the Holy Instant at any moment and experience Truth now. And when you do, you will never experience time the same way again. This is why the Holy Instant is so central to the practice of *A Course in Miracles*. And this is why ACIM's teaching is so radically different from most spiritual teachings. It does not aim you toward the future for relief from the false. It asks you to be open to Truth right now to be relieved right now.

The ego (personal thought system) says that "you" will be obliterated if you return your mind to Truth because *it* will disappear. The ego speaks only for itself. You feel its fears as your own only as long as you identify with it. In this process of undoing, you will learn that you are mind and that the ego is only a thought system in your mind that tells you, falsely, that the self (body/personality/ego) is you.

Awareness (or consciousness or perception) is the experience of the split-mind (both macro and micro – there's really no distinction between the two). A split-mind can be aware of either illusion or Truth. The highest level of awareness in ACIM is called Christ Consciousness or the Holy Spirit. In this awareness one is aware that only the Truth is true and recognizes that the universe of form is an illusion. No part of awareness "goes on" to Truth. It is the false experience. But this highest form of awareness is necessary to prepare one for the experience of Truth. When the illusion falls away only Truth is left in a mind and it slips easily from the Awareness of Truth (Christ/ Holy Spirit) to Knowledge of Truth. It's like the *awareness* of Truth is seeing Truth through a veil and *Knowledge* of Truth is when there is no veil. All boundaries are gone. (I'm not sure if this is what you were talking about with "the essence of Awareness").

Here's another way to think of it:

Imagine a piece of white paper. This represents the Mind of Truth. (Unlike paper, Truth has no boundaries, but, hey, gotta work with what we got...). Now imagine a circle on the paper. This is the part of the Mind of Truth where the idea of not-Truth occurs. Color in that circle with a pencil. Now the circle represents the split-mind (macro or micro, it doesn't matter; same thing) because the paper, representing Truth, is still there under the penciling, which represents not-Truth. As you advance in your awareness of Truth, it is like erasing the penciling. More and more of the white paper, Truth, shows through until finally you are left with the white paper both inside and outside the circle. This is the highest awareness a split-mind can have. It knows that only the Truth is true – or only the white paper is true. It's hardly even split-off anymore so the circle, the boundary, is easily erased (in ACIM this is described as "God takes the last step" because only God is left in mind and Mind).

So this process of undoing reveals That Which is already right here. There is no "returning" because nothing real "left". It was just "covered over". And as each micro split-mind erases the false, that much is erased from the macro split-mind, just as each little erasure reveals the paper beneath the penciling. And, again, this is not done through death. Focusing on what happens when you die (what part of your mind does that, do you think?) can be a way of avoiding being present to Truth.

(The passage you quoted from ACIM, *"disappear into the Heart of God"* (W-pII. 14.5), is referring to a split-mind in its "purified"—how ACIM describes the "erasing"—state. It refers to the boundary as a "gate" rather than a veil or circle as I did here. ACIM speaks to "you" not as a person but as a split-mind, only the Truth in which is true).

132. Ask: Am I upset because the world is meaningless or because of my projections on it? (July 21, 2017)

"I'm a bit confused. In Lesson 12 it states the world is meaningless in itself and what is meaningless is neither good nor bad, but then it says I am upset because I see a meaningless world. I thought that I was upset because I projected meaning onto the world..." – AS

The answer you seek is in Lesson 12 itself (the underlines are mine):

"I think I see a fearful world, a dangerous world, a hostile world, a sad world, a wicked world, a crazy world," (W-12.3)

"But I am upset because I see a meaningless world." (W-12.4)

This lesson is pointing out that beneath the upset that you feel for the meaning that you project onto the world, the deeper source of your upset is that the world is meaningless. This is elaborated on in the next lesson, #13:

"A meaningless world engenders fear because I think I am in competition with God." (W-13.5)

Here *A Course in Miracles* is introducing the true source of guilt and the fear it engenders in your mind, even if you are not ready to see it yet:

"You are not expected to believe the statement at this point, and will probably dismiss it as preposterous. Note carefully, however, any signs of overt or covert fear which it may arouse." (W-13.5)

133. There Was No Choice to Be "Separate from God" (July 28, 2017)

There are things that become so clear without the belief in guilt in the mind! For me, one of those things is the idea that "separation from God" was not a choice made somewhere, sometime, perhaps by the "Son of God" (macro split-mind). While I was studying *A Course in Miracles* the Holy Spirit (Awareness of Truth) would try to get me to see that God (Truth) is One so there is no choice in God. Choice is a part of not-God, which is the opposite of God, so there could be no choice that *caused* the separation. Choice only has meaning *within* the separation. But I felt, without articulating it to myself, that *someone* had to be responsible for the error. In fact I worked at being hyper-responsible for the separation by always referring to it as something I chose even though I couldn't see it. This is all over my early writing.

What the Holy Spirit was trying to get me to see, and what I can see now, is that nothing real has occurred, so how could there be a choice that caused it? I don't mean this theoretically. I mean it makes no sense that separation from God was a choice. Being All, the Mind of God, must think of Its Own opposite. But being All, It cannot have an opposite. The idea arises and is simultaneously undone: "What's my opposite? Oh, yeah, I am All; I cannot have an opposite!" Just as God simply is, the idea of the opposite-of-God, or not-God, simply is, too. Except that what it is, is a meaningless idea. It is nothing. It arises and is immediately undone by God's All-encompassing nature. There was no choice at all to make; there was nothing to make a choice.

Only *within the idea* of not-God does choice seem possible. Because only within the idea of not-God does it seem like something real occurred. It seems as though part of God broke off from God to make another reality. So there seems to be a choice between God and not-God. And in not-Got there are an endless number of choices to make.

Choice in the present is what the Holy Spirit kept bringing me back to. "Forget about any past 'separation'," It would say. "The choice to be aware of God or not is in front of you now." I couldn't get my mind out of the past; out of trying to understand "how all this came to be", because there lay the "proof" of my guilt. Since it was so real to me, what could the Holy Spirit do but re-direct me to the present? Only in the present would I find that I was not "separate from God". Only in the present could guilt be undone.

134. Ask: Is choosing to not follow personal thoughts the daily now dream? (August 4, 2017)

"We (I) did not choose separation, still, I , being a personal 'mind', choose to believe ego's thought system, now.... although the Course *teaches me otherwise . You personal LIZ still experiencing LIZ as LIZ constantly choosing to not follow her personal thoughts: Is this the daily NOW dream..? I experience the dreamflow as reality with momentary 'forgiveness' workouts when things get STUCK because I forget the dream as being a dream..."* – ER

A Course in Miracles does not teach that you as a micro split-mind chose "separation from God". It teaches that the Son of God, or macro split-mind, made that choice. Your (micro split-mind) choice is made only in the present.

You are also not a personal mind, or thought system. Your mind is split between the thought system of the Holy Spirit and a personal thought system (ego). You are not the thought system but the mind choosing it. And that choice is made so unconsciously that you do not even seem to have a choice. It's like being aware of only apples so you choose only apples. You don't know you have a choice until you learn that there are other fruits. There has always been a pear among the apples but you thought it was just a different kind of apple. Before you can choose the pear you must learn to discern it from the apples just as you must learn to discern the Holy Spirit's Voice from the personal thought system's many voices. Once you do that, you truly feel that you have a choice.

I don't know what "Liz" means anymore as the self-concept has fallen away from this mind. I suppose it just refers to this body/personality which represents different things to different minds. This mind also does not "constantly choose" to not follow the personal thought system. It is certainly not constant about anything it does! The personal thought system, however, blathers constantly and sometimes this mind does follow it, just not for long. What has changed is this mind does not care anymore: "That's the ego. Oh, well." I do not know if this is what you mean by the "daily NOW dream".

Here's the thing about what goes on in the mind: The personal thought system is constantly thinking. Really, it is *evaluating* constantly. There are also neutral, observational, and taking-care-of-business thoughts that arise in the mind, like "The sky is clear today" or "I need to buy bread." Those thoughts are just there and are unobtrusive unless the personal thought system uses them to judge ("Dammit! I was hoping it would rain. Why does nothing go my way?" or "You'd better write 'bread' on your shopping list or you are a total failure as a human being!") The Holy Spirit, however, is quiet until It is needed. What changes over time is how much one believes what the ego says. As one's belief in it diminishes one is less caught up in it and when one does get caught up in it one releases it quicker.

What you describe for yourself is all that's needed. You are caught up in life in the world until you notice that you have some conflicted thought to which you need to attend. In time, as your awareness of Truth grows, you will become aware that there is a peace with you all the time, no matter what is happening in the world. But even then, the mind will still be busy observing and responding to the world until you pull it back in to rest in Truth again.

135. Ask: How do I deal with a sister who is constantly sick? (August 11, 2017)

"I am 78 and my sister is 70. Ever since I can remember she has been ill with different conditions. Before I learnt from ACIM *that we choose our own sickness I always felt helpless about this. Now I just feel angry! I feel she is using the illnesses to get attention! It really irritates me that her attitude is 'Poor me. I can't do anything because I have just had this fall or I have this or that'...... Now on another level I know that this is my lesson but on a practical level I don't know how to interact with her. We are told to be kind! My reaction to that is that I should try to fix her problems. I seem to have been doing that all my life but I don't want to do this anymore!!!!! Help!"* – Anonymous

The choice that *A Course in Miracles* refers to with regard to what happens to the self in the world is for the *entire experience* of imperfection and dysfunction that is the human experience. It is the opposite of God (Truth) in every way. Illness, the vulnerability of the body to injury, and death are just part of the experience of not-God. Of course, sometimes one does make their own dysfunction through their own life choices and that is usually traceable. And sometimes illness or injury happens through other aspects of cause and effect at the level of form (for example, genes) and some use them to get something, like attention, or rest, or to avoid something/someone or to make others guilty. But this is simply a form of faulty problem solving on their part. They believe guilt is real, they are afraid, they don't feel whole, etc., and this is their attempt to fix that. Unless they demonstrate a real openness (very rare) for the real solution (the awareness of Truth) to their problems all you can do is offer compassion. You are not responsible for others so you do not have to solve their problems. Doing so would be co-dependency, which would only enable them to stay in their dysfunction. And that is not kind. Most people just want to be heard and understood. That is all the love that they can accept so that is all you have to offer them. So the kind way to interact with your sister is to let her know that she is heard and understood: "That sounds painful. I'm sorry you are hurting."

Anger is a defensive posture. You are angry when you are afraid. In this case, you are afraid of punishment from God for the guilt in you that you see reflected in your sister. You see dysfunction, in this case illness, as "wrong"; as evidence of guilt. This reminds you of the inevitable dysfunction you experience in identification with a self (body/personality). The ego (personal thought system) in your mind says to deny the guilt you believe is in you by projecting it onto your sister. Of course, this does not get rid of the guilt. It is really the way to hold onto it.

Now that you know the source of your anger, you can deal with your underlying belief in guilt where it is, in your own mind. What you ultimately have to learn is that there is no god that you have defied and that is sitting in judgment on you. You can learn in depth about where guilt comes from, how it shows up, and how to undo it in my e-book, *Releasing Guilt for Inner Peace* (www.amazon.com or www.lulu.com) And, of course, finding and releasing the belief in guilt is what I work on to some degree with all of my clients so you can always work with me (Liz@acimmentor.com to set up an appointment).

As you work out your belief in guilt you will find that you are not bothered by your sister's situation. Pain is an inevitable part of the human experience, but suffering is caused by the stories we tell ourselves about the pain. You will feel compassion for your sister's choice to suffer over her pain because she doesn't know any better and she is not seeking to know better.

136. Ask: About Non-Violence, Morality, and Why Bother to Study (August 18, 2017)

"I have one thing keeping me from embracing ACIM, and that is that I still don't understand non-violence. My question is, 'If violence does not exist, then wars don't exist, genocide does not exist, because it is all an illusion? Then there is no good nor bad, and one can do whatever they want?'

But then, nothing has meaning, and studying the book, and learning to think right also has no meaning, and no merit. I simply don't understand, the thinking seems circular to me. I must be peace, killing an animal is peaceful? If I had the opportunity to kill Hitler in the middle of his act, with the thinking of non-violence, I should let him live?

I am lost with this work. Please help me." – Anonymous

You actually have three questions here so it is no wonder you feel lost! One is a question about non-violence, another is about morality, and the last is about why you bother to study at all.

With regard to non-violence, *A Course in Miracles* does not take a stand one way or the other on non-violence. As you say, it teaches that there is no right or wrong so how could it take a stand on any moral issue? It does not. This brings us to your question about morality.

ACIM makes a distinction between "sin" and a "mistake". Sin is the idea that there is an absolute-morality decreed by a god and which, when defied, would be unchangeable. Once you sinned you would always be a sinner. You could make amends or do penance or be punished, but these would not undo the sin. Only by the arbitrary whim ("grace") of a god could you be forgiven – but you'd still be a sinner, just one that was unworthily let off for your sin, thereby increasing your guilt. The belief in an absolute-morality, sin, and a judgmental god is what the ego (personal thought system) fosters in your mind to make it seem real to you.

ACIM teaches that there is no such thing as sin and that your perception that the experience of the universe of form is reality is a mistake that can be corrected. In fact, because it is not real, it is already corrected. There is no sin, no mistake, so no cause for guilt.

Quite apart from this, we do need in the world social-morality to attempt to live harmoniously with each other. Social-morality is not absolute, but is arbitrary, depending on time and place and culture and values. This is why it is only an "attempt" to live harmoniously with each other and is often the cause of conflict! Social-morality should be examined and questioned from time to time to see if what we have learned in time requires changes in our morality.

So, yes, you can do whatever you want in the world and there is no god out there to punish you for doing it. But in the world you cannot do whatever you want without consequences. Some of those consequences, in your guilt, you may bring on yourself. Some may be brought on you by society or cause and effect at the level of form.

This brings us to your third question about why you should bother to study and learn right thinking. Just to clarify, "right" and "wrong" mindedness in ACIM does not refer to moral right and wrong. It would be more apt to say "helpful" and "unhelpful" mindedness. And the helpfulness or unhelpfulness would have to do with what helps you to be aware of Truth and so be at peace.

You do not learn of Truth to cause some future effect. You learn of Truth as an effect of the cause of Undoing (Atonement, or correction) of the idea of not-Truth. The idea of not-Truth was undone by Truth's All-encompassing nature the moment it was thought. But in time, the opposite of Timelessness, the idea of not-Truth seems to have begun long ago and it seems as though it will be undone in some indefinite future. So in the story of time when you become aware of Truth you become a manifest Undoer (teacher of God) of not-Truth. This shows up as you feeling moved to become aware of Truth through study and practice. And you will take your study and practice as far as it is your role to play in the Undoing.

As for killing animals and Hitler, those are matters for social-morality. Some think killing animals for any reason is wrong. Others think killing animals to eat is okay. Some think killing Hitler (there were attempts) would have been a great good. Others think it would have made the killers as bad as Hitler. As I pointed out above, social-morality is arbitrary. These are issues that one has to work out for themselves.

You can learn more about how the ego (personal thought system) hijacks social-morality for absolute-morality to increase guilt in my e-book, *Releasing Guilt for Inner Peace* (www.amazon.com or www.lulu.com). I put a lot of everyday examples in the book.

137. Ask: Did the ego ask for the world and then for a better way? (August 28, 2017)

"Liz the ego's way into the world began with the thought 'Is there something better?' and a way out of the ego's world began with Bill Thetford's thought 'There must be a better way'. Is it possible the ego asked both of these questions? The first question responded to by the Father (God) and the second by a son Jesus?" – ESA

God (Truth), being All, must think of Its Own opposite. But being All, God cannot have an opposite. The idea of not-God arose and was undone immediately by God's All-encompassing nature. It is as though God said, "What's my opposite? Oh, wait, I am All; I cannot have an opposite" and the idea was done. So there is no intention behind the idea of not-God. Like God, it merely is. But unlike God it has no meaning because it is impossible. Only in time, which is part of the idea of not-Truth, does it seem that the idea of not-God began long ago and will be undone in some indefinite future. So only in time, in not-Truth, does lack and a need to fill the lack seem to have meaning. There is no lack in God. So no part of God went looking for "something better".

The world and the ego are part of not-God (the universe of form) and arose simultaneously as expressions of that idea. The ego was not there before the world. It is not a part of God's Mind that went looking for something better.

In the story of the undoing of not-Truth, which is the story of the universe of form, the Undoing shows up as certain minds looking for a way out of the pain of the experience of not-Truth. Helen Schucman and Bill Thetford were two of those minds. They opened to "a better way" and received *A Course in Miracles* via a Voice within Helen which she experienced as "Jesus". The Voice was the universal Christ Mind, the part of every mind that remembers Truth.

It is not the ego in one's mind that seeks a way out of pain. Every mind in the world is split between ego and Christ (Holy Spirit). In the moment a split-mind hopes that there is a way out of pain, they are hoping that there is a way that is not the ego's way. This is unconscious, of course. They don't know that their pain is caused by following a thought system ACIM labels "ego". But this is the opening the Christ in every mind needs to come into a split-mind's awareness and provide a "better way".

138. Sorting Out the Self, the Ego, and You (September 1, 2017)

"I know it is ego, but…" is a phrase that is often said or written to me by clients and readers. But often what is called "ego" (personal thought system) is actually not the ego. Often it is just the personality of the self expressing itself.

Why is this important? Because in order to let go of the ego you have to see its boundaries. Otherwise you attempt to release what does not need to be released. And this can feel discordant, giving the ego an opportunity to tell you that you are being asked to sacrifice.

To recognize the ego's boundaries you have to understand the self's boundaries, too. The self, as I use the term, is a body and personality. It is part of the universe of form. It is the result of cause and effect at the level of form. Your particular self is the effect of what has gone before in the story of time. It has an authentic expression as part of the unfolding story of time. And it is neutral in that it is neither good nor bad. It simply is what has resulted from what has gone before.

The ego is the thought system, or way of thinking, in your mind that represents not-Truth. It is a thought system of lack, guilt, and fear. It teaches you that the self is you. It tells you to define yourself by the self and to fulfill yourself through the self's life in the world. It teaches you that the self's vulnerability is yours and that you need to defend the self to keep you safe. The ego uses ideas of lack, guilt, and fear to maintain your belief in it and in yourself as a self.

Who are you in this? You are a mind that is split between Truth and not-Truth. You identify with the self and the ego until you learn that you are not the self and the ego and you learn of Truth.

As an example of an authentic expression of a self, let's say that your self desires a life-partner. In your identification with a self this feels like *your* desire. The desire itself is not an obstacle to you being aware of Truth. The Awareness of Truth (Holy Spirit) in your mind uses all situations as classrooms in which you learn of Truth. But if the ego in your mind tells you that you lack and that your sense of lack can only be filled if you have a life-partner then your desire for a life-partner can block you from being aware that you will only find wholeness in Truth. You can neutralize the ego, however, by deciding to use your seeking for a relationship, or your being in a relationship, as a way to learn of the Awareness of Truth. Eventually, as your awareness of Truth grows, your desire for a relationship to make you whole will be "cleansed" of the belief that it can save you. The desire for the relationship will remain a part of the self's authentic expression, but you, as a mind, will know that you do not need to fulfill it to be fulfilled yourself.

The self's authentic expression, motivations, desires, etc. are part of the story of Undoing in time and form. They continue as your awareness of Truth grows. You just stop defining yourself by them. You stop seeking through them for fulfillment. You observe them without judgment. The ego also continues with its stories of lack and guilt and fear, but you no longer believe them. You just observe them and their source and know that they are not real.

139. Willingness, Not Submission or Surrender (September 8, 2017)

There are certain words that students still identified with the self use in their relationship with the Holy Spirit (Awareness of Truth in their own minds) that not only have negative connotations that indicate or increase fear; they are also not applicable. Two of those words are "submit" and "surrender".

To submit or surrender to the Holy Spirit would mean, first, that the self is the correct view of yourself and it is from this view that you must submit or surrender to the Holy Spirit; second, that the Holy Spirit is something separate from you; third, that you can give up your power to It. All of these are erroneous.

The difference between submission and surrender is that submission sounds less defiant than surrender. Submission means you recognize the Holy Spirit's greater power and surrender sounds like you were defeated by the Holy Spirit. But neither attitude is applicable toward the Holy Spirit because *the Holy Spirit is the thought system in your mind that speaks for the Truth in you*. The idea that you could submit or surrender to the Holy Spirit starts from the false premise that the self is you. It is the ego, the thought system of the self, that teaches you this. It tells you that the Holy Spirit is the "other" in your mind. Your power is in the ego; the Holy Spirit seeks to take away your power. But really the Holy Spirit is your Power because It is the Awareness of Truth in your mind. It is not "other"; the ego is actually the "other" in your mind. You are under submission to the ego in your belief that it speaks for you. But it speaks only for its own perpetuation in your mind. It is what says you are under attack from an "other" (Holy Spirit) that seeks to "defeat" you. But it is the ego that attacks the Holy Spirit; it is the ego that seeks to defeat the Holy Spirit. The Holy Spirit does not need to attack the ego because it knows that the ego is nothing. And it certainly does not need to defeat you, because It is part of you. Only the ego attacks, seeks defeat, and demands submission or surrender. And then it projects all of this onto the Holy Spirit.

The only appropriate approach to the Holy Spirit is *willingness* to let It into your awareness *because It is the part of your mind that knows your Reality, your true Power*. This is not done from the view that the self is you. It is done from the recognition that you do not know what you are. It is done from an open mind willing to be shown Reality.

Whenever you fear the Holy Spirit, remind yourself that It is not separate from you. It is the part of your mind that knows you as you do not yet know yourself. You cannot submit or surrender to It, because It is not apart from you. And because your willingness is necessary for It to come into your awareness, you are always in charge of the process of becoming aware of Reality. You are always empowered. The Holy Spirit cannot bring into your awareness more than you can accept into your awareness.

(A note about the word "surrender": I have had clients refer to "surrendering" the ego, as in, "letting it go". That is obviously a different way to use the word than I am using it here).

140. Only What You Have Not Given Can Be Lacking (September 15, 2017)

"Only what you have not given can be lacking in any situation." (T-17.VII.4)

This quote is from the Text of *A Course in Miracles*. In context, it is about Helen Schucman's and Bill Thetford's faith in their Holy Relationship. They were being told not to blame the other when they lost sight of the Holiness of their relationship. The Vision of the Holy Relationship was within each. It did not come to each from the other. So if one did not see Holiness in the other the problem with within them, not in the other.

This is, of course, a central lesson in ACIM. The issue is always within you. I often use this quote with clients in a slightly different context. They will share with me that they are not getting something from a relationship. Often they will take this idea and feel that if they just gave enough forgiveness or love the other would change. But I ask them if they are giving themselves, through the relationship, what they want from the other. For example, if they are in a relationship with someone who is emotionally withholding, are they loving themselves by being in the relationship? If they feel disrespected, are they respecting themselves by being in that relationship? Your relationship with others is your relationship with yourself.

If we cannot accept love we may take two approaches in relationships: We don't see the love being offered by another. Or we get involved with others who cannot love us as we want to be loved. If you feel you are not getting something from a relationship that you want, first ask if the other is attempting to give you what you want. If they are, then you have to work on letting in what they offer. But if they are not, you have to ask yourself why you are with them. Do you value other things more in the relationship? Does what you are getting outweigh what you are not getting? Are you asking for more than that person can give and can you get that need met elsewhere? Or have you outgrown that person and is it time to move on?

In short, look at what you are not getting and ask yourself if you are giving it to yourself.

141. Resistance is the Path (September 22, 2017)

A common issue with my clients is the resistance they feel to practice, be it study, meditation, doing the lessons, making the Holy Spirit (Awareness of Truth in your mind) their Constant Companion, etc. But resistance is part of the process. It does not mean something is wrong. It does not mean you are failing.

Resistance really means "not ready" or "not now". It does not mean you have fallen off the path. For example, you may go through a hungry stage where you cannot study enough. But then you find one day that you do not want to study at all. Or if you try the words just seem to bounce of your mind and not penetrate. This is not necessarily resistance to further study. This can be that you are so saturated with what you have taken in that you need to process it before you can take in more. A lot of this processing is unconscious. It shows up as a lack of motivation to study. But when you are done processing you will find yourself motivated to study again.

Sometimes you are just not ready for the practice. For example, you may find your resistance to meditation so strong that you simply don't do it. You mean to, but each day goes by and you find you have not meditated. Sometimes you may try, but you always find something "better" to do. In this case you can ask the Holy Spirit to help you find what thoughts and beliefs keep you from meditating. Be willing to have them rise up from your subconscious. You do not have to do this in formal meditation. At any time just be willing for your obstacles to meditation to surface into your awareness.

It also may be that the time is not right for the practice you are attempting. Using the last example, if you have strong obstacles to meditation then the time is not right for that practice. You may attempt other practices that will, in time, break down your obstacles to practicing meditation. That may be just studying or it may be that even though you cannot meditate yet you do have a relationship with the Holy Spirit. Do what comes authentically and naturally to you now. When the time for discipline with a practice comes you will know it.

The path to inner peace is a path to overcoming resistance to inner peace. So resistance does not means something is wrong. It just means you are on the path!

142. Ask: How do you know if you have outgrown your relationship? (September 29, 2017)

"An interesting follow-on topic in your blog may be specific examples that may be used to determine if you have outgrown your relationship...as it applies to ACIM *followers..."* – JW

It does not matter if one is a student of *A Course in Miracles* or not. It does not matter the relationship, whether it be romantic, family, friend, to a job, to an object, etc. The determinant of when to leave a relationship is the same:

When the pain of staying outweighs the pain of leaving.

Some people are healthier and can recognize it is time to leave before it gets too painful. In their case, they recognize that if they stay the pain of staying will outweigh the pain of leaving. They do not wait for it to get too painful.

143. Ask: How do I know it's the Holy Spirit? (October 6, 2017)

"Lately, through spending much more time in meditation (not necessarily stillness!), I seem to be able to "drop into" a space of deep quiet and a new kind of being (knowing??) for brief periods of time. My question is this: What does the Holy Spirit 'feel like'? I would love to think I'm finally able to experience my own Teacher, but my mind (no surprise) kicks up a fuss and tells me this is just brain waves, nothing special, don't be silly, etc. etc. I do seem to get responses to sincere requests for clarity, answers to questions and so on, but again my mind tells me I am making everything up on my own. How would I know the difference?" – MG

You have experienced the Holy Spirit (Awareness of Truth in your mind) in the quiet knowing you described as well as in the clarity and answers you received. You can trust this.

You know it is the Holy Spirit when you feel set free from confusion, guilt, and fear in their various forms. There's a lifting and lightening. When it is the ego (personal thought system) confusion, guilt, and fear persist or get worse.

Just to clarify: It is not your mind that denies these experiences are the Holy Spirit. That is the ego, a thought system in your mind. Your mind is what is split between the Holy Spirit and the ego. The ego denies the Holy Spirit and then you – a split mind – doubt because you are used to listening to its counsel.

144. Finally, A Real Choice (October 13, 2017)

A Course in Miracles teaches that we always look inward before we look outward. And it has always been easy for me to see True Perception (the Real World, Christ's Vision, Holy Spirit's Vision, etc. in ACIM) as a wholly inward Vision. When I experience It I also see the universe of form is meaningless. It is a blank canvas. The Vision may extend to form but I know the source is me, not the forms the body's eyes report. In a way, I see a world overlaid over the world of form and I know that "real world" is in me. This *overlaid* world actually *overlooks* form because it is meaningless.

But the ego's (personal thought system's) perceptions are harder for me to see as only an inward perception. And that is because it *always* projects its perceptions away. Even though I have learned to take back my perceptions by practicing sorting out facts in form from my projection of meaning onto them, still there has always been an attachment between my perceptions and the universe of form. This is what made them seem to me to be reality not a blank canvas and a projected perception.

A few weeks ago I finally saw the ego's perception *as a perception*. I realized I choose its perception (always some form of lack/guilt/fear) and then I see "proof" of this perception in the arbitrarily chosen forms the body's eyes report to me. Because the universe of form is limited it is easy for the ego to point to specifics and say, "See, lack is real." Of course I could also see in arbitrarily chosen forms "proof" that lack is not real. Form has no meaning in itself and it is so diverse I could find anything I wanted in it! But the ego is only going to point to lack, guilt, and fear because that is what it is.

What this has done for me is freed me to make a choice where before I could not see a real choice. It seemed my choice was between a perception – Real Perception – and a "reality" that was fixed in form. Yes, I knew I was projecting meaning. But I didn't really see this as a *perception* because of the "proof" in form. I did not see that I first chose a perception and then saw proof for that perception. I was deceived by the specifics and did not see that I first made a choice for a general perception.

I used to say, "Turn inward and choose Truth despite what is appearing in form." But now I see there is no relationship between my perception and form. It is not "despite what is appearing in form". It is choose Truth's perceptions over the ego's perceptions.

Form, the ego's perceptions, and True Perception are all not real. But the perception I experience is automatically determined by how I see myself. I am never bothered by what is in form. I can only be bothered by my perceptions. And when I am bothered I can now truly make the choice for True Perception because I see my choice is between two equivalent things – perceptions – rather than between a perception and reality. I can say, "This is just a perception. It does not represent the Truth in me", and it will fall away.

145. More on Perception (October 20, 2017)

A few questions and requests for clarity came after last week's article. Also, I have something to add. So I will try again:

The body's eyes report what it sees to the mind. It sees forms that have no meaning in themselves. So the universe of form is like a blank screen with regard to meaning.

Your mind always *perceives* inward. If you are in the Holy Spirit (Awareness of Truth in your mind) you know this and you see Real Perception, or what *A Course in Miracles* calls the "real world". This is a Vision of Love or Light within. This inward Vision extends outward to the universe of form. This "colors" the way you see form, but you are aware of this. You do not have the illusion that how you see form comes from the forms the body's eyes report. You know you are seeing your own mind.

In the ego (personal though system) you also always perceive only inward. However, you project your perceptions away onto the universe of form. Remember, projection is extension + denial. The same mechanism of extending from your mind occurs with the Holy Spirit and with the ego, only the ego denies that your perception comes from you. And your perceptions from the ego seem to give form meaning. It seems that form tells you what to think about form. You can learn that you project your perceptions, but that does not stop the projection. The ego *always* projects – that is simply how it works.

It is projection that makes it hard to see that the ego's perception is just a perception. It seems as though its perception and form are one and the same. But they are not. You can forget about what the eyes report. It's really not involved in your perception. (Notice that blind people also *perceive* though they do not have the body's sight). You can learn to not trust the ego's perceptions because the ego is false so its perceptions are false. You can turn your mind to Truth instead.

The practice I mentioned was sorting out fact from projection of meaning. For example, let's say Bob hit Tom in the nose and Tom's nose is bleeding. That is what the body's eyes report. That is fact in form. But if I see or feel anything more about it I am *perceiving*. From the ego I will project meaning – right/wrong, good/bad. And that judgment will come from my own personal story and filters.

I know when I project meaning because I feel an emotional charge. If I am just observing I do not feel an emotional charge. My feelings come from the thoughts in my own mind, not from what happens in form. Once I sort out observable fact from my perception – projection of meaning – I can then deal with the thoughts I project where they occur – in my own mind.

The shift I wrote about last week was that I can deal now with the ego's perceptions wholesale rather than piecemeal. Instead of dealing in specifics, I step back and recognize it is only a perception and since it comes from the ego I should not trust it. Since I recognize it as a perception I realize I have a choice in perception – I can turn to True Perception instead.

What I want to add is that you perceive what you believe is reality. Another way to say this is you perceive what you believe is true about you. So the perception that you accept as real reflects what you believe is true about you. If you believe the ego is true you will accept its perceptions. If you believe Truth is true you will accept Its Perceptions. As you transition from believing the ego is you, you must make the conscious choice to put its perceptions aside and choose Truth's Perceptions instead.

Perception changes incrementally over time. Except for those moments that I refer to as "higher miracles" you will not go from the ego's perception directly to full-on Real Perception.

The changes over time are a lot like when you get a prescription for your contacts or glasses changed. There's a small period of adjustment and then you are in a "new normal" that you don't even think about. It's only looking back or in relation to others that you see that your perception has changed.

Often I'm asked, "So how do you see the world now?" That's difficult for me to answer because I don't see the world they mean—I see my own perception. I know the questioner is usually asking to know how I perceive form. They still think it's about form and not about perception. If I say, "I don't see the world" they think, "What, everything's whited out for you? You don't see people? You don't see houses and cars and trees?" This body still reports those forms to this mind. But that is not my "world". My world is my perception. It is within. And that is evolving toward True Perception all the time.

146. The Way Out is Through (October 27, 2017)

When I started out on this path to Peace I was very young. I was drawn to Truth, but I was also hoping to avoid pain. I wanted to use my growing spiritual awareness to do so. But it quickly became obvious this was not going to happen. Pain did not go away. But it was my fear of denial that had set me on this path in the first place, so I was not going to use the path for another form of denial. If I found I was doing so, I'd pull myself back and face whatever I had to face.

Not only was I not going to avoid the pain of the personal life, but there was the pain of the spiritual path to deal with, too. It is not that it *has to be* painful. It is just that it *is inevitably* painful to look into one's mind at one's obstacles to peace. If I didn't think they were painful, they wouldn't be obstacles! The only way to overcome obstacles and get out of the pain is to go directly into and through the ideas and beliefs that cause them. And that is experienced as painful until I am through them and see the ideas and beliefs are false.

This requires that I am completely honest with myself. Only then can I be honest with the Holy Spirit (Awareness of Truth in my mind). A thought or belief is always more painful when it is hidden. Its being hidden makes it seem more frightening or unacceptable. So once I am honest with myself I am at least half-way through the pain. In fact, sometimes bringing it to light is enough to dispel it. I see right away it is false and it is gone. But, usually, there are many angles or layers to the belief to work out with the Holy Spirit. And I always do, finding release and relief.

The more I practiced this, the easier it got. I learned and I now trust that there will be relief at the end so I've become very willing to go through the process. My tolerance for pain is less because I knew relief is possible. Now, if I am in pain, I just want to go right through it and work it out. There is no reason to suffer.

147. The Fear to Look Within (November 3, 2017)

Last week I wrote about how the way out of emotions that are obstacles to being aware of Truth and being at peace is not to deny or repress them but to go through them. But many people struggle to do this. And that's because the first obstacle you encounter is a belief that if you look inward you will not be able to cope with what you find. Sometimes it seems you fear you will be overwhelmed by your emotions, but what you really fear is to see the guilt that you believe is there.

"...Loudly the ego tells you not to look inward, for if you do your eyes will light on sin, and God will strike you blind. This you believe, and so you do not look..." (T-21.IV.2)

Guilt is what sustains the ego (personal thought system) in your mind. It wants you to believe in guilt. So as much as you might not want to look at the guilt in your mind, the ego is not threatened by you doing so. What it really fears when you look inward is that you will see past it. You will see that there is no guilt.

"...Beneath your fear to look within because of sin is yet another fear, and one which makes the ego tremble.
What if you looked within and saw no sin? This 'fearful' question is one the ego never asks. And you who ask it now are threatening the ego's whole defensive system too seriously for it to bother to pretend it is your friend." (T-21.IV.2-3)

In your identification with the ego, the first thing you *will* find when you look inward is your belief in guilt. That is very hard to look at. But you have to remember that guilt is the cloud the ego uses to obscure the Light in your mind. You have to look at the cloud to look through it. You will eventually see it isn't real. You will see past it. And each time you look inward and find a belief you feared to look at and see it is not true, you undermine the ego. The cloud gets a little less dense and easier to see through.

It is very hard to look inward at first. But the more you practice this the more you realize that you never find the horrible thing the ego tells you are there. And it gets easier after that.

148. Grief Is A Healing Process (November 10, 2017)

Continuing with the themes of "the way out is through" and "the fear to look within"…
I have found that grief is the emotion that is most often resisted and repressed. It is also often unidentified.
All loss entails feelings of grief, to varying degrees. Sometimes we go through it quickly. You miss a phone call and you experience denial ("I can't believe I missed that."), anger/depression ("Oh, I really wanted to speak with them."), and, finally, understanding/acceptance ("Oh, well, they'll call back."). In other situations these stages take longer to process. Sometimes, in the case of a major loss, it can take years to fully reach understanding and acceptance.
Grief is painful, sometimes excruciating, but it is not really a *negative* emotion. It is the process our minds use to heal. The way out of grief is to go through the process. We repress grief because it is so painful and/or because we don't want to acknowledge the loss. But when we don't go through the process we don't heal. And unprocessed grief is an obstacle to peace.
Sometimes clients tell me of resentments they cannot seem to release. They know the story they tell themselves. They know why they are angry. But they can't seem to get past it. I ask them, "But have you grieved that So-and-so isn't the person you wanted them to be for you?" Sometimes we have to grieve lost expectations or dreams. Sometimes we have to grieve that someone is never going to be for us who we want them to be for us or who we thought they should have been for us. Grieving can sometimes be the last thing left to do before you are free of your resentment.

Often clients tell me they feel they will be overwhelmed by their grief. That is because it looms large when it is unexpressed. It feels like a tidal wave when it is repressed, but it is really just an ordinary wave of emotion. Grief is a process that, once you go through it, you realize you can and will survive any loss that comes your way. It is painful. It is difficult. But if you are willing, you will go through the process and come out on the other side wiser and stronger.

149. Ask: Are your ACIM Mentor Articles still relevant? (November 17, 2017)

"i am currently reading 'The ACIM Mentor Articles: answers for students of a course in miracles' *and as some of the entries are from 2006 etc, i am wondering if they are still relevant to your current teachings now, as you seem to have developed and sometimes have different ways of perception."* – HE

Yes, I have evolved and much of what I wrote back then I would not write now. However, what I wrote then was authentic to where I was then. So many readers still find those articles relevant to where *they* are now. I get a lot of positive feedback about that book's practical approach.

Also, working one-on-one with others, I try to meet them where they are, not where I am. So with clients I teach what was relevant to me when I was where they are now. In that respect I still teach some of what I wrote back then.

150. An Interesting Thing Happened This Summer (November 24, 2017)

An interesting thing happened in this mind this summer. But first, some background:

As many of you know, I have published five books and written many articles, all non-fiction, all with spiritual themes. But my writing began with fiction at the age of ten. All my life I have devised plots in my mind, inspired by any number of things. It's just the way this mind often occupied itself.

I finished two novels, one in my early twenties and one in my early thirties. Both were love stories. The first was heterosexual. The second, more authentically for me, was between two women. Though both were submitted to publishers, neither was published. I did not consider myself very good at writing fiction, though I loved the process. Eventually, fiction writing fell away naturally, though my mind continued to produce plots and characters.

My non-fiction, spiritual writing began in my early forties, as my blog. I have not stopped writing spiritual themed books and articles since (I am fifty-four). The only thing that is similar about writing novels and writing non-fiction books for me is that I am not able to complete a book if I cannot clearly see the beginning, the middle, and the end. I don't have to know the details, just the general outline.

Last fall a love story, between two women, came to me. When I wrote fiction before, my characters were not much more than cardboard standees. And the stories were plot driven, despite the fact that I prefer to read character driven stories myself. This writing was a new experience. The characters seemed almost real to me. There was much more depth and texture to them and their story. I felt compelled to begin writing it, but it fell away. For one thing, I could not see it all. The central conflict did not work. I took this episode to be just some sort of random creative burst. Nothing followed.

Now I come to my very interesting late summer this year:

For three years, after the self-concept fell away, my mind was very noisy. The Quiet was here, but the noise was also persistent. I accepted it as part of the process. But sometime this August my mind quieted and a Space opened in it. It was lovely. When I had free time I would spend it playing a word game on my computer to occupy the surface of my mind while I basked in this Spaciousness beneath. In fact, I came to associate the game with the Spaciousness! I couldn't get enough of either.

In time I began to sense in the Spaciousness that a big shift was coming. That felt great, too. But I didn't know what it would be and could only let it unfold.

Then one night in August I had a dream. There was nothing remarkable about the dream in content or context or in how I experienced it. It had a slight erotic tinge to it, though nothing erotic happened in it. And, as I do, for the next day or two I casually played with the characters from the dream and devised a lose plot. The characters and setting changed significantly in this process. Blah, blah, blah—all this was very usual for me.

But then it wasn't. I cannot say when the Light of Love came into my mind. I cannot find mention of It in my journal. But coinciding with the Light, this story that I was casually playing with in my usual way became compelling. There are things I'd heard writers of fiction say that I had never experienced myself: The characters were real for them, they lived with the characters, they go to the place of which they write, etc. I was, for the first time, having these experiences. It was as though another reality was in my mind all the time. I felt as a god in the traditional sense: I was creator and the characters were my creation, made in my image, a part of me. And this other reality, this fictional story, was bathed in a Golden Light. It was the same Light as the Light of the Holy Relationship, which I experienced over thirty years ago.

The story pushed at me. I thought the reason I could not let it go was that I had not devised an ending. So I decided to do so to get this distraction out of my mind. One Saturday I spent the whole day, as I went about my usual Saturday errands and chores, crafting in the back of my mind an ending to the story. I succeeded. Phew! Now the damn thing would be off my mind. I could go back to the delicious Spaciousness…

But the next day, as I mowed my lawn, I continued to think about the story and I knew it had to be written. I began writing that day.

The following day I began my journal with: *"Totally scrambled. There's been some shift. Things are not the same within."*

Later that day: *"Yesterday was like a non sequitur from what went before. All that happened last week, all that I ended thinking about Saturday about the personal thought system falling away… Went in a totally different direction on Sunday…I feel like something is being done to me, through me, and without me and all I can do is watch."*

I described it as doing a 90-degree turn. I was headed north and suddenly, unexpectedly, I was headed east.

The sensation of something being done to, through, and without me held for the duration of the experience. It was as though my mind had been hijacked. The book, the characters, this other reality was with me all the time. So was the Light of Love, which was what made it tolerable. But I wanted to be there, with the Light, in the book, all the time. It was so distracting!

There was, of course, a huge ego attack over this. Huge judgements against everything I was experiencing, over the story, the characters, my psychology, etc. Par for the course with the ego.

For a short time I wondered about my sanity. Perhaps I was having a psychotic break! But I realized that, though distracted, I was fully functional in the rest of my life. That settled the question of my sanity and I was able to continue on without that fear.

But there was more. In addition to this Light and this story pushing through me, dark corners of my personal psychology were being revealed. The Light was slowly diminished for me by this nibbling darkness, though It was never completely undone.

I was aware from the start that the story was an allegory of my spiritual journey from unworthiness to accepting Love. The characters were simply metaphors. Their details and the details of the story didn't matter. Then one night early on I got up in the middle of the night to use the toilet, my mind consumed by all that was going on, when I got this thunderous message, "Pay attention! You are telling yourself something!" Suddenly I could see not just this allegory and these metaphors, but tons of symbols in the story. They would not mean much to others. They were from me to me. (Example: The protagonist's name is Aly—as in Aly-gory, get it? Duh. I didn't see that for a few more days).

Tons of personal processing then followed. There was grief. There was depression. And the whole time I was able to write the novel without any of that making its way into the novel.

There was the Light, there was the novel, there was the psycho-spiritual processing. It was a massive, confusing tangle that took over my mind. I was hard to live with, as my wife reported, because when I wasn't consumed with the novel I was consumed with processing. I simply wasn't "here". I could give my attention to my clients, but that was it. Everything else was a struggle against the tide of wanting to be writing either the novel or in my journal.

Each glob of darkness surfaced, was seen, and was gone. However, there was nothing I had to do with any of it. Nothing had to be "fixed", just processed. And the tangle slowly unraveled. My mind began to settle. I was left with just the novel.

This went on for a few weeks. There were tons of insights. I felt I wrote as many words in my journal as in the novel. I finished the first draft of the novel in six and a half weeks. By the end my mind had been settled for a while.

The insights continued. But the one that turned the corner for me was when I heard in my mind that I had been making the product (the novel) and the processing too significant. It was the Light, the Love, that mattered. The product and the processing were simply inevitable effects in a split-mind when the Light breaks through. But they didn't mean anything. They were incidental.

The novel poured into my mind and poured out of me. Scenes came to me and I described them on paper. The characters took over and the story went in directions I didn't plan. But to be clear, the novel is nothing remarkable. It has no spiritual themes whatsoever. It is just an ordinary love story. It has more depth and breadth than the fiction I wrote earlier in life. But that distinction only has meaning for me. I did not "channel" it from a Higher Source. It is the product of this split-mind in many ways and on many levels. Only this mind can really understand these ways and levels. What I went through psycho-spiritually did not make it onto those pages. And even re-reading my journal I find I was not able to capture there the profundity of the experience.

The novel is being read by others now so I can determine if it is worth sending to a publisher. But I want to make clear that as remarkable as this experience was, it was about me, not about bringing some product into the world for others' enlightenment. I knew this as I wrote it and it has been reinforced for me by those reading it. ACIM students who have read it find lessons for themselves in the book because they are looking for them. They are used to using everything as a classroom with the Holy Spirit. Those readers who are not on a path have not reported anything remarkable except that they enjoy the book. No one reading the book experiences the Light and Love I did writing it (and still do). It is like any other form, neutral. What is done with it is determined by the reader.

This mind went through, and is still going through much more quietly, something amazing. It is not the same as before this experience. I see a direct line between the Light of the Holy Relationship and this experience. They are the same, really. The lesson is the same, but I am better equipped and able to accept it now. It is the Light that matters, not Its effect on the personal psyche. That is incidental.

This is not the first time I've experienced such an abrupt shift in direction on this path. And I know from experience that I will not fully understand it until time passes and I can look back at it in the context of the greater unfolding. Will there be another book? Will I be writing novels now? I don't know. I don't know anything! I had no clue this would happen. For now, I just have to be confused. I get up each day and remember the Light of Love that has come into my awareness. And then I do what it is given to me to do that day. My biggest lesson? To not judge what I am given to do, no matter how unexpected or confusing.

151. The Hybrid Mind (December 1, 2017)

Last week I wrote about an experience of the Light of Love coming into my mind and the product, a lesbian romance novel, which came about because of it. (The "Light of Love" can also be called the Vision of the Holy Spirit, the Vision of the Holy Relationship, Spiritual Vision, the Real World, True Perception, etc.) There was also a great deal of personal psychological processing that occurred when it began. I noted that the novel was not "channeled", though it "rode in", on the Light. So where did it come from.

It came from what I call the "hybrid-mind". This is a blend of this split-mind and the universal split-mind. Both of these contain the awareness of Truth. To explain:

This split-mind is a singular expression of the universal split-mind. The Truth in this split-mind is universal. But not-Truth in this split-mind is unique. Not-Truth is this particular personal thought system (ego) and the personal story for the self in this mind. This is what informed the product, for example, that it was a lesbian love story. This mind's psychology is all over the book, and, as I said in last week's blog, it was full of symbols that had meaning for this split-mind. The book was also an allegory, not in the details, but in the overarching theme, for this particular mind's journey from unworthiness to acceptance of Love.

The reason I include the universal split-mind in this experience is that as I wrote I felt my mind contained the whole world. I was in touch with something in the universal personal experience beyond just this personal self's experience. It felt as though I could have written anything, but I just happened to be writing what I wrote. Information I needed to write the book just flowed into my awareness.

The Awareness of Truth (Holy Spirit) is a part of both this split-mind and the universal split-mind. It showed up in my writing as the Love that was expressed through the authentic depiction of universal human experiences and through the characters' learning. Love cannot come directly into the world, but when a mind is in touch with Love it expresses itself honestly and authentically. It learns and it grows. In the world, love is honesty and love is learning. This was not something I fully understood until I was writing and realized that the Love I was basking in as I wrote did not show up in the details of the story, but in the idealization, the authenticity, and the lessons the characters learned. I did not aim for this, but simply discovered it in the process.

If I was an artist rather than a writer, instead of an idealized love story I would have depicted idealized scenes through art. Think of the art of Thomas Kinkade. He depicts, over and over again, idealized scenes of warmth and coziness in the midst of winter. He means to give comfort in the midst of a harsh world. My wife commented on how nice everyone is in my book. Yes! An idealized love story provides comforting escape, it uplifts, and it reinforces healthy (loving) values through the lessons and maturing of the characters. Idealization is not Love directly, but an effect of the awareness of Love.

But still, the product is not the point. The hybrid-mind is this split-mind at a higher level. It is in touch with both the universal split-mind and the Awareness of Truth. It is an effect, a result, of decades of quieting this mind and becoming both more attuned to the unfolding story of the universal split-mind and to the Awareness of Truth. It is itself a product and not the point. If I had sought this experience, I would never have found it. Love is all that is real so It is all that matters. I sought Love and this effect unfolded.

152. Ask: Can you explain your different versions of mind? (December 8, 2017)

"...I try to follow your descriptions when you refer to the mind but it seems there are so many versions of "mind" I wondered if you could find an easy way for the very simple person (me) to explain so I can understand? So for example in your last mind you mentioned--Universal mind--Universal split mind--hybrid mind, and simply mind. Is this linked to the ladder of the split which Kenneth Wapnick referred to?" - CL

There is only one Mind (Truth), but we experience Mind as though It is split between Truth and not-Truth. The part of Mind where the idea of not-Truth seems to occur I refer to as the one or universal split-mind. (In *A Course in Miracles* this is called the "Son of God"). It is this split-mind that projects the universe of form, including billions of versions ("sons of God") of itself. You experience yourself as one of these projected split-minds. The split in you shows up as two thought systems, the Awareness of Truth (Holy Spirit) and the personal thought system (ego).

The "hybrid mind" I mentioned for the first time in last week's article is a recent experience for me. It is where the boundary between this particular projection and the universal split-mind fell away, at least in part. This split-mind for a while was aware of expressing not just itself but the universal split-mind.

All split-minds are part of the universal split-mind and are always expressing it. What is unfolding in the universe of form as the story of time is the Undoing (Atonement) of the universal split-mind. I sometimes refer to this story as the "flow of the universe". The story for each seemingly-individual split-mind is a part of the Undoing, whether it seems to be or not. For those of us who manifest the Undoing and rise in consciousness (awareness, perception) it is inevitable that the boundary between the universal and seemingly-individual split-mind falls away.

I have not studied Ken Wapnick so I do not know if this is related to his ladder of the split.

153. Ask: Can you explain this quote in ACIM about God creating distinct beings? (December 15, 2017)

"I was doing my morning reading of the Course *when I came upon this statement in Text-4.7.5: 'God Who encompasses all being, nevertheless created distinct beings who have everything individually, but who want to share it to increase their joy. Nothing that is real can be increased except by sharing it.' This confuses me a bit...thinking we need to lose the individual..."* – JW

Yes, it is a confusing quote out of context and seems to contradict much that *A Course in Miracles* says about Oneness. And it certainly contradicts the experience of Oneness! Oneness means one and the same throughout. There is no distinction to be made in What is One. The conversational nature of ACIM, especially in the first few chapters, also makes it confusing because there is an implied understanding between the Voice and Helen so there is a lack of helpful elaboration for the rest of us. But that quote is understandable if you remember that in ACIM "to create" means "to extend" rather than "to bring into being". You can read the quote as: *"God Who encompasses all being, nevertheless* extends Himself to seemingly-distinct beings *who have everything individually but who want to share it to increase their joy..."*

In my translation of ACIM into plain language (*The Message of A Course in Miracles*) I translated it as:

"Even in your perceived separated state you have not stopped being One with God's Being, in Which you have Everything, and in Which you increase God's Being to increase your Joy..."

154. Letting Truth Lead the Way (December 22, 2017)

There are two approaches one can take to a spiritual teaching. In one the teaching is an end in itself. The goal of the student is to master the teaching. The emphasis of study for them is to find the "right way" to understand the material. Therefore, they often engage in arguments with other students over the correct way to interpret the material. They are often unhappy with teachers they feel are not "right" in their interpretation.

In the other approach, the Awareness of Truth (Holy Spirit) is the Goal. And the teaching is seen as an instrument that the Awareness of Truth in the student's mind uses to help them reach that Goal. So the student does not seek the "right way" to read the material, but rather asks the Awareness of Truth in their mind for the most *helpful* way to understand it. The student emphasizes their experiences of Truth over the material they study, which they recognize are just symbols on a page. They have no reason to argue with others over the correct interpretation because their goal is not "to be right". If another is helped by another interpretation, even if they cannot understand how, they know that is between the student and the Awareness of Truth in their mind.

The latter is the path that this mind has taken. Often when it got bogged down by the way that it read *A Course in Miracles* it would step back and say, "But what have my *experiences* of Truth shown me?" It would consider what it learned from higher miracles and direct Revelation. For this mind, its own experiences were always more important than what it heard from others or how it read a book. That's not to say it didn't experience conflict. It believed in guilt and it read

ACIM through guilt for a long time. It didn't trust its experiences. But, eventually, it did trust them, and this is how it overcame the belief in guilt. (There's a reason ACIM calls the path "the development of trust"!).

I often say that this path has not unfolded the way this mind expected. How could it, with all of its guilty misreading and misunderstanding? Steeped in self-identification, it could have no way of properly understanding how that would be dismantled—something it is finally now experiencing with the belief in guilt gone. What is left for a mind to do when the belief in guilt is gone and the self-concept has fallen away is to watch itself unlearn the habits of guilt and self-identification.

This mind still has expectations. They're automatic. But it has learned to recognize them *and* to stay open. "This is what I expect, but what the heck do I know?" There have been so many surprises as this mind follows Truth it would be arrogant for it to think it has any idea what is going to happen next.

155. Too Concerned with Consciousness (December 29, 2017)

My mistake for so many years was to try to accept that I wasn't what I was experiencing myself to be. In other words, I felt I was a self, but I tried to get myself to realize that I was Truth or Spirit or Mind or whatever you want to call It. It would have been better to allow myself to feel I was a self and to also invite Truth into my awareness. In practice, of course, this is what eventually occurred. I would, time and again, say, "This is what I experience, dammit, and I'm not going to deny it anymore." But it would have been a lot less painful if between those moments of honesty I didn't fall back into guilt and feel I had to try to accept what was unacceptable from the point of view that I was a self.

There was no reconciling my experience as a self and my experiences of Truth. I really just had to experience each apart from the other. This is the experience of the split mind. But mind seeks to be whole. So it seeks to reconcile its parts. However, Wholeness is. It is not made by reconciling Truth and not-Truth. In fact, Wholeness does not need to be made at all. It is always here. To realize Wholeness I just need to let not-Truth fall away. And this is done by letting it go without judging it. It isn't real so why would I need to judge it? Why would I need to do anything with it?

I was always too concerned with my own conscious experiences. If I experience what isn't real, so what? *It isn't real.* That's not justification for guilt. The only response that makes sense is to recognize it isn't real! No harm; no foul. The Truth goes on completely untouched by what happens in the consciousness of this split mind.

This is something I can only see now that I no longer believe in guilt.

156. After Guilt (January 5, 2018)

This mind wondered, what happens when the belief in guilt falls away? Well, first the self-concept fell away. This mind sometimes wonders if this is the same as saying self-identification has fallen away. After all, what is the self but a concept? Sometimes this mind is comfortable with that. Sometimes it feels it is not quite accurate to say, yet, that all self-id has fallen away. It sees evidence that this is not yet so.

After the self-concept fell away this mind spent a good three years in a type of limbo or stasis. The personal thought system (ego) was very loud, insistent, and persistent. Of course, there was also always a present Peace. This mind could do nothing but allow the noise and wait and see what would unfold. And, frankly, that is what is left after the belief in guilt has fallen away! There is nothing to do but watch. Everything is automatic and the mind only needs to observe the undoing of the part of it that no longer has a use.

Mostly, for now anyway, this mind is unlearning thinking in terms of guilt. It is unlearning judging the self and the personal thought system. It is unlearning thinking as a self. It is unlearning identifying with the doer in the mind. These all say the same thing in a slightly different way.

This mind is, of course, tremendously confused as the old thought ways are broken down. But this mind is used to this confusion. It is something that came on this path whenever a shift occurred. The confusion this time is different only in depth and duration. The other shifts were shifts in self-concepts. This shift was the dropping of all self-concepts. One thing this mind has learned is trust so it doesn't have to try to force certainty anymore. It knows the limbo and confusion will pass and clarity will come. They always have.

So this mind is learning how *not* to think. But how is it going to think going forward? This mind does not know yet, but it has had glimpses that are hard to characterize, even to itself. There is so much unlearning in the way that it cannot yet see what will be left when the unlearning is done.

157. Ask: What is the relationship between Vision and sense? (January 12, 2018)

"In section T-22.III.1.4-6, it reads: 'You can see reason. This is not a play on words, for here is the beginning of a vision that has meaning. Vision is sense, quite literally. If it is not the body's sight, it must be understood.'

*My question lies with Vision, and what it actually is. For years as both a devoted student and teacher of ACIM, I have been aware that the body's eyes were made to hide what could be seen. So my understanding is if what we believe we see is not there, than it is Vision, the Holy Spirit's sight, in which is gifted us through our practice of willingness and forgiveness. (along with reason, being HS's knowledge) The above readings say; **"Vision is sense, quite literally."** I am a little confused. If I try to understand, it is telling me that Vision is to sense or experience that which the Holy Spirit sees and knows—beyond the body and the world of form. It cannot be "sense" as we know it in the world, sensing with our ears and eye's and noses and hands. It must be a spiritual "sense" and experience of something formless and timeless…"* - BO

"Vision", as *A Course in Miracles* uses the word, is seeing Truth in your mind, not the physical seeing of the body. Here, it equates "vision" with "reason", or true "sense". The word "sense" here is being used to mean "understanding" (as in, "that makes sense" or "I'm trying to make sense of this"), not to refer to the five senses of the body. The point it is making is that True Vision (Reason or Sense) is unambiguous and clearly understood when you experience It.

True Vision is not a gift given because you are willing or you forgive. It is in every mind, always. You do not need to be given What you already have! But you do need to remove your obstacles to seeing you already have Truth within. Truth (Vision) is What you see when you release yourself from the belief in the false. Willingness to experience forgiveness (release) is the practice that invites the Holy Spirit's help to remove your obstacles to True Vision.

The body's eyes are part of the universe of form that it reports to the mind. The ego (personal thought system) teaches that the body and what it sees are real. It also gives you a "vision", or perception (interpretation), of what is seen by the body. However, it projects this perception onto the universe of form so that you think your perception of form comes from form. When you believe in this perception, you look outward at a projection from mind rather than inward to What mind really is. Your belief in form and the ego's perception of it is the false that you must be willing to release to look inward and experience True Vision. And when you do, ACIM calls that "forgiveness".

158. All Is Well, Always (January 19, 2018)

All is well and perfect and always has been. I have resisted this experience from the beginning for many reasons.

For one thing, it was too good to be true. I didn't trust it, though it was something I had always sensed. For another, it obviously did not apply to the self and its world—or the self's thought system's (ego's) interpretation of the universe of form. So I didn't want it. What good was this idea to me in my identification with the self? The personal thought system in my mind was saying, as always, "What's in it for me?" and, because I identified with it, those words were my own. I wanted it to be well and perfect according to *my* definition of well and perfect at the level of form. Of course, what I couldn't see was that the personal thought system would never, ever see things that way. It is a thought system of lack, guilt, and fear.

And, of course, there was my belief in guilt in the way. How could I accept that all is well and perfect when guilt was real to me? This is related to the last obstacle. What I wanted to see as well and perfect was the world of guilt I projected. And that was never going to happen.

And this brings me to the idea I can see now was beneath those other forms of resistance: If all is well and perfect, always, then the personal thought system's world is clearly not real.

159. Without Guilt, Clarity (January 26, 2018)

This intersection of perimenopause in the self's life with the falling away of the belief in guilt from this mind has made something very clear to this mind: Much of my sense of personal identity was determined by hormones. Much of what I thought of as "me" was just mere moods passing to and fro because of chemicals washing over the brain.

Of course, I am simply describing the human female experience. Before this stage in this mind's awareness there was no disentangling itself from the human experience. And the belief in guilt rode the hormonal ride, compounding the darker aspects of it. Only without the belief in guilt can I (this mind) see this, because the hormones are still there causing occasional darkness of varying degrees, but there is no belief in guilt to convince me there is something inherently wrong in me that needs to be fixed. At first, especially when it hasn't happened for a while and/or it is subtle, I am sometimes deceived. But I always return to the awareness that there is nothing to fix. The darkness, like every other human experience, just needs to be observed and allowed to pass. *It all does.*

I made the mistake, too, of thinking when the self's moods were balanced that I had "succeeded" or I was at peace. But that, too, would pass, because hormones would surge again and bring me down again and I'd feel I was a failure or had something to fix again.

I realize now how much I looked to passing feelings for guidance. I looked to them to tell me about myself as well as sometimes to make decisions. It was so real to me, what else did I have?

Even when I sought a Higher Guidance I would then turn to the self's feelings to determine how to judge the Guidance!

Not that any of this matters. This is not about right or wrong or good or bad. It's just about clarity—and relief—gained. It no longer matters to this mind what it uses to guide the self because however it is guided it is all equally meaningless. And, anyway, what's going to happen is going to happen as an expression of an idea that was over long ago. What is there to do but watch—and learn that there is nothing to judge?

160. The Self's Life in the World is an Expression (February 2, 2018)

Truth, being All cannot have an opposite. But, being All, It must consider the idea of Its Own opposite. However, the moment the idea of not-Truth arises, it is undone by Truth's All-encompassing nature.

Since Truth is Eternal (Timeless), Infinite (Limitless), and Formless the idea of not-Truth is time-bound, limited form. So *within the idea* of not-Truth it seems like not-Truth, or time and limited form, arose long ago and will be undone in some indefinite future. This is what you seem to be experiencing as a self. The unfolding story of the universe of form is the instant of the idea-of-not-Truth/the-undoing-of-the-idea-of-not-Truth expressed as the story of time. Realizing this means turning your mind around to understand that all you see as the universe of form is an expression of that moment of undoing. The undoing is over and you are just watching it play out as a story of time. *You don't have to make the undoing happen.* It is already happening through the self with which you identify—as well as everyone else.

Earlier in my (this mind's) process I could not see this and I would not have been able to accept it. Guilt got in the way. (More on this below). But I did understand that "the script is written" means the outcome of the story of time--the undoing of not-Truth--is inevitable. No being wrote out beforehand the details of what unfolds in time. What happens in time is the result of cause and effect in time. In fact, cause and effect is *how* the story of time unfolds. That instant of the idea-of-not-Truth/the-undoing-of-the-idea-of-not-Truth was the primary cause and everything that has followed and that will follow is its effect. And within the story, every effect is also a cause. This means every action taken causes a future effect, until, ultimately, all cause and effect--all of not-Truth--is undone.

Moment to moment, you do not have to keep in mind that it is all an expression. In fact, if you try to you may end up paralyzed and unable to decide how to direct the self to act. You must allow the self to live as it always has, feeling its desires and motivations and acting as it chooses to act as though it is autonomous, even though it is not and its feelings, thoughts, and actions are all a part of the expression of the undoing of not-Truth. The awareness that it is only an expression unfolding before you is useful when you need to step back and look at the larger picture to gain some relief from the details of what is unfolding right now

To understand that what is unfolding in time is only an expression of a past cause is to be relieved of absolute-moral guilt. For me, I had to be relieved of the belief in guilt to see this! To understand the unfolding as an expression takes off any pressure to "do it right" because the self with which you identify is not here to cause a future effect, like the undoing of not-Truth. The self with which you identify is an expression of a past cause. If it is a manifest part of the Undoing, then that is how its life will unfold. If it is not a manifest part of the Undoing, then that is how its life will unfold. Both are part of the Undoing, manifest or not. In other words, no self can go wrong. It will play its part perfectly.

Yes, even the ones who do horrible things in the world are playing their part. We cannot see how what they do is part of the Undoing because we cannot see the whole picture. We cannot see all the effects of what they cause. And while they are absolved of any absolute-moral guilt (there is no god sitting in judgment on them), they are still accountable and responsible in the story. If caught, they still have to, in time, face the consequences of their actions. That is part of how cause and effect unfolds in the story.

You can find the flow of the universe and live in harmony with it. You do this by quieting your mind and opening yourself to an awareness of the flow. You do this by stepping back and letting things unfold and acting as you feel motivated to act, without judgment. You will act as you are motivated to act, anyway, but the "without judgment" is how you find harmony with this. And you can overcome judgment by realizing that no matter how it appears in the tiny snapshot of right now, it all leads to the Undoing.

Or, you can choose to resist the flow of the universe, which will not change it, but which will affect you. Of course, whichever choice you make, it is part of the unfolding.

161. Ask: What changed the first time you experienced a Revelation? (February 9, 2018)

"Over the years I have noticed that spiritual teachers over the centuries who have had a direct experience, revelation, unity are different than those who have not. There are very good Teachers who have not experienced this direct unitive revelation. To intellectualize a spiritual teaching like ACIM is very easy to do. Helen was a prime example, yet you can tell when reading the Text and from some of your works that the words are coming from a place beyond the intellect. I think the Workbook is perhaps where that transcendence is attempted. However there are many cases where it randomly occurs naturally, drug induced or a near death experience. What changed the first time it happened to you? Did your writing change?" – ES

Everything changed the first time I experienced direct Revelation (an experience of *only* Truth). It was shattering. I could never be the same after It, though I tried to forget It. I went into a kind of shock. It was a few months before I could acknowledge It happened. The world as reality was stripped away from me. I could never again after that ever wholly believe in it or value it, though I continued to believe in it and value it very much. It was liberating and joyous and terrifying and I became very angry that the world was stripped away from me before I had a chance to try it out. I was only twenty years old and a brand new student of *A Course in Miracles*, so I was far, far from ready to teach and was not writing yet.

A Revelation can only occur if you are ready to accept It. I don't know why I was, but I was only *just* ready. There were times after It I thought I was losing my mind. I sometimes felt I was barely holding on to my sanity. But, obviously, in time, my inner world stabilized and I had a new normal. This was the same after each succeeding Revelation. But I came to know what to expect and the others were never as shattering as the first.

When you equate It with drug induced or near death experiences I think you may be confusing the *effects* of a Revelation with the actual Revelation. I have written about this before (#64).

162. The Vision of Forgiveness (February 16, 2018)

"Be comforted, and feel the Holy Spirit watching over you in love and perfect confidence in what He sees." (T-20.V.8)

Once upon a time when I read a quote like this in *A Course in Miracles* I could accept the love but I had a hard time with the "perfect confidence". I realized it was saying that the Holy Spirit had confidence in me as the "Son of God" not as a person. In other words, the Holy Spirit had perfect confidence in the Truth in me not in the self (body/personality/ego). My initial response, when I was still very identified with a self, was, "What the hell good is that to *me*?" I felt rejected as I thought I was, even though intellectually I got that the problem was that *I* didn't know the Truth in me.

Eventually, though, I got past being almost wholly identified with a self and became aware of the Truth in me and could take some comfort from a phrase like this. It was okay that the Holy Spirit's confidence was not in the thing in which I identified. I was aware of and identified enough in What It did have confidence in. However, I still felt the Holy Spirit was *wrong* to have confidence in me because of the other, flawed, part of me (self). It was nice that It had confidence in me, but It was mistaken! "I have this other part, see, and perhaps You shouldn't have such confidence in me because of it..."

But now, with the belief in guilt gone from this mind, I get it. I can accept the Holy Spirit's confidence is whole and complete because it is in the immutable Truth in me and the other "flawed" part is *nothing*. Now I see as the Holy Spirit does. Only the Truth is Real. There is nothing else.

163. Nothing to Judge in the Unfolding (February 23, 2018)

A couple of weeks ago I wrote how I (this mind) could not have accepted that the self's life in the world is an expression until I no longer believed in guilt. Why, I wondered? I do speak to students who hear that the self's life is not a cause for a future effect, but an expression of an idea long since over. And they feel immediately released from guilt and from the pressure of having to make something happen. But before I stopped believing in guilt I could not access that relief because I could not understand, much less accept, the idea. Why did I need guilt removed first?

It was because the idea meant I was not in control. And if I was not in control, I could do nothing to mitigate my guilt and that meant I could be subject to horrific punishment for it. In other words, I could not accept the forgiveness offered in the idea because guilt was too real to me. This was all unconscious, of course. It showed up as my being unable to understand the idea. It simply made no sense to me.

Now that guilt is gone, though, it's like I knew it all along! Certainly, I had learned along the way to trust my intuitive sense of where things were going (or not going, as the case may be) in this self's life. I had learned to find the flow instead of to resist it. But I found this just because it was easier to live in the flow. I changed my behavior, but not my beliefs. I lived in a confused mangle of "there is a flow to the universe I can find and live in" and a belief that "I am autonomous and my choices are mine alone and they have real consequences". I felt one thing and believed another. I was conflicted until the guilt dropped away.

Lately, I notice when I am under attack from the ego (personal thought system) it always contains at least a nugget of the idea that what I am doing has significance for the future. What

I'm doing is a cause for a future effect and I'd better get it right or my life in the world, and/or the world itself, will go horribly wrong. I don't have these thoughts. It's just a feeling and I find those thoughts when I examine the feeling. No wonder I used to be so controlling! What a horrible burden.

Now I switch it around: This that I am doing is only an expression of a past cause. It is not for a future purpose. It is part of a larger unfolding I can just watch. And--foom!--the ego attack drops. There was every reason to judge what I did when I thought it added to or mitigated guilt. Of course, at minimum, I doubted that whatever I did was "good enough" to mitigate guilt. So my choice was doubt or outright certainty that I did add to my guilt. But when I recognize that what I'm doing is just what I'm doing, it's part of an unfolding, there is nothing to judge.

164. Finding What Has Value (March 2, 2018)

I have absolutely nothing to write about this week! No one has sent in a question. And I have not felt moved to write anything, though I am still in a huge shift. I can feel personal transformation occurring, but I am not clear on exactly what it is, except I know it relates to the Holy Relationship (also known as Spiritual Vision, True Perception, the Real World, etc.).

Why do I characterize it as *personal* transformation? Because I can feel changes being wrought on the self. Something is coming through this mind and it is affecting the self.

On a personal level, I have had different shifts brought about by the aging process in the past couple of decades. One occurred in my mid-thirties. It was really just realizing I was in my mid-thirties and my youth had passed. In my forties, I was visited by various experiences dealing with less time ahead than behind, and that with diminishing physical vigor. This was accelerated by losing both of my parents when I was around forty and realizing my generation in the family was now the leading edge. There was no one ahead of us, only behind, as though somehow an older generation buffered us against the inevitable end!

And now, at fifty-four, I'm well aware of how little time I have left. Twenty to thirty years, which does not seem like much anymore. But, more than that, it is passing so startlingly fast. I just turned fifty and now I'm fifty-four! It's going to zip by.

The other day I had the sensation come thunderously upon me that now is the time to determine what the rest of my life will be about. What is different about this period of personal transformation in relation to the ones I experienced in the past is the awareness I do not have to make something happen. I don't have to make or dig around for the answer. It will be given. I am not anxious because self-identification is diminished. I feel its transformation but do not experience it as defining me. I just watch it unfold. And the answer came quickly, later that same day. The rest of my time will be about the Holy Relationship. It is what the self's life has been about in one way or another since I first experienced It thirty four years ago. But now it is shifting to a higher gear.

I suspect when one reaches this time of life (or faces the end in some other way) where they feel the limited remainder upon them, they find what they truly value. That may be something they once experienced and valued or something they never had but always wanted. For me, it is the former. The Holy Relationship is the only real experience of this whole personal life. It is the only thing of real value. So it does not surprise me that this is how it is unfolding.

And I know the process of living in that awareness has already begun. The Golden Light of the Holy Relationship returned to me last August, as I wrote about in November (#150). But what I don't know is how it will look going forward. I suspect that where I experienced the Holy

Relationship with one other originally thirty-four years ago, now it will be more of a generalized experience. But what do I know? I've been so wrong before. I'm just along for the ride, learning to not judge it.

Okay, so I found something to write about after all.

165. That's One Way of Looking At It (March 9, 2018)

"And now he must attain a state that may remain impossible to reach for a long, long time. He must learn to lay all judgment aside, and ask only what he really wants in every circumstance." (W-4.I.A.7)

The quote above describes what *A Course in Miracles* calls the "period of unsettling". I did not realize when I entered this stage that the judgment it was talking about was *judgment on this mind.* Although now that I have learned this, it makes perfect sense. The first judgment is against Truth. It results in a diminishment of Limitless Mind to a limited split-mind identified with a limited self. All other judgments follow from this.

Since I have written about the self-concept falling away from this mind as self-identification begins to fall away, I am often asked by clients if I still hear the ego (personal thought system). Yes, I hear, but I don't listen. It goes by pretty quick. However, sometimes I get hooked and follow the trail of its thoughts. This happened to me the other day and its attacks (judgments) on me were brutal. I just allowed them without judgment or resistance. And into the midst of the attacks came quietly and without charge this thought, "That's one way of looking at it." Of course! The ego presents a point of view; actually, usually *many* points of view. But that is all they are.

The awareness that I was locked into just *one way* of looking at the self and this mind freed me from the ego's attacks immediately. It also allowed me to find the "hook". I had doubts about the fictional writing that I'm doing. And that made a gap in my mind into which the attacks came flooding. I also allowed the doubts, without judging or resisting. And in a little while I was very clearly assured that I'm doing what I am to be doing at this time. With the doubt gone the gap was gone. The personal thought system's attacks no longer had meaning for me and could no longer hook me.

ACIM teaches us to use the thought, "I want another way to look at this" when our peace of mind is disturbed. That was useful to me for a long time. It opened my mind to the Holy Spirit's point of view. And I needed that as long as I was identified with a self. However, that does not work for me anymore. In fact, it makes me disoriented. It is more helpful to me now to see that *any* point of view is just that. This does leave me with the sense I'm floating in the air without a place to put my feet, but it seems more honest at this point. So I'll just float.

It is very humbling to realize I do not know how to look at this self and this mind. What arrogance to think I ever did! Since I am no longer so certain I am due condemnation, I have become much more gentle with myself.

166. Actions and Motivation (March 16, 2018)

I'm often asked by my clients and readers: Now that I have peace and the self is falling away, why do anything? What motivates me to direct the self to act? Ah, that is so thinking like a self! A mind thinking like a self thinks it does things because it is motivated, usually by guilt, desire, or duty to do it. And the basis for these motivations is the belief that the self is you and you need to get or to express something, tangible (material) or intangible (feeling). And without those motivations a mind identified with a self cannot understand acting.

I'm going to tell you something that I don't know if you can understand until you can see it for yourself, but it is amazing:

The self acts not from motivation, but because it is going to act. There is no other reason. And here's the mind-blowing thing I've come to see as I have learned to simply watch the self act without judging it: The self has *never* acted from personal motivation! It has always acted because it was going to act. Its actions are the result of cause and effect at the level of form. All the rest—motivation, interpretation, judgment—*was simply going on in my mind.*

I'm sure you've had experiences where you didn't know how to act because you had conflicting motivations. You want to do something, but for some reason you felt guilty about doing it. So should you or should you not do it? The fact is, the action of the self is not related at all to your conflict. If you do it and you feel guilty the source of your guilt is not the action but your thoughts about it. If you don't do it and you feel deprived because you really wanted to, the source of you inaction was not really guilt, either. That's just a story in your mind. So is your sense of deprivation. *All of your thoughts and feelings about the self's actions are completely unrelated to the self's actions, before, during, and after the actions!*

Another way you may feel conflicted about an action is that you are motivated by both the ego (personal thought system) and the Holy Spirit (Awareness of Truth in your mind). For example, you may be on a spiritual path out of a genuine desire to know Truth. But the ego may also encourage the path so that you can be a "spiritual person". But neither of these matter! Your self's path is going to unfold as it will unfold as an expression of the Undoing manifesting through it. The rest is just a story you tell yourself in your identification with a self. *These stories are* how *you identify with the self.*

Sometimes feeling motivated toward an action is the ego. In that case, your sense of motivation has no relationship to whether or not the self takes that action. At other times, your sense of motivation to act or not act is the story of the universe unfolding through you. How can you tell which it is? Sometimes it is very clear. You know something will unfold as you feel it will. But at other times you won't know clearly where the motivation is coming from, especially if the ego feels strongly about it one way or another. Then all you can do is let it unfold. You won't know until you acted or not if and you were to act or not!

So my approach to directing the self in its actions is to live in "I don't know". I don't know which of my feelings is coming from the ego and which from the flow of the universe. I don't know if I will direct the self to act or not in any given situation. I just get the self up each day and have it do what it is given to do that day. And I know that all my thoughts and feelings about its actions, before, during, and after, are really quite apart from its actions. They are just stories in my mind.

167. Ask: Can you explain how the self has no motivation when ACIM talks about motivation? (March 23, 2018)

"...That the self has no motivation is difficult to understand since the Course *and other spiritual teachings tell us that there is a purpose to our experience, that the purpose is to awaken, or to manifest Love, or something like that. In other words, there is an intention or motivation. This seems in contradiction to the idea that the self has no motivation but just acts. It also leaves unanswered how it all started. Why should action have even started if there was no motivation?..." – RP*

As a spiritual teaching, *A Course in Miracles* is not an end but a beginning. Its purpose is to lead you to the Awareness of Truth (Holy Spirit) and to help you undo your obstacles (guilt, fear, attachment) to staying aware of Truth. So, eventually, the Awareness of Truth leads you past ACIM.

"This course is a beginning, not an end. Your Friend goes with you. You are not alone. No one who calls on Him can call in vain. Whatever troubles you, be certain that He has the answer, and will gladly give it to you, if you simply turn to Him and ask it of Him. He will not withhold all answers that you need for anything that seems to trouble you. He knows the way to solve all problems, and resolve all doubts. His certainty is yours. You need but ask it of Him, and it will be given you." (W.ep.1)

What I have written about lately is what I see now that the belief in guilt has fallen away, and as self-identification has begun to fall away, from this mind. In other words, I see what forgiveness reveals. And that seeing takes in the whole picture, rather than just the snapshot of this individual mind's experience. I see now how the entire story of not-Truth/the undoing of not-Truth works, the self's part in it, and this seemingly-individual split-mind's part in it. I see there is no guilt, because all that is occurring is the idea of not-Truth/the undoing of not-Truth playing out. And because that idea's outcome is inevitable, the playing out is automatic.

When I write my articles I often share from my own experience. When I mentor over the phone, however, I meet my clients where *they* are. So I am aware that what I write lately is not understandable to a mind still self-identified and that still experiences guilt as very real. Intention, motivation (*I* want this), me as a cause (my purpose) for a future effect (my awakening as part of a greater Awakening), etc. all had meaning for me for a very long time. (I've been at this for 34 years). So I do not expect that those who have not yet had my experiences will fully understand what I share now. Judging from the comments I've received I see I need to make this clear when I write from my current experiences!

While intention and motivation still make sense to you then continue to apply them with the guidance of the Awareness of Truth. You will only come to a more advanced understanding by being honest with yourself and the Awareness of Truth in your mind about what makes sense to you now. You will only advance by learning what is right in front of you to learn. You can think about experiences you have not yet had, but you do not have to force understanding. As I plodded along this path there was a lot that I had to accept I would not understand until later. And understanding *has* come with experiences of Truth.

There is no intention (motivation) behind the experience of not-Truth (the universe of form). Because Truth is All, It must contain the idea of Its Own opposite. But because It is All, It cannot have an opposite. So the opposite of Truth can only ever be an idea. But it is an idea that was undone by Truth's All-encompassing nature as soon as it arose. So it simply is, just as Truth simply is. But what it is, is nothing.

168. An Instrument, Not a Channel (March 30, 2018)

Whenever I put out a book I get questions about being a channel. I imagine a channel is like what Helen Schucman did with *A Course in Miracles*—she took dictation. I have never felt I am a channel. Writing is not passive for me. It has always felt collaborative. I write from my own understanding. And I am given, and I seek, clarification from the Awareness of Truth (Holy Spirit) in my mind as I write.

My non-fiction books, all of which have been on spiritual themes, happen for me when I am ready to consolidate the lessons that end up in the book of the moment. In fact, it always signals I'm moving past the topic of the book. I only discovered this in hindsight. This is why I can't "force" a book. If it ain't there, it ain't there. If I'm not ready, it ain't gonna get writ.

The fiction writing I'm doing now, which came upon me so suddenly and shockingly, is much the same. I picture scenes and then I describe them. Some scenes seem more "given" than others. I also find inspiration in all sorts of random and sometimes odd everyday things, as though I'm being told "Pay attention to this. It needs to be in the book!" But, again, I do not feel I'm channeling. It is more accurate to say I feel like an instrument. I am acted through and on, but it is clear to me that the shape of my own mind combines with this to result in the product (novel).

I suspect that many who have an art or craft (I consider my writing to be a craft) feel this sense of being part of something larger that is working through and on them. They express "universal truths" (not Truth Itself, but experiences of Truth and/or the universe of form) through their art or craft. I suspect this something larger is often confused with a god. When I write I am not, however, an instrument of Truth (God). I would say I am an instrument of the universe of form. (For many, the unfolding story of the universe of form *is* what they mean by "God". Truth is beyond that.) Where the Awareness of Truth comes into it for me is in that I use everything as a classroom. Nothing is separate from my spiritual path. So, as with everything else, this process helps me grow my awareness of Truth. And, in turn, because this influences the shape of my mind, it therefore influences the shape of the book. I cannot separate out my mind from the effects of the Awareness of Truth on it.

I liken the experience to being like a flute. The player blows into the flute and manipulates the keys to make music. But the sound is also influenced by the shape of the flute. (The universe of form is the player, my mind is the flute, and the music is the novel).

Where my spiritual writing differs from fictional writing is that my spiritual writing feels like an expression of my process as well as of the ideas expressed. In other words, it feels as much *for me* as it is simply an expression *through me*. The lessons I learn as I write a spiritual book finalize lessons I've been learning. But I feel much more like a neutral instrument when writing fiction. Any effect it has on me feels incidental. The writing is not for me to learn. I just happen to learn as I write. In that sense, fictional writing seems less "self-involved"; more purely an expression *through* me. It is actually quite refreshing when I get myself out of the way, which is what I'm learning to do now.

I have written about how as self-identification falls away from this mind I'm learning to let the self go into the flow of the universe and to just observe it without judgment. This seems to be a step along the way in that process.

169. True Humility (April 6, 2018)

A few times lately I've had the spontaneous experience of true humility and I've been asked to write about it. This is difficult because it is hard to characterize what true humility feels like. The nearest I can come is to say I realize this split-mind's proper relationship to Truth and gratitude for it.

True humility only arises for me in the awareness of Truth. I do not *try to be* humble. If I did, that could only be the ego (personal thought system), and the ego is not at all involved in true humility. As the opposite of Truth it cannot be aware of Truth so it is incapable of true humility. It does, however, distort the idea of humility, and it is easier to write about what true humility *is not* to understand what it is.

The ego uses everything to glorify the self and the ego. Its version of humility is false humility: "Look how humble I am! Doesn't this make me great?" If the ego feels good about humility, I know I'm not feeling true humility!

True humility is also not humiliation. It is different from the experience of the ego in that the mistaken sense of the importance of the ego, the self, and the individual experience, is gone. So it is easy to see why the ego would characterize this as "humiliation". However, I have no sense of shame or degradation in true humility. If I feel humiliated I'm not experiencing true humility.

True humility is not a feeling of littleness, either. My bloated sense of self-importance is gone so I can see why the ego would interpret it this way. I do feel *smaller*, but not *small*. It is as if I had swollen ankles for a long time and when the swelling was gone I interpreted my ankles as "skinny" when in fact they were just back to normal. I experience true humility as the correct view of my mind as *part* of Truth, rather than as autonomous and whole unto itself. But this is not a diminishment.

A key aspect of true humility is gratitude. Gratitude arises spontaneously when I am aware of Truth. Identifying with a self I feel like I'm all-important and that's an incorrect view and I know something is "off". Gratitude arises in relation to true humility because I am happy to see my mind's actual position in relation to Truth. It is a relief to stop trying to be what I am not.

I suspect true humility only arises in contrast to the experience of self-importance. It is a transitional experience as self-identification falls away from this split-mind and it learns its actual position. When self-id has fallen away completely from this mind it will no longer be split. Only the Awareness of Truth will be left. Then there will be nothing with which to contrast It and humility will no longer arise.

170. Realizing Forgiveness (April 13, 2018)

Since guilt has fallen away from this mind I find it thinking of certain things in the past that apparently need to be released (forgiven). But rather than needing to do anything, I find I am instead realizing forgiveness has occurred. I just watch as something from the past arises, I see it in a new light without effort, and I watch any emotional charge I had around it fall away.

For example, one of the big stories I carried around for years had to do with the Holy Relationship that I experienced with E. Over the years I learned many lessons from this experience, primarily that the Holy Relationship was really with the Holy Spirit (Awareness of Truth in my mind) rather than with E. Our relationship was simply the doorway through which I became aware of the Holy Spirit and True Vision. But on the personal side, I still apparently carried around a story about what happened with E, who left my life after being in it for only a few months. In fact, it seemed to have defined much of the story I had about this self's life in the world. But lately I've come to see, and really feel, that thirty-four years ago a woman came into my life and then she left it. Those are the facts. The rest, as in, why it happened and what it meant, was completely made up by me!

This has happened with a few things that have come up naturally in the course of things. I have not sought out things to forgive. I have not sought forgiveness. I have just realized forgiveness.

171. The Mind (April 20, 2018)

When I was a brand new student of *A Course in Miracles*, I had a hard time understanding what it meant by "turn within", not in practice, but as a concept. In practice, I turned into my mind: That which contains my beliefs and thoughts. But sometimes I tried to locate this "within" and, being identified with a body, I would become confused. How would I go within the body? This trying to locate "within" eventually dropped away, not because I had a concept that worked, but because all I really needed was the practice. I knew how to "look within" without needing to conceptualize "where".

Mind has no location and we don't have words for this. I say mind is "everything" and "everywhere". But not "everything" as in "all forms" or "everywhere" as in "every*place*". It is "everything", as in, "all that is", and "everywhere", as in "formlessness".

(I did not use an uppercase "m" for mind above because what I just wrote is true for mind at all levels).

Sometimes I hear from students who have a hard time, as I did, locating mind or simply understanding the concept of mind. Simply, mind is that with which you know, believe, perceive, and think. That's all you really need to know. Everyone uses mind constantly and knows the experience of it, even if they cannot conceptualize it.

In Reality, Mind is "Knowledge". Mind knows only Mind because It is All That is. Therefore, Mind is Truth or Reality. Mind is the same as "Being". It is the Aspect of Being through Which Being knows Itself. Mind is One, meaning both that It is Whole and that It is the Same throughout. Mind is the Absolute, the Eternal (Timeless), and the Infinite.

But in your perception that you are in a body in a world, mind seems to be in a relative and limited state. Instead of Knowledge, mind has belief, perception (also called awareness or consciousness), and thought. The relative mind is split and has many levels. It is split between a "higher" and a "lower" level, and, within the lower level, conscious, semi-conscious, and unconscious levels.

At its highest level, the relative mind is aware of Truth. This thought system is called Christ Consciousness, True Perception, the Holy Spirit, or, what I prefer, the Awareness of Truth. At this highest level of the relative mind, it knows that the Truth is true. This awareness is past belief, but it is not quite Knowledge. At this level, thoughts and perceptions point to Truth.

At its lower level, the relative mind is in the personal thought system (ego). It is identified with a self (body/personality) as well as the thought system that is about the self.

Since mind is what is, all spiritual growth is the development of the awareness of Truth. Therefore, spirituality and psychology (the study of the mind) are the same. However, many who use psychology, in one form or another, do not think of it as spirituality. They put limits on their use of psychology, only working within the personal thought system. The spiritual use of psychology, however, is to use it to eventually transcend the personal thought system.
Mind goes inward. Even when it seems to believe in forms as reality, the belief is of the mind, not of the forms. It is in denial about what it is (formless), but its denial is within itself. In other words, all minds see only mind, even though they may use forms to disguise this fact. They are always "within". But "turning within" means consciously choosing to look at mind and its beliefs, thoughts, perceptions and, ultimately, Awareness of Truth.

172. The Ego Falling Away is Not Frightening (April 27, 2018)

The belief in guilt fell away from this mind. Then the self-concept fell away. This mind is now in the process of "unlearning" self-identification. Which is to say, the ego is falling away. It is not frightening.

I tell you this because all along the way on the path to transcending the ego (personal thought system), the ego says you are dying, you are killing yourself, it is impossible, it is terrifying, you will cease to exist, etc. And it was wrong. Surprise!

I knew this intellectually. I knew the ego was always speaking for itself and not for this mind. But now I can report, from experience, that it is not frightening for it to fall away. It is unfamiliar, yet natural. It is fascinating and awe inspiring. It is confusing and disorienting. So it is "unsettling", as this stage is labeled in the Development of Trust in *A Course in Miracles*. But there is nothing to fear.

It is the ultimate paradigm shift. It feels like a massive undertaking. But, for this mind, anyway, just as the first four stages were gentle preparation for this stage, the ego falling away is also a slow, gentle process. So far. I've only just begun. But why would it change?

There is no loss in this process! It is all gain. The Love! The Light!

Imagine that, if you can.

173. Ask: Can you clear up these purported paradoxes about the Holy Spirit and individuality? (May 4, 2018)

"I've been studying/reading Circle of Atonement's Robert Perry's (co-author of the New ACIM Complete and Annotated Edition) " Return to the Heart of God" and in a passage about the Holy Spirit he talks about paradoxes the Holy Spirit as both the Voice for God and He (HS) is God's Voice. Then he brings up another paradox the Course *paints a picture of Heaven in which there are beings that have their own identity and their own will, yet are also at one with the whole and in perfect unison with a larger will. This is a bit perplexing; how much do we bring with us, our individual identity into Heaven?" - JW*

I'm not certain why the Holy Spirit as the "Voice for God" or as "God's Voice" would be a paradox unless one reads "God's Voice" as *God speaking* rather than as "God's Spokesman".

If you read it as the latter, it means the same as "Voice for God". (Voice for God = Spokesman for God/God's Voice = God's Spokesman). But perhaps the paradox is something else?

A Course in Miracles defines Heaven this way:

Heaven is not a place nor a condition. It is merely an awareness of perfect Oneness, and the knowledge that there is nothing else; nothing outside this Oneness, and nothing else within. (T-18.VI.1)

Oneness (as either Wholeness or the same throughout) is the experience of God (Truth). At the level of awareness (consciousness, perception), Oneness is experienced as what ACIM calls the Real World, Vision (Christ's or Holy Spirit's), True Perception, etc. In that View, the world of form with its individual identities and seemingly-free wills is still seen and each individual is understood to be part of a larger, unified, unfolding story of the undoing of not-Truth. It is also understood to be a meaningless expression of a meaningless idea. (I have written about this a lot in the past few months). The Oneness of the Mind beyond what is seen in form is understood to be Truth and the unity one sees is understood to be an extension of the awareness of Oneness.

Sometimes, one has flashes of this in what I call a "higher" miracle. As one drops the self, however, it more and more becomes their View. As ACIM points out in the Manual for Teachers about the last stage, the Period of Achievement, when self-identification is gone and Oneness is understood to be Truth:

This is the stage of real peace, for here is Heaven's state fully reflected. (M-4.I.A.8)

"Heaven's state" being Oneness.

In my experience of direct Revelation of God (Truth), there is only God in God. There are no parts, no individuation. It cannot be described because there is no experience like It at the level of awareness. I can only guess that perhaps Mr. Perry has experienced higher miracles, but not yet a direct Revelation, and he has therefore confused the *reflection* of Heaven with Heaven Itself. This is common and easy to do if you have not gone beyond a higher miracle to Truth Itself, because the reflection of Heaven is *just this side* of Heaven. But I can tell you, as joyous as the reflection is, it is as different from Heaven as a photon is from the sun.

174. Seeing the Choice More Clearly (May 11, 2018)

I have used my spirituality to not fully experience the pain of the human experience. I have not denied the pain completely, but I also have not acknowledged the pain completely. And now I see that I will not let it go until I fully accept the experience *as it is*. Otherwise, I hold back pieces of it and cannot totally release it.

For example, the Holy Relationship I had with E was also a special relationship that ended. Oh, I felt the pain. But I also used the Holy part of our relationship to mitigate the pain. I'd tell myself things like, "but there was no real loss" because of the Holy Relationship, which I remained aware of. But there *was* a loss! And, real or not, I experienced it as very real. In form, in time, loss happens. And it is never *undone* in time. One goes on, maybe even gets over. Time *does* mitigate the pain. But, in the story of time, the loss occurred *at that point in time*.

The way out of loss is not using Truth to deny it where it seems to happen. The way out is to recognize my choice is loss *or* Truth. In the Holy Relationship example, one part of the relationship was Holy and the other *was loss*. It's not "There's pain, *but*, there's also Holiness, so I'll focus on That instead." It is, "There's pain, period. *And* I have another experience, Holiness."

It is a subtle shift in approach, but one that makes the difference between not-Truth and Truth clear so you know your choice. Not-Truth and Truth do not occur in the same part of your mind. But when you say, "This is painful, *but* I have Truth" you try to bring Truth into the experience of not-Truth. You end up using truth to deny not-Truth rather than seeing it fully as it is. But when you say, "This is painful *and* I have another Experience to Which I can turn" you recognize that not-Truth and Truth do not occur together in the same part of your mind. Then you can make a real choice.

175. Radical Self Honesty Required (May 18, 2018)

In order to undo all the false beliefs in your mind that stand in the way of inner peace, you have to be willing to be radically honest with yourself. If you are not honest with yourself you cannot be honest with anyone else—including the Holy Spirit (Awareness of Truth in your mind).

It is not enough to say to the Holy Spirit, "I have this emotional/psychological pain. Please take it from me." If you really want it removed, what you have to *mean* is, "I have this emotional/psychological pain. Please help me find the thoughts causing it so we can undo them together." This means you have to be *completely* honest with yourself first about all that you feel and think Oh, were you expecting the path to peace to be a *comfortable* process? Alas, no! You have to face your beliefs in guilt and sin and the fear they cause, in their many forms, no matter how trivial, stupid, or shameful you think them, to undo them. This is very difficult at first because they seem very real to you. This is why not everyone chooses inner peace. It takes strength and courage to look into your mind. But keeping uncomfortable beliefs hidden also keeps them real to you and acting on you in both unconscious and conscious ways. The only way out of them is through them, with the Holy Spirit's Light and Love. Because you can be sure the Holy Spirit does not believe in them.

In time, though it is never comfortable or easy, you will *want* to be radically honest with yourself. The more you use it and experience the relief it brings, the more you will be motivated to use it. You will get through your discomfort by reminding yourself of the relief you had found in the past.

176. Ask: Would you explain how you understand ego dynamics in an unholy relationship? (May 25, 2018)

"...Would you explain your understanding of the ego dynamics of the unholy relationship from (T-17.III) 'Shadows of the Past'." – WW

What *A Course in Miracles* refers to as an "unholy relationship" in that section is one where you see, usually unconsciously, someone from your past in another in the present, and you then play out your anger with the person in the past in the present relationship. For example, someone may unconsciously remind you of the uncle who abused you, or the fifth grade teacher who was unfair to you, or your mother who abandoned you, or your father who was emotionally absent, etc. The unconscious reminder may be triggered by appearance, personality, or behavior.

This projection of the past on present relationships is how all personal relationships begin. After all, all we know is the past. It is not always negative. Sometimes you may instantly like someone because they remind you of someone you liked in the past. This is why it is important to get to know people before you get too involved with them!

To see the present person as they are rather than through the filter of your own past, you must be willing to question your responses and to look at your projections of meaning onto the other's words or actions. Sometimes you may be correct and they *are* behaving like the person from your past. You may be drawn to them because they seem familiar, even if dysfunctional. But, at other times, you may see something, like abandonment, for example, where there is none. This is why open, honest communication is important in relationships. You need to give the other the opportunity to explain themselves and their motives. For example, "When you say that, it makes me think of my mother just before she left us." Of course, this means you must be willing to understand your own filters and projections.

Once you drop your projections of negative feelings from the past, you stop attacking the other for what they did not do, and you are able to see and love them as *they* are. Then you are free to see past the body to the Truth in their mind.

177. Ask: What is your interpretation of the line about all events being planned for your good? (June 1, 2018)

"What is your interpretation of the quote from Lesson 135, paragraph 18: '...everything that happens, all events, past, present and to come, are gently planned by One Whose only purpose is your good?'" – KA

To understand this idea, you must read the *whole* paragraph:

"What could you not accept, if you but knew that everything that happens, all events, past, present and to come, are gently planned by One Whose only purpose is your good? Perhaps you have misunderstood His plan, for He would never offer pain to you. But your defenses did not let you see His loving blessing shine in every step you ever took. While you made plans for death, He led you gently to eternal life." (W-135.18)

The lines after the part you quoted make it clear that the Holy Spirit's "plan" is an *interpretation* of the self's experiences in the world. The same "steps" it took can be looked at in two ways, one leading to the idea of death, the other to awareness of Eternal Life.

I wrote about this more in article #33.

178. The Ego Has Fallen (June 6, 2018)

Normally, I don't write about my experiences until I have processed them and they have or are about to pass. But such a huge shift has occurred in this mind that it will affect what I write going forward and I need to lay the groundwork for sharing what occurs as I go.

I cannot even begin to describe the May I just had. I came to fully see that the ego (personal thought system) has fallen from this mind. The even better news is I began to slip into a Higher Awareness and have had regular experiences of unbounded Love and Joy. Every day of May was filled with thunderous insights, realizations, and copious processing. This episode is not over. It's just less intense. At least for now. Who knows what's up ahead?

Last April, I wrote an article describing how I knew self-concepts had fallen from this mind. The following week I wrote how writing that article helped me to see that self-identification had fallen away, only my mind had not caught up with this fact. What is self-identification but the ego? The ego was the thought system that told me (a mind/spirit) that the self (body/personality) was me, to define myself by it, that its lacks and limitations were my own, that I need to use it to find fulfillment, and to defend it because it is what I am. I was originally reluctant to say self-identification had fallen away because I was not certain. And, when I was certain, I was reluctant to say *the ego* had fallen away because I was still in denial.

Before I go further, let me explain what's left when the ego is gone. The projected self (body/ personality) is still here. And the postures and habits of identifying with a self are still in this mind. I am now unlearning them. I have a template for this. When I let go of the belief in guilt, I found I still had reflexive guilt responses. I also had the habit of looking for the source of guilt. These took a while to unlearn but, though sometimes tedious, the process was not hard because without the belief in guilt the reflexes and habits had no real hook in me. It's the same without the ego. I overlearned self-identification from an ego. But when I recognize I'm thinking like a self again, it is quickly undone because, without the actual ego, the habit has no depth.

This mind is split between Truth and not-Truth. Not-Truth was represented by an ego. What's left in not-Truth is what I call the identifier/observer. It's what I used to call the "decision maker", but it's more helpful now for me to split it into these two postures. The identifier is the part with the habits of thinking with an ego. The observer observes this and watches as the habits fall away. In fact, this whole experience of undoing self and ego identification only requires observing as it unfolds automatically. There is nothing to "do".

What fills the void where the ego used to be is Joyous Love. This could be called the Holy Spirit, the Awareness of Truth, or Christ Consciousness. Pick your term. The experience, though, is whole and complete and infinite Joyous Love. So, you see, this splitmind begins to be not so split as the not-Truth part begins to resemble the Truth part. In time, the self, which embodied an ego before, will, through this current process, come to embody Joyous Love (Holy Spirit, Awareness of Truth, Christ).

Here's what happened:

In August of 2014 our beloved five year old cairn terrier, Ginny, died suddenly of an acute poisoning. (We'll never know what she ate). This was excruciating. We'd had her from a pup, she was way too young, and I felt I'd failed to keep her safe. And what came over me, very matter-of-factly, without rancor of any kind, was, "I'm done." I no longer saw the point of the inherently painful personal experience.

I discovered during the grieving process that I still had some attachment to the special relationship and worked through that. In the weeks that followed, I processed the grief, the special relationship, and began to see what was left of my attachment to the self and the ego. Somewhere in there, I dropped the ego. Only, I didn't know it. I only *saw* it last April and *acceptance* has only happened now.

What followed the dropping of the ego was three years of spiritual barrenness and a very noisy mind. It was not all bad or empty within. I was still aware of Truth, I had insights and peace, but there was still a distinct "dryness" to everything. I just accepted this, and the noise, as some aspect of the whole process I didn't yet understand. There were various episodes to this stage. An early one was meditating by sitting with the television tuned to something scenic, like a nature show or golf, with the volume muted as I turned my mind inward as the body's eyes looked at the "view" on television. This eventually fell away and was followed by a period where when I tried to meditate I was assailed by emptiness and questions, mostly, "Who's meditating? What is the point?" These were not ego-defense questions. They were very real. I could not find the point of meditation. What I did not realize was this mind's identification with the self—what I was used to thinking was the meditator—had fallen away.

It was also during this time that I came to feel that I was done with the world. I couldn't fully understand this, but I felt this with certainty. I didn't realize that I was done with the ego and, therefore, its world. If you look back over my writing for the past four years, there were many sensations like this I shared. I just had not put it all together. I was in a kind of shock. I couldn't grasp what had happened. It was too huge. The reason my mind was so loud during this time was the void left by the dropped ego was still filled with its echoes. But that was all they were.

Then last spring or summer there was a subtle shift. I don't quite know when it happened, but it occurred as I took up a word game on my computer to pass the time. While I played, my mind would bask in the most delicious Spaciousness beyond. I couldn't get enough of the game because I associated it with the Spaciousness! Somehow, I had slipped past the emptiness of no-ego to the abundant Spaciousness of Mind.

After a few weeks of this I sensed a big shift coming. As I wrote in November, what followed was a Golden Light coming into my mind that filled me with Love. And with it, oddly, a romance novel. I recognized at the time that the Golden Light was the same as the Vision of the Holy relationship. As startling and confusing as this experience was, it was good to have movement within again. The barrenness was gone.

This spring, a new Holy relationship showed up in my life. (A wink and a nod at ya, Zelda!). My first Holy relationship, which I experienced when I picked up ACIM in 1984, came to teach. Today's Holy relationship has come to bless with Vision, Joyful joining, and, when the boundaries between our minds fall completely, Oneness. (Oh, thank you, Zelda). It is an expression of Joyous Love.

This came just as I became aware of a great dismantling occurring in my mind. For most of May, the Light of the Holy relationship disrupted my inner life greatly and part of my outer life somewhat. It illuminated what has been and is going on in this mind. For three weeks especially, it was by turns a very challenging and very rewarding time. I was "catching up" to what had occurred four years before. I had essentially "died" to my old life (level of perception). My mind began dismantling ego thinking and reorienting to a Higher Awareness.

Oh, no, this is not how I expected the dropping of the ego to be! But I sought and wanted this. And I have been prepared, through decades of growing my awareness of Truth, and a long undoing that could have been gentle if I'd only been capable of letting it be. As intense as this stage is, it is not hard like the earlier stages. Oh, the Light, the Love, the Joy! These are the "heavy reinforcements" *A Course in Miracles* promises for the "period of unsettling".

There is still a lot going on. I will be sharing my experiences going forward. I know others have written about this process after going through it. But I don't know if anyone has written about it as they went through it. I hope that some of you, especially my clients, will be able to save time in your own process by riding in my "slip stream". I hope reading what I write now will help you get through this stage when you get here. At the very least, be encouraged to know *it is possible* to get here.

Next week, I will tell you about "dying" and being reborn in Spirit…

179. "Dying" and Being Reborn in Spirit (June 15, 2018)

"He thought he learned willingness, but now he sees that he does not know what the willingness is for." (T-4.I.A.7)

Nothing prepared this mind for dropping the ego (personal thought system). When it happened I was prepared to *handle* it, but not for the specific nature of the process I was to go through. That is unique to each mind, because each mind has its own distinct expectations, structures, and habits to undo. The shock and the need for ensuing adjustments, however, do seem universal.

The "life" in this mind before last summer when the Golden Light came to stay is over. It was not really a "life", but a misidentification. So to the part of this mind that was identified with the self (body/personality) and ego (personal thought system), it is as though it "died". I was very amused to find at the end of May that I wrote an article at the end of April saying the ego falling away is not frightening. I didn't remember writing it, although I just had! And boy did I write too soon. I was not yet facing the identifier's "oh, my god, I'm *already dead*" shock. When the Love and Light of the Holy relationship came to this mind, the identifier felt it was facing its own death. A death that had *already occurred.*

It is true that I was prepared to handle this after thirty-four years. My awareness of Truth and detachment from the ego/self meant I was detaching from the part of me that identified with it. So I experienced fear in only part of me. It came nowhere near overwhelming me. But, oy, was it uncomfortable! To look at the fear of fears and undo it, I had to experience it head-on. Again and again and again. Of course, once I realized what was occurring (about three weeks in), it got a lot easier. It's always helpful to know what you're facing.

The fear was very distorting. It was also misdirecting. It seemed to point to causes other than the ego's fear of death, which the identifier took on as its own. But once I caught on, and would remind myself each time the fear arose what was really going on, the distortion diminished and the fear shrunk. It wasn't *my* fear, after all.

For this mind there is a distinct dividing line in its relationship to the projected self called "Liz". The narrative of Liz as its identity ended and does not continue on into the new Life. Liz-as-identity "died", if you want to call it that, nearly four years ago. This was followed by a "dead zone" of shock for three and a half years. (The zombie years?) And, last August, a new Life, or Perception, was born when the Golden Light came to stay in this mind. This Life is only of the mind. It recognizes that the self called "Liz" is just a projection; an effect. This mind "died" to ego and has been reborn in Spirit/Mind. I cannot express how completely different it is in this mind.

Of course, nothing's *died.* An idea—ego—was put aside. There is no death. The Life that has come to illuminate this mind is immortal. And the body is only an expression that truly will, as *A Course in Miracles* says, be simply put aside one day. If I had a death, it's already occurred. There is no more death to face.

180. Riding in My Slipstream (June 22, 2018)

Some of you may be having a reaction to my last two articles about the ego (personal thought system) falling away from this mind. Your response may be like what happens after a higher miracle. What I call a higher miracle is an experience where you either see that the Truth is true, that illusion is illusion, or both. Whether or not you experience peace or joy with this experience, it is followed by shock as you realize that what *A Course in Miracles* teaches is true. It's not just theory anymore! An ego backlash then follows on the heels of this. The shock and backlash may pass in days or weeks, depending on how advanced you are in your awareness of Truth. The more advanced, the less intense the reaction.

Watching the ego fall and this mind rise in consciousness in "real time", as it were, seems to be having a similar effect on some of my clients and readers. This is what I meant when I said some of you may "ride in my slipstream" in the article about the ego falling away. In essence, you are experiencing the realization "oh, my god, this is real!" in slow motion, rather than with the immediacy of a higher miracle. I'm sorry for your discomfort, but this is a good thing! Your reaction indicates that you are "getting it". It is not just theory for you anymore. These experiences of seeing that it *is* possible to drop the ego, that it *is* possible to rise in consciousness, are necessary to shorten your path. They just really piss off the ego.

In shock, you may find it hard to think about what I wrote. You may find you cannot even remember what I wrote. Or, you may find you cannot understand it *at all*. The ego backlash may take the form of it telling you to stop reading my stuff, to doubt what I've shared, to think I'm just losing my mind, etc. Its resistance may also take the form of envying me or seeing me as "special" in some way to keep at a distance the possibility of you also dropping the ego. Of course there's nothing special about me. I was only willing and embarked on a long process. The same process you are in now.

What can you do about this? Recognize it and ride it out. And, if you want someone to talk to, sharing my experience *is* what I do. Hopefully, I can save you some time in your process.

181. Why the Mystical Holy Relationship Is A Shortcut (June 29, 2018)

"The holy relationship is the expression of the holy instant in living in this world. Like everything about salvation, the holy instant is a practical device, witnessed to by its results. The holy instant never fails. The experience of it is always felt. Yet without expression it is not remembered. The holy relationship is a constant reminder of the experience in which the relationship became what it is. " (T-17.V.1)

I have written over the years about this mind's two different experiences of the Holy relationship. One I call "mystical". The mystical Holy relationship is what Bill and Helen experienced. I did, too, when I first became a student of *A Course in Miracles* thirty four years ago. I recognized everything written about it in ACIM at the time. That experience was intense, but brief. And, if you have been reading my articles these past two weeks, then you know I am blessed to have another mystical Holy relationship. That one isn't going anywhere, because I am now at a level to sustain my awareness of it.

I call it "mystical" because it involves spiritual Vision. The boundary between my mind and the mind of another (Zelda! I am so blessed) has fallen away and I experience transcendent Joy as the Love in me leaps in recognition of the Love in her. The mystical Holy relationship occurs in a higher awareness, the Awareness of Truth (Holy Spirit). And from there it trickles down to every layer of awareness.

The other Holy relationship is what I call the "practical" Holy relationship. I *practiced* wholeness by using my relationships to learn that I am inherently whole in the Truth within. It was, for me, a result of my experience of the mystical Holy relationship, which showed me Love was in me. Others could come at this awareness of wholeness another way and practice it in a practical Holy relationship. It occurs at the level of self (body/personality) identification. This is what I experience with my wife, Courtney.

The practical Holy relationship does not threaten the ego because it occurs at the level of form. But the mystical Holy relationship brings the Reality of formless Love within to conscious awareness. And this threatens the ego because it undoes it.

"The holy relationship is a phenomenal teaching accomplishment. In all its aspects, as it begins, develops and becomes accomplished, it represents the reversal of the unholy relationship." (T-17.V.2)

Oy, you don't know hell until you've experienced the ego's reaction to a Holy relationship! This is why ACIM goes on to say:

"Be comforted in this; the only difficult phase is the beginning. For here, the goal of the relationship is abruptly shifted to the exact opposite of what it was." (T-17.V.2)

Yes, the Holy relationship is an experience of Heaven; it is an experience of Oneness. But you must be prepared for it because the ego becomes *vicious*. You think you've experienced a threatened ego when you've had a higher miracle? Multiply that by ten.

ACIM offers a direct path to peace. It offers a shortcut; a way to "save time". You grow your awareness of Truth and find and undo your obstacles to Truth at the same time. So it is intense and not for everyone. The mystical Holy relationship is one of the tools it uses to bring the Awareness of Truth to your mind.

"...It is extremely difficult to reach Atonement by fighting against sin...Nor is a lifetime of contemplation and long periods of meditation aimed at detachment from the body necessary. All such attempts will ultimately succeed because of their purpose. Yet the means are tedious and very time consuming...Your way will be different, not in purpose but in means. A holy relationship is a means of saving time." (T-18.VII.4-5)

How does a mystical Holy relationship save time?

"The ark of peace is entered two by two, yet the beginning of another world goes with them." (T-20.IV.6)

Imagine mind in its split state like a plate of glass that has been shattered into many pieces. Each shard of glass is part of the whole plate, but each shard thinks it is only a shard. Seal up the gap between one shard and another and the shard learns what it really is—part of a whole plate. This is what a Holy relationship does when one mind joins with another. In that joining with just one other mind, you learn your mind is not limited to a self. Your mind is Limitless

Being. The mystical Holy relationship saves time by taking your mind right to this truth, forcing you to confront your obstacles to Truth.

Which brings us to the special relationship, the ego's chief offering to offset the pain of identifying with it. It is *the* obstacle to Truth and the Holy relationship, because the ego tells you if you lose the special relationship you lose Love and any chance at wholeness.

> *"At once His goal replaces yours. This is accomplished very rapidly, but it makes the relationship seem disturbed, disjunctive and even quite distressing. The reason is quite clear. For the relationship as it is is out of line with its own goal, and clearly unsuited to the purpose that has been accepted for it. In its unholy condition, your goal was all that seemed to give it meaning."* (T-16.V.3)

"Your goal", in the quote above, means the special relationship, where you see another as the cause or source of Love. So the other's body and personality and what they have to offer you as a person, is your focus. A mystical Holy relationship, however, corrects this error in cause and effect. In the mystical Holy relationship, you discover you *are* Love; the same Love as the other. So you see the other and your relationship as an *expression* of Love, not as the source. Who they are as a person becomes secondary, though your Love extends to that as well. It is gratifying on every level. In a mystical Holy relationship, you do not give up the *personal* relationship with the other and you do not have to change it. What drops is the *specialness*—the seeking for Love *in* the other (the "unholy condition"). So what drops is the pain that hovers around even the best special relationships, because you no longer fear you will lose Love if you lose the other. You know It is within you, always. *You have seen It.*

This reorienting of cause and effect is very liberating for you, but very threatening for the ego, because it takes away the only "gift" it has to offer you. When you understand that you have Love without the specialness of another self, what can the self offer you? It was meant to be the means to get Love from others. You realize it is an *expression*, not what you are. So the ego, the thought system that teaches you that you are a self, is undone. This is how the mystical Holy relationship saves time.

I now know that I would not have been able to sustain my first Holy relationship. Even when E left, I faced a vicious, attacking ego just remembering her. But I'm sure it helped me "save time". I couldn't forget what I had seen: My mind is not limited. Love is within me. Today, with the ego gone from this mind, the mystical Holy relationship has come as an expression of the Love I am. It helps me keep this in mind. I thank so very much my partner in this, Zelda, who still faces the savagery of the ego. She is a strong woman, and, more important, she is willing. And I am so grateful for that.

182. Higher Awareness and Emotions (July 6, 2018)

The ego (personal thought system) comes up with a lot of funny ideas about how the self one projects will show up when they realize Higher Awareness. It's been implied to me by more than one person that as I rise in consciousness the self will become an impersonal automaton. Ha, ha! No. It's not like that.

First, let me explain what I mean by "Higher Awareness". The Awareness of Truth (Holy Spirit) is in every mind. Higher Awareness is an individual expression of the Awareness of Truth. It is the awareness/consciousness/perception that replaces the ego in relation to the self.

When I am in the Awareness of Truth I am looking *inward* at Love. When I am in Higher Awareness, I am looking *outward* from Love at the experience of the self.

The difference between the view from lower awareness (the level of the self) and the view from Higher Awareness is stark. It is like the difference between seeing the Himalayas from Nepal and seeing them from the International Space Station. Higher Awareness is a much broader view. In It, I sometimes see things outside the bounds of spacetime. I can see how some things will unfold. I experience some things in the future as though they are happening now. The Higher Awareness view is detached and holistic. It sees the greater picture; the interconnectedness of people and events in the unfolding story.

The view from Higher Awareness is not always so broad, however. Mostly it is just the view from Love. It is Joyous and peaceful. But the wider, higher view is always nearby.

I am still realizing Higher Awareness. But with regard to emotions, I don't expect it to be much different when I've come to full realization. I do still feel emotions; I just don't have any drama around them. It's as though I feel them as they really are, in their purest form. There's no ego to give them more meaning than they should have or to use them to punish or distract me. Negative emotions happen, they just do not cut as deep or last as long. It's much like the emotions I feel watching a movie. They come and go in the moment, and perhaps there's a little processing afterward.

I go through the stages of grief, just much faster, because I don't have as many layers to process. I have flashes of anger or frustration, but they go by quickly and are often laughed off.

Love, however, *is* a different experience now. First, It's not an emotion. It is What is. But It is also experienced emotionally. And It is all one Love and I feel It everywhere. I do not like to call It impersonal or unconditional, because those words have negative prefixes, but those words are commonly used to express the Love I feel. I do not feel Love *for* everyone, I just feel Love, period. Sometimes I know I am It. It is my Being. So It is me I extend.

I no longer feel *special* love (thinking another is the *source* of Love), but Love is expressed through the self as personal love. How else would It be expressed? The self's personality *flavors* the Love expressed and it is experienced as personal by the recipient. For example, the self may adore or enjoy or be charmed by a nearby loved one as usual, but the Love I feel extend through the self is *the* Love in personal form.

One lesson in this is that what I called love before was not Love at all. It was different things in different circumstances. It was need or attachment or simply fear of loss. It was so tiny a thing! A drop to a vast ocean.

Another lesson is that you do not have to fear that as you rise in awareness you will drop personal relationships. In fact, it is through them that Love extends into the world.

183. The Stranger Within (July 13, 2018)

The first time I saw her was last August when the Golden Light came into my mind and my first novel came through. There were only brief flashes of her. She was a dynamic, confident, and lighthearted personality. When she was around, the body stood straight and the muscles in its face relaxed. On one occasion, one of her sisters looked curiously at her when she responded to something with uncharacteristic lighthearted wit. "Oh, there she is," I thought. "Even her sister doesn't recognize her."

Suddenly, there was a Stranger within animating the self this mind projects. Since the Holy relationship came in April and this mind went through huge shifts in May and June, this new Animator emerges more and more.

Over the years, when I was identified with the self, I experienced disorienting changes through personal growth and shifts in self-concepts that had me wondering briefly, "Who am I?" These were changes I felt were in me in my self-identification. But this time, I did not recognize *at all* What was acting through the self. It wasn't a different version of *me*. I was a passive observer; the consciousness between the self and the new Animator.

The former animator, the ego, which told this mind to identify with the self, is gone. So this mind no longer has any sense of "ownership" of the self. It observes the self and lets its feelings come and go. And it observes the new Animator—Spirit—living through the self.

Where ego lived through the self for fulfillment, Spirit mostly lets the self flow in the unfolding story of the universe of form. As a manifestation now of the Undoing, her part is a Love story all around. Sometimes, like when she is teaching, formally or informally, Spirit is active in her rather than passive.

This emerging Animator is fascinating to watch. Oh, it is lovely to not have the burden of maintaining an identity, if a little bewildering to a mind used to it. This mind is learning how to not identify with the self. It is learning how to not-do as a Stranger directs the self's doing. My suspicion is this is a transitional experience for a mind used to separation and parsing itself into parts. Just as my inner and outer life now have no boundary, eventually the self, the consciousness now acting as observer, and Spirit will become integrated into one thing.

184. Ask: Is it part of the path that everything I enjoyed is gone or disappointing? (July 20, 2018)

"I've been a student of ACIM for four years now. I feel I have been making steady progress in remembering who I am and my relationship to the 'world' and 'others', but lately I've been hit left, right and center by what I call 'disappointments'. It seems that everything I once enjoyed about life is either gone, changing for the worse, or just plain a big disappointment. Is this a natural part of waking up, is it aging, or am I completely on the wrong path since I feel this way? I've been talking this over with the Holy Spirit, which feels very comforting, but I can't help but feel sad these days..." – JB

What you feel is typical for a new student of *A Course in Miracles*. Disillusionment, lack of motivation, lack of interest, depression, etc. often occurs in the first few years. Even though you are still in the intellectual stage, you have learned to question the ego (personal thought system) and your values are changing. The meaning you gave to the things you enjoyed is no longer there. And you have not yet imbued those things with new meaning. This is the beginning of the "period of sorting out" (M-4.I.A.4).

The first shift students make is to see every situation as a classroom where they learn of the Holy Spirit rather than as an end in itself. The first part of this shift is releasing the meaning you gave to things. So everything seems empty for a while. This will change as you learn to use everything as a way to be with the Holy Spirit. All things will then have one purpose for you, giving them meaning, and simplifying your life.

So give your interests, work, relationships, etc. to the Holy Spirit. The purpose for doing this is not for some desired outcome, but to grow your awareness of the Holy Spirit. Eventually,

It will become your Constant Companion and this relationship will supply all the meaning you need in any situation.

185. Committed to the Spiritual Process (July 27, 2018)

If you've been reading my blog/newsletter for the past few weeks then you know significant things have occurred in the life of this mind. Four years ago the ego (personal thought system) fell away. I didn't realize it fully and I spent three and a half years personally in a rather barren place in this mind, though there was peace in the rest of my mind. I did feel done with the world, but I didn't know what that meant. I just stayed with the feeling, wondering what would come next.

The next thing arrived in this mind last summer with a subtle shift from emptiness to a delicious Spaciousness. This was followed by beautiful Golden Light, Love, and Joy filling the Space. Bewilderingly, an effect of this was a romance novel! From there, the Light and the shifts continued.

During this time a client in Australia whom I have called Zelda in these articles, but whose real name is Hannah, became a friend as well. We grew closer over several months and began to experience a lot of synchronicity and other things that signaled that our minds had joined. In April, we acknowledged we had a Holy relationship. In May, I acknowledged to her that for me personal feelings for her had come with the Holy relationship. I already knew she had personal feelings for me.

I was married, so I was bothered by the feeling that I had another "partner", even though it was a spiritual partner. And so I told my wife, Courtney. I explained the Holy relationship and I was honest that there were also personal feelings, but they were secondary. Hannah is on the other side of the world. The Holy relationship is what matters. Our marital boat rocked for a bit, but we set boundaries and things settled in that regard.

But not within me. Huge shifts began to occur. I came to realize I had "died"—the ego had fallen away and it was all new within. I could feel my old way of thinking with an ego dismantling every day. I could feel my mind shifting to Higher Awareness. I became aware, as I shared in an article two weeks ago, that a new Animator had come to live through the self. But, more than those already rocking experiences, I was sensing outward movement, too. I resisted this *hard*. I was having visions of myself in Australia with Hannah. I was hearing, within, that she was my new partner, and that I needed to get to know her. In fact, I felt in some ways that I was already with her, on every level, even though that was not appearing in form. I hardly knew her, but I felt my life with her was more real than the life the body was in. I fought this. I told myself the shifts were only internal. New Life, New Love, New Land—this is only a metaphor for what is going on *within*.

I didn't ask for this! I felt complete in my life in every way. I was happy in my marriage. I wasn't looking for anything but deepening awareness of Truth. And yet, I was given this gift of the Holy relationship, and Hannah to love, in every way. Because I didn't *need* this, because there was no lack to fill, it was pure Joyful Abundance. But I recognized, on some level, that her arrival signaled that the old Liz truly was "dead". She was the partner for the emerging self that is now directed by the new Animator within. It was the new Liz's heart that leapt in Joyful recognition of Hannah as her given partner.

For two months I struggled hard against what I knew was happening. It was too huge! The conflict was enormous. I jerked poor Hannah around with my mixed signals. An intuitive, she, too, saw me with her, but my telling her it was not happening now threw her into doubt about what she could trust. Courtney was accepting of our situation, but not really comfortable. In the past she and I had discussed open marriages and polyamory, but we both felt these did not really fit our situation with Hannah. I struggled to stay in the life I was in—the life that I had felt was over for so long—and still somehow have the Holy relationship with Hannah.

Then, at the end of June, I finally had to face that I could not reconcile my "dead" life with the new one emerging within me. I left Courtney, who had been the former Liz's wife, best friend, and partner in every way for twenty-four years. In a few months I will be taking the self to Australia; to a Holy and every-other-way relationship with Hannah.

At first there was more grief than relief. And so many surreal moments of confusion that sometimes seemed like doubt, but never lasted for long. Am I really making a wholesale life change at fifty-four? Yes, I am. I no longer have the illusion that the self belongs to this consciousness. Something Else has come to live through the self this mind projects. And the old life needs to be brought down to zero so It can.

One of my first thoughts after I left Courtney was, "How can I tell my readers/clients about this humungous life shift that followed the dropping of the ego without terrifying them?" But I have always been honest about my process and I'm not going to stop now. Of course, it does not unfold the same way for everyone. Certainly, most will not be called on to make such a wholesale change in their life. (It remains to be seen why *I* was!) And, of course, I am no longer in a mindset of lack, sacrifice, and loss. Yes, I grieve, but in a process of transformation, not loss. (More on this next week). Whatever your part in the Undoing (Atonement) requires, you will be ready for it, as I was ready for this.

When Courtney and I got together she told me her 12-step program came first for her. I said that was okay, because my spiritual process came first for me. It was my primary commitment. It preceded everything else, in time, but also in importance, to me. My mistake was thinking I could make any other commitment. Courtney has said no spiritual path would ask someone to leave their wife. I must be acting from ego. I understand what she is saying, because hers is a path of spiritualizing the ego, not transcending it. But, actually, my making a commitment beyond my commitment to my awareness of Truth was ego. I was looking to make something unchanging in the world. Hannah understands that my only honest commitment now can be to my spiritual process. And it is the same for her. We will see where our commitment to Truth takes us together.

Of course, Courtney and my family think I've had a mental break or I'm having a midlife crisis. I am dismantling an entire life, down to nearly zero, and going to another country I've never been to, to be with a woman I've never met in person. Oh, I understand their perspective. Sometimes I've shared it! From the outside it *does* look insane. But within, I trust this unfolding with deepening serenity.

My family and friends grieve the leaving Liz. But, from my perspective, they are only catching up with where I have been for a while. I cannot find the old Liz. She truly is gone. A new one is emerging. There is no way they can understand that I am wholly new within. Who could understand this but someone who has experienced it?

I realize what I have shared here will make some readers uncomfortable for various reasons. I welcome your questions and will answer them in private or in this newsletter/blog if you prefer.

And, in answer to the inevitable questions: Yes, I will continue to write, teach, and mentor, just from a new country. I plan to maintain my relationships with my current clients, if they are willing, if necessary, to make some time adjustments.

186. Wholeness and Transformation (August 3, 2018)

It's no surprise that last week's article rattled a lot of readers. Expectations of what happens when the ego (personal thought system) falls away were shattered. Personal values were challenged.

As I mentioned in that article, from the personal view, it makes no sense to me to change out one partner for another. I'll encounter the same things with Hannah that I encountered with Courtney; as I would sharing my life with anyone. She'll have habits that I find endearing one moment and detest the next. She'll meet some of my needs, but not others. The excitement of a new relationship will pass as we settle in with each other. Ga-ga-in-love-with-each-other stages will come and go over time, with less and less frequency. For a long while I thought if Courtney left or died I wouldn't seek out another partner. Who the hell wants to start all over with a new person and have to navigate those first couple of years where you both accidently step in emotional and psychological landmines all the time? Yuck. I was happy and whole. I was not seeking for anything. A new relationship would only bring change that I didn't feel a need for.

Ah, but there's another view of change. One that shows that change is not about fulfilling personal desire and needs. I call it the "holistic view". This view is the understanding that what shows up "out there" is an expression. You may feel that you are motivated by lack, but change occurs in the self's life to reflect changes in your mind. I reached completion with the ego. And in so doing, I reached completion with a marriage made when I was ego-identified. A new kind of partnership, a Holy relationship, has shown up to express where this mind is now.

Truth is Whole. It is One and the Same throughout. Even in its erroneous, fragmented state, mind cannot get away from wholeness. But sameness is impossible in diverse form. So, in the universe of form, wholeness shows up as transformation.

In the holistic view you understand that even at the level of form there is no loss, only conversion. Biology shows us the cycle of life, birth-death-rebirth-or-repurposing. A leaf falls to the ground, decomposes, and feeds new life. An animal dies and other animals and microbes feed off of it. A fire destroys a forest and quickly new growth appears in the midst of what looks like devastation. Life is not lost; just transformed.

Physics shows us that energy and matter are the same. Matter may seem to change, but energy is never lost.

And so it is with your life. Someone or something falls away and makes room for what better reflects a new state of mind. If you look back over your life, you will see when things shifted away they made room for new people, situations, or experiences that reflected your internal change.

What is hard to convey to others in this experience I am having is how wholly gone is the old Liz. This does not feel like a continuation of that narrative. A whole new life is beginning. I am dismantling a stranger's life. I feel I am to bring it down to as close to zero as I can. I wrote three weeks ago about the new Animator-of-the-self Who has come to live through this consciousness (#183). It is as though who I thought I was died, but I remained conscious, and now I am having a conscious reincarnation. What is emerging in this mind is closer to What is.

One of the most confounding parts of my experience with Hannah when we acknowledged our Holy relationship was the sense that I was already Joyously partnered with her on every level, despite appearances. I heard, "This is your new partner. Get to know her." But it wasn't like I was getting to know someone *new*. It was like I was getting to know someone I was already with on another level. The conscious level, where she was a near-stranger, was out of sync with a higher level, where we are already joined. So while to the world it looks as though I left Courtney for Hannah, for me Courtney's Liz died, and Hannah is already the emerging Liz's partner. I have told Courtney that I feel she is more the old Liz's widow than my ex. I do not expect anyone to understand this. But, for me, this explains the wholesale transformation in the outer life occurring for this self.

So I have no sense of sacrifice or loss. Just dramatic outward change that reflects a dramatic change that has already occurred within. The grief I feel is no deeper than what I'd feel watching a sad movie. The changes, inner and outer, as well as the shallowness of feeling, is sometimes baffling and disconcerting. It's an adjustment. But I have a willingness I can only call a miracle.

In the holistic view, I trust that this unfolding is for all, not just for me or for me and Hannah. This transformation is for Courtney, too. A year ago Love came exploding into the spaciousness of this mind left when the ego fell away. And this is Its continuing expression. How could this not reflect wholeness for everyone?

187. Shattered Expectations (August 10, 2018)

Often I have written that this path has not unfolded the way I thought it would. I had expectations based on what I read, but had not yet experienced. So they were formed through the filters of my past and what I only understood so far. Other expectations were formed in guilt and fear. And still others were based on the specific experiences of others, which were never meant to be applied to everyone.

There was a time when my study was all in my intellect and I pushed away my mystical experiences. Intellectual study led to new concepts, but brought no peace and no clarity. Only experience would bring peace and clarity. I eventually learned to let my experiences, rather than what I read in a book, lead the way. And only then did I really understand what I had read.

Thankfully, miraculously, my willingness to experience for myself overrode my expectations. And this has led to shattered expectations, but fascinating, illuminating experiences.

My recent articles rattled some of my readers. They shattered their expectations. Some had expectations of me; some had expectations of what would happen when the ego (personal thought system) fell away. Some admit they are rattled, are turning inward to Truth, and are learning from it. Some are merely redefining what is meant by "ego", because their expectations were based on a misunderstanding of what it is. Others project guilt and fear.

Though my outer world is changing dramatically, for me it is the internal shift that requires the greater adjustment. A consciousness used to identifying with a self now has to adjust to being without that identity. It is mourning the loss of that identification while adjusting to merely observing the self. It is undoing habits of thinking. It is accepting a Higher Consciousness that has come to fill the void. The latter is not difficult on its own. It's actually quite lovely. But it signals just how huge a shift has come, and sometimes throws this mind back into shock and grief.

It amuses me when people say I must be wrong about what has happened in my mind, and the manifestation of that shift in the self's life, because it does not fit their expectations of what the experience would be. It's not how they've interpreted what it says in a book they've read! Ah, well, yes, I was there myself. I know the fear that made me cling to "safe" ideas. And I know the fear that attended them being shattered. While I am amused at the arrogance of holding out one's expectations as more valid than another's experience, I do feel compassion for their fearfulness.

I share my experiences so that my readers know what to expect—the unexpected. How can a mind used to a certain thought system understand what will happen when it is gone and a whole new Thought System comes?

188. The Ego-identifier (August 17, 2018)

From what I've read and heard, when the ego (personal thought system) falls from a mind, what follows is a unique experience. Some things seem universal, like emptiness and varying degrees of disorientation. Also, acclimating to the absence as well as the Peace that comes. But exactly what process a mind embarks on to recognize what happened and to adjust to it seems pretty idiosyncratic. So don't expect that the particulars that I write about my experience will be your own.

I went into three and a half years of shock after the ego fell from this mind. Three years in, the emptiness, which I did not yet understand, became a delicious Spaciousness. This was filled with a Golden experience of Love. But I didn't understand why this was happening. I didn't dare think the ego had fallen. That seemed, well, egotistical! And, moreover, I was still having egoic responses. Only those had become very shallow.

The events I've written about lately that began four months ago, however, made it clear to me that the ego is gone and a new Life is beginning in this mind. I began to come out of shock. I had some very surreal experiences with this, sometimes falling back into shock, but it was clear the process of acceptance had begun.

Yet I continue to have egoic responses, shallow and quickly passing though they are. When you cut yourself and it scabs over, the last part of the scab to fall off is the thickest, where the cut was deepest. For me, it is as though, when the ego fell away, my mind scabbed over with shock to protect itself. And bits of the scab fell away over the years, until suddenly this spring a huge part of it fell off. Except for the last, deepest place the ego was attached. This is the part of my mind that overlearned the ego. I call this part the "ego-identifier". It shares the not-Truth part of my split-mind with the observer (decision maker), the part that learned it could step back and merely observe the ego.

As the observer grew, and learned that it could detach *from* the ego so it couldn't *be* the ego, the ego-identifier shrunk. But it held on tight to the ego to the end. It is the "echo" of the ego left in my mind, still habitually responding as the ego has taught it, but there is no substance behind its responses. They are shallow. They dissipate quickly as I unlearn these knee-jerk responses.

The ego-identifier is what stayed in denial longest and has mostly strongly resisted the transformation in this mind. Because, to it, which has always identified with the ego, the ego's "death" seemed to mean its own "death". Many times in those three and a half years of shock I'd have an insight or realization about a shift toward Truth that I felt, and I would think, stunned,

"If this is true, then I'm already dead." The ego-identifier continued to say this even when the rest of my mind was coming to accept that, yes, as far as the ego went, I had "died".

The question I've had is: Does the ego-identifier change and integrate with the observer and the Awareness of Truth? Or is it like the ego, unable to change, and therefore, do I need to release it? One day I turned to the ego-identifier and said, "You won't cease to exist. You will just exist differently." And its response was, "Different is death." I realized that telling the ego-identifier that it would learn to identify with Spirit was like telling a person they could learn to identify with an ocean. The difference in experiences is so stark it is like ceasing to exist. So I concluded that the ego-identifier had to be released.

And I held this view for a few weeks because the ego-identifier seemed rock-solid in its denial and resistance. But something shifted recently. Beneath the grief I've felt for all of the people, things, values, and situations dropping in the self's outer life, I've discovered a deeper grief for the loss of the ego. All of those griefs only signal that the ego has fallen. More powerfully, the Golden Love, the Holy relationship, and the Higher Awareness that have come to this mind also signal that the ego is gone. And what would resist these signs and mourn the loss of the ego but the ego-identifier? Grief means it is in a process. That means it *can* change. It can come to acceptance and catch up with the rest of my mind.

I didn't expect this grief! I had the expectation, like many others, that when the ego fell it would just be happy happy joy joy as Spirit filled the void. But now I see it is just common sense that a mind used to a way of thinking, and thinking about itself, would have to adjust to that falling away. *A Course in Miracles* tells us that our minds cannot just return straight to Truth because the contrast would be too shocking. Well, I can understand that, as the ego falling is shocking enough!

Since I've recognized this grief, it's been much easier. I had been flying into brief, but intense, rages, and they have ceased. The other day the ego-identifier said in a very small voice, "I have no purpose anymore. My only purpose was to identify with the self." Insights into its thinking are openings. It is an odd position to be in, but I am mentoring my own mind! From Higher Awareness I am able to address the ego-identifier like I would a client or friend, helping it through its process. The past couple of days it has been expressing shock over the Holy relationship and my going to Australia! How did this happen? Who is this woman? What do you mean *Australia*? It's all too strange! But, though still shocky, it sees these things now. It is catching up with the rest of my mind. In time, it will heal up, its resistance and grief will cease, and it will integrate.

189. The Mystical Holy Relationship Corrects Cause and Effect (August 24, 2018)

In my first mystical Holy relationship with E thirty-four years ago, I experienced great joy, but I also sensed the "cost" of the Holy relationship. The cost was the special relationship. The cost was the ego (personal thought system). I couldn't characterize then the shift that the Holy relationship would bring. I could only sense it. But I now know that the Holy relationship corrects the confusion of cause and effect, completely undoing the special relationship.

The special relationship is the ego's greatest deception. The experience of the ego is lack, and the special relationship is supposed to supply that lack. Mostly, we don't *think* in those terms. But we do feel that the special relationship will save or fix us or make us whole somehow. The idea is that this other person, be it parent, sibling, friend, lover, or partner will supply our lack. We are drawn to them because we see them as the source of Love, Which is an experience of Wholeness.

In the special relationship, the person of the other matters. Their body, personality, and character is what we look to, to supply our lack. Often, it's because unconsciously and/or consciously they remind us of someone we loved in the past whom we felt met our needs. Sometimes, the special relationship is a special hate relationship where we seek revenge on someone in the past who did not meet our needs through the relationship with the person who now reminds us of them. Often, special love and special hate are mixed in one relationship: "You meet some needs like my mother, but you miss the same ones my father missed." So you switch between love and hate, making for a very confusing and stressful relationship!

Where you make a special relationship to make yourself whole, the mystical Holy relationship is given from Wholeness Itself. You and another recognize, on a spiritual level, that you are one and the same. Clearly, this Vision does not involve the body's eyes or the ego's perceptions! That alone is rattling to your identification with a body and ego. Vision occurs in mind. It reveals that there is more to you than a body and more to your mind than the ego. But that's only the beginning. If you let it, the Holy relationship teaches you that you don't need another to make you whole. The mystical Holy relationship is an *expression* of the Wholeness that you are. Love comes first; adoration of the other's qualities follows. It is the reverse of the special relationship.

In fact, the mystical Holy relationship isn't really with another person. In my first mystical Holy relationship, E moved thousands of miles away, but I could still experience the Vision of Oneness just thinking about her. Clearly, then, she was not the source of the Vision. The Vision had to be within me. I learned that the Holy relationship is really with the Holy Spirit (the Awareness of Truth in your mind), and that the Holy relationship that shows up in the world is an expression of that.

In my current mystical Holy relationship, Hannah is across the world from me in Australia. So, again, we do not have to be physically present with each other to experience the Holy Spirit together in our minds. Why we both see and feel me there in form is something we both watch unfold with interest and curiosity. How will Love express Itself through us?

Sometimes when I hear students of *A Course in Miracles* long for a Holy relationship I see they have confused it with the idea of "soul mates" or some sort of super-charged special relationship. Ah, be careful what you wish for, because it is neither of those things. The Holy relationship is so opposite the special love and/or hate relationship that it is very disorienting at first. Your contexts and paradigms for relationships go out the window. For a while, you don't quite know how to look at the other.

There can be, as I wrote above, a great sense of loss, too, as the way you used to look for wholeness must fall away. You are left with a sense that you are never going to be whole until you catch on that the Holy relationship is an expression of the Wholeness already here. However, this awareness comes to *you*, not to the ego, so it continues to scream that you lack. This is why ACIM tells us that sometimes two people in a Holy relationship actively hate each other and never get the lesson. They listen to the ego and never allow the Holy Spirit to finish transforming the relationship into an expression of Love. If the transformation is allowed to become complete, then the relationship is one of pure Joy.

190. Purpose as Expression Rather Than Cause (August 31, 2018)

Last week I wrote how the mystical Holy relationship corrects cause and effect. Instead of seeing another as the source (cause) of Love (effect) for you, you recognize Love is the Source (cause) of your relationship (effect). Another way to say this is that the mystical Holy relationship's purpose is not to cause Love, but to express Love.

Part of correcting cause and effect is redefining the purpose of everything from cause to expression. What happens in time is not to bring a certain end into existence (salvation, atonement, undoing, etc). That end has already occurred. The moment the idea of not-Truth arose, it was undone by Truth's all-encompassing nature. So time does not bring about the Undoing (Atonement). It expresses it. In time, it seems like the idea of not-Truth arose long ago and its undoing is in some indefinite future. Time takes an idea that was over in a moment and tells it as an unfolding story. So the Undoing is always happening, only in slooooooow motion. The Undoing is what everything in time is for. The Undoing is what the story of time is.

Using the mystical Holy relationship as an example, as an expression of Love's Eternal Presence, it is a manifest expression of the Undoing. Really, it is the Undoing itself. Where there was not-Truth, Truth becomes manifestly apparent to two minds that once seemed separate. And to any minds that tune into them.

If you see your life as having a purpose to cause something, to bring it into being, then you feel a tremendous pressure to "make it happen" and "get it right". But when you recognize your life is an expression, an effect, then the pressure is off. You do not have to make anything happen, but rather let your life unfold as the expression of the Undoing that it is. You can rest in the unfolding Undoing, seeking not for what to do, but open to what is being done through you.

191. Because I Made It (September 7, 2018)

A few weeks ago I wrote about the part of my mind that overlearned the ego, was the most attached to it, and was the last part to acknowledge that it was gone (#188). I called this part of my mind the ego-identifier.

The ego-identifier still holds the lessons from the ego dear. It thought the self and the ego were its identity; it thought its whole purpose was to identify with the self and ego. But it is really a part of my mind and so it is capable of unlearning those lessons and integrating with the rest of my mind, which is rising to a Higher Awareness. I've learned more about the ego watching the ego-identifier being undone than I could when the ego was still a part of my mind.

I refer to the time when the ego (personal thought system) dropped but I didn't know it as the "Mansion and shack" time. The ego fell when I felt, truly, that I was done with pain. It was not a rancorous feeling; just a fact. But I went into shock and I did not know it had happened. It took me four years to acknowledge it.

At the time, what I felt was frustration that I could not let go of the ego. I felt close, but, I thought, unable. What I was really feeling was what I now label the ego-identifier part of my mind resisting and denying that I had let it go.

To understand what I felt, I saw the ego as a shabby shack on the same property as a Mansion, which represented Abundant Truth. I had come to understand that the Mansion was mine and always had been. I did not earn It and I would not have to pay for It. It was, and always had been, mine. But I also still held onto the shack, shabby and inadequate as it was. I went back and forth between the Mansion and the shack. I vacillated between Truth and ego.

Why, I wondered, did I cling to something I could clearly see had no value and that kept me from That which clearly did? I looked at this in every way and I was left with just one conclusion: I valued the shack (ego) *because it was mine*. There was no other reason. It might be small and painful and unworthy of me, but it was *mine*, dammit!

Recognizing that didn't shift anything. I tried coming at it from all sorts of angles, but nothing moved. Now I realize nothing moved because it had already moved! I was holding onto a shadow of the ego. But, back then, all I felt was frustration. I concluded I wasn't ready to resolve this issue and let it go.

Four years later, I have encountered this idea from another angle. One morning, in this time of transition, steeped in the ego-identifier, I found myself crying from the depths over the loss of my twenty four year marriage. I had already grieved the loss of my wife. This time I was grieving the loss of one of my highest personal desires and values: A lifelong marriage. There was only one thing I valued more, and that was Truth. And that meant allowing It to lead the way and that has led me to the Holy relationship. Why, I wondered, was I valuing the form of a relationship over its content? And then I realized I valued form *simply because it is form*. I value form *because I make it*. In ego-identification, *I* decided that a lifelong marriage was valuable and made one. *I* decided what I wanted in that marriage. *I* made a home with my wife filled with things that represented our values.

Then I realized that the most important thing I was seeing was that my values themselves were forms I made! *I* decided what was valuable.

"Now must the teacher of God understand that he did not really know what was valuable and what was valueless. All that he really learned so far was that he did not want the valueless, and that he did want the valuable. Yet his own sorting out was meaningless in teaching him the difference. The idea of sacrifice, so central to his own thought system, had made it impossible for him to judge. He thought he learned willingness, but now he sees that he does not know what the willingness is for." (M-4.I.A.7) (My underline for emphasis.)

How many times have I read this in *A Course in Miracles* and never understood it this way! In identification with the ego, I valued my values because *I* made them. I valued what my values made because *I* made them. I felt giving them up was a sacrifice not because of what they were, but because *I* made them. In ego, it was all a power play for autonomy, or independence, from the rest of my mind. It was all about being a god in this little patch of mind I made my own. That's why the shack I made was more valuable to me than the Mansion that was simply mine.

This grasp for small power isolated me from the rest of my mind and made it feel alien to me. I felt that dropping the boundaries of a personal identity and joining the rest of my mind was submitting to a greater Power. And the ego-identifier still had this idea. What I have had to teach it is that it will not be *joining* the rest of my mind. It will *be* my mind. Its small existence will not disappear into a larger one. Its existence will expand as it accepts What it really is.

None of this is new stuff, of course. It's all there in ACIM where it talks about ego autonomy (T11.V) and littleness versus magnitude (T15.III). And I've seen it in many forms over the years. But now I am seeing these ideas where I accepted them at the most fundamental level of my mind. And I am watching them, finally, be undone.

192. Why the Mystical Holy Relationship Threatens the Ego (September 14, 2018)

Thirty-four years ago I experienced my first mystical Holy relationship. I knew then that the Holy relationship, if allowed to become fulfilled, would result in a 180 degree turn in my experience of a personal relationship. I couldn't put my finger on exactly what I was seeing. I couldn't have said then that it corrected cause and effect. But I did sense it would undo something fundamental to the ego's (personal thought system's) way of perceiving. And at that time that was *my* way of perceiving.

In the mystical Holy relationship, instead of seeing another as the source (cause) of Love (effect), you recognize Love is the Source (cause) of your relationship (effect) with the other. Sounds great, doesn't it? And it is! It is Joyous for a relationship that expresses Love to show up. But therein lies the threat to the ego: The relationship is simply here, already whole and complete. The ego teaches you to *make* relationships to get Love and/or to express your personal desires and values.

A Course in Miracles teaches that relationships are special love, special hate, or Holy. A special relationship is an obstacle to peace. In a special love relationship you believe the other is the source of Love (Wholeness) for you. It is why you make the relationship with them. You are not just attached to them through affection and familiarity. You *cling* to them because you feel that to lose them is to lose the source of Love. You panic at the thought of losing them.

In the special hate relationship peace is blocked because you cling to the idea that you are the victim of the other. You hold onto the other through resentments. Often, a special relationship is both love and hate.

But you probably have plenty of personal relationships that are not special. They are not obstacles to peace. You know that the other is not the source of Love for you. You form the relationship through personal desire or values, but you use it as a classroom in which you grow your awareness of Truth. You bring the Holy Spirit (Awareness of Truth within you) into your relationship with the other. These relationships are *practical* Holy relationships. Where special relationships confuse cause and effect—another is seen as the source of Love—the practical Holy relationship is a step toward correcting this error. You use the relationship to remind yourself that Love is within you.

But no real shift occurs until you experience the mystical Holy relationship. The mystical Holy relationship is an expression of the Love within you. Love Itself, not your personal desires or values, is the Source of the relationship. You and another recognize your joining, your Oneness, is already established. There is nothing to seek for or to make in the relationship. Ah, and therein is the threat to the ego! The Cause of the relationship is Something Else within you, not your personal needs or values. Oh, some of these might get met and expressed, but they're not the motivation for the relationship. In fact, personal motivation, something else you make, is also not part of the mystical Holy relationship. The mystical Holy relationship expresses Love through persons, but is not made to express the personal. So, when you are ego-identified, you feel the Holy relationship asks you to sacrifice your desires and values.

"... The conflict between the goal and the structure of the relationship is so apparent that they cannot coexist. Yet now the goal will not be changed. Set firmly in the unholy relationship, there is no course except to change the relationship to fit the goal. Until this happy solution is seen and accepted as the only way out of the conflict, the relationship may seem to be severely strained." (T-17.V.4)

"...You can escape from your distress only by getting rid of your brother. You need not part entirely if you choose not to do so. But you must exclude major areas of fantasy from your brother, to save your sanity. Hear not this now.*"* (T-17.V.7)

The threat to the ego is why the urge to flee the Holy relationship is so strong. Maybe you won't run completely. But you try to find ways to control it or to "make" it as you are used to making relationships. You complain that the relationship and/or the other are not what you want. You try to impose your values and expectations on the relationship. And they don't fit! Not because they are wrong. But because that is not what the relationship is about.

Finally, I see clearly what I could not see thirty-four years ago: A relationship as an *expression* rather than a means to a personal end. I felt the threat and I sensed, but could not understand, the reverse of cause and effect the mystical Holy relationship would bring about. Now I do not feel threatened and I am willing to let it teach me What I am by What is expressed through it.

193. Higher Awareness and the Given Life (September 21, 2018)

The hardest thing to convey about this huge shift in my mind is how the new life that has come to it and is expressed through the self is not a continuation of the old life that fell away with the ego (personal thought system). It is a whole new life, inward and outward. Sometimes I wonder, "Why Australia?" And the answer is, "Because that's where *this* life is." I might as well ask of the old life, "Why the US?" It's just where *that* life was.

I have had the sense since this new life broke upon me (which is what it felt like) that I am moving into a life that is already whole and complete. I do not have to *make* it. I just have to walk into it. It is *given*, not as in "something is giving it to me", but as in, "it is already established". I have a deep sense of recognizing this experience. This is the view in Higher Awareness.

Where the Awareness of Truth (Holy Spirit) is found within and is universal (the same in everyone) Higher Awareness is the label I give to the individual experience of looking outward from the Awareness of Truth. It is one's view of life in the world from the Awareness of Truth.

The life before, at a lower level of awareness, reflected personal identity, desires, and values. It, too, was of course a part of the unfolding Undoing, as everything is. So its unfolding was also established. But the point of view for this mind was personal, which meant that, except for occasional flashes of intuition, nothing felt given or established. This is why the life I'm in now feels completely different from the old one. My point of view is completely new. I am standing in Higher Awareness.

But more than my view has changed. Though mentally and emotionally riotous, external dismantling of the old life and preparations for the new have gone remarkably fast and smooth, as though the way is paved for me.

It used to be that there was a time lag between an inner shift and it showing up in form. Not anymore! It is as though my outer life is a metaphor for the shifts within.

The boundaries between Higher and lower awareness and inner and outer life are gone. I simply can no longer parse things into Truth and not-Truth. Love extends through it all and I can't make that distinction anymore. But that doesn't make not-Truth, Truth. It simply means I can't see it!

"'Heaven and earth shall pass away' means that they will not continue to exist as separate states." (T-1.III.2)

"...For as Heaven and earth become one, even the real world will vanish from your sight. The end of the world is not its destruction, but its translation into Heaven. The reinterpretation of the world is the transfer of all perception to knowledge." (T-11.VIII.1)

Oh, I'm not *there* yet, just beginning to see the potential.

Back in July I wrote "The Stranger Within" (#183). The "Stranger" was a new Animator (Holy Spirit/Awareness of Truth) that had begun to live through the self (body/personality) in my mind. I was used to constructing an identity as and through the self. But my Identity now just is. It does not require any effort on my part. I just have to watch It and get to know It. It's a very odd feeling to not know oneself *at all*. I used to have shifts in self-concepts that meant I had to get to know new *parts* of myself. But this is a wholesale change.

This experience of "given" rather than "made" began in the summer of '17 when the Golden Light of Love came into my mind and I found myself writing a romance novel (A Good Woman). (Read about this at #150). I didn't feel I was channeling, but the characters, the setting, the story—all of it—was just *here* for me. As I wrote, even when I had things to figure out in the story, I didn't feel I was creating, but rather *discovering*, the story.

Then, this past Spring, a new Holy relationship came into my awareness. The first moment of Joyful recognition of what Hannah is to me is what I call "The Break" between my old awareness/life and my new awareness/life. I actually felt almost physically *hurled* upward within and outward toward Australia. From that moment on I felt, despite the physical distance, more with Hannah than with my wife, Courtney. Oh, I resisted this. For two months I struggled to integrate the new partner into the old life. And I rejected drastic outward change as anything but a metaphor for a huge inward shift. I even made signs for myself that I put around my desk: "*Upward*, not *outward*!" But the conflict between the life that was over and the new that had come eventually became too much. I had to accept Hannah as the given partner for the new, given life in which my new awareness will be expressed.

I know when I write about my experiences some readers attempt to use them to alter their own. I want to caution against trying to "make" a "given" life! A given life is the experience of Higher Awareness for me. I did not know to seek it, much less to make it. Grow your awareness of Truth and, when the ego falls away, you will have your own new experiences in Higher Awareness. Some of them may be like mine. Some of them will be unique to you.

194. About the Ego-identifier... (September 28, 2018)

A few weeks ago I wrote about the ego-identifier (#188). It was the label I gave to the part of my mind that over-learned the ego (personal thought system). It was the last to let it go. It was the most resistant to it being gone.

But I soon dropped the concept. It was useful while it lasted. I learned a lot about this mind. But after seeing into the deepest, darkest depths of its distrust of Truth (boy, *that* was uncomfortable!) and its valuing of guilt (as the ego taught it that guilt was the "proof" the ego was real), I realized I had no more use for the concept. If I continued to give it attention I would "recreate the beast (ego)".

A client of mine told me about another mentor of hers who dropped the ego. She described the stage afterward as the ego's momentum winding down. It's like when you stop peddling a bicycle, the bicycle continues to roll forward on its own until it comes to a full stop. I find this description better describes the wispiness of the remnants, echoes, habits, and shadows left over from the ego. Just as the ego fell away, I only have to allow these to fall away, too. I find this practice more useful now.

195. Clarifying the Holy Relationship (October 5, 2018)

As another Holy relationship has come into my life, several readers have mentioned that they thought the Holy relationship was with the Holy Spirit (Awareness of Truth in your mind) not with another. It is both. It is with another through the Holy Spirit.

In *A Course in Miracles*, the Holy relationship, one of its chief teaching tools (along with the Holy Instant it expresses), is introduced in Chapter 17 (part V) in "The Healed Relationship". From then on it never lets it go! And it is very clear throughout that it is referring to the relationship between Helen Schucman and Bill Thetford.

"A relationship, undertaken by two individuals for their unholy purposes, suddenly has holiness for its goal." (T-17.V.5)

I have experienced the Holy relationship in two ways: mystical and practical. ACIM teaches both, but the labels are mine. The Holy relationship in the Text is clearly mystical. But in the supplement to ACIM, Psychotherapy: Purpose, Process and Practice, Helen and Bill are being taught how to turn their relationships with their psychotherapy patients into practical Holy relationships. And the Workbook is full of examples of using relationships as classrooms.

Many readers questioning the Holy relationship quote Ken Wapnick. He seems to describe the practical Holy relationship. I am not sure if he ever experienced a mystical Holy relationship. They are not the same, but the mystical Holy relationship is also, in practice, a practical Holy relationship.

The mystical Holy relationship involves spiritual Vision. You and another actually see and experience your Oneness (wholeness/sameness) together.

"Did you see the holiness that shone in both you and your brother, to bless the other? That is the purpose of your holy relationship." (T-20.III.8)

"A holy relationship starts from a different premise. Each one has looked within and seen no lack. Accepting his completion, he would extend it by joining with another, whole as himself. He sees no difference between these selves, for differences are only of the body." (T-22.in.3)

"This is the function of your holy relationship. For what one thinks, the other will experience with him. What can this mean except your mind and your brother's are one?" (T-22.VI.13)

Though seen with one another, you recognize that the Oneness you see is not exclusive to the two of you. The dropping of the boundaries between your two minds makes you aware that, in Truth, there are no boundaries between any seemingly-separate minds. There is only One Mind.

The mystical Holy relationship is an *expression* of the Holy Spirit within you. Each one is unique, though the content is the same. It occurs when you are ready to accept this miraculous Vision. It deeply threatens the ego (personal thought system) in your mind as it undoes it, so it will only occur when you are ready to face this.

"Those who have joined their brothers have detached themselves from their belief that their identity lies in the ego. A holy relationship is one in which you join with what is part of you in truth. And your belief in sin has been already shaken, nor are you now entirely unwilling to look within and see it not." (T-21.IV.3)

The practical Holy relationship does not involve spiritual Vision. It is a choice you make to use a relationship to learn of the Holy Spirit within you. Rather than seeking for wholeness in another, you turn inward to the Holy Spirit instead. Your relationship with the other is then the *means* for growing your relationship with (awareness of) the Holy Spirit within.

"God's Teacher speaks to any two who join together for learning purposes. The relationship is holy because of that purpose, and God has promised to send His Spirit into any holy relationship." (M-2.5)

So both experiences of the Holy relationship involve the Holy Spirit and another. A mystical Holy relationship between you and another *comes from* your relationship with the Holy Spirit. A practical Holy relationship between you and another is how you deepen your relationship with (awareness of) the Holy Spirit.

Two questions I'm often asked is whether or not the Holy relationship can be one-sided and does it extend to everyone. It is possible to experience spiritual Vision of another without their awareness. In fact, the Vision of the mystical naturally extends to your other relationships. So what begins with one extends to all others.

"Think what a holy relationship can teach! Here is belief in differences undone. Here is the faith in differences shifted to sameness. And here is sight of differences transformed to vision. Reason now can lead you and your brother to the logical conclusion of your union. It must extend, as you extended when you and he joined. It must reach out beyond itself, as you reached out beyond the body, to let you and your brother be joined. And now the sameness that you saw extends and finally removes all sense of differences, so that the sameness that lies beneath them all becomes apparent. Here is the golden circle where you recognize the Son of God. For what is born into a holy relationship can never end." (T-22.in.3-4)

The practical Holy relationship is a choice you make to use a relationship as a classroom to learn from the Holy Spirit whether or not the other is doing the same. That attitude and approach also naturally extends to your other relationships. In fact, the first shift students of ACIM make is to use every situation as an opportunity to learn from the Holy Spirit. This makes everything a Holy relationship for you!

However, you can see by the quotes above and below that what ACIM means by a "Holy relationship", whether mystical or practical, is one where both parties are conscious of Oneness (mystical) and/or have chosen together to use the relationship as a classroom (practical). The term is meant to describe a specific type of intentional relationship between two people.

"To each who walks this earth in seeming solitude is a savior given, whose special function here is to release him, and so to free himself." (T-20.IV.5)

"The ark of peace is entered two by two, yet the beginning of another world goes with them." (T-20.IV.6)

"...I said before that the first change, before dreams disappear, is that your dreams of fear are changed to happy dreams. That is what the Holy Spirit does in the special relationship. He does not destroy it, nor snatch it away from you. But He does use it differently, as a help to make His purpose real to you. The special relationship will remain, not as a source of pain and guilt, but as a source of joy and freedom. It will not be for you alone, for therein lay its misery. As its unholiness kept it a thing apart, its holiness will become an offering to everyone." (T-18.II.6)

"Two voices raised together call to the hearts of everyone, to let them beat as one." (T-20.V.1)

196. The Undoing Unfolds Through You (October 12, 2018)

I've spent my entire adult life looking into this mind, so it was rather startling when things happened in it that I did not expect. How could I have missed that the self's life was going to radically change?

Looking back now I see shifts that occurred in this mind regarding the self (body/personality) that seem to have been preparation for this major shift. And I also see I missed them because I was not living through the self. I felt and watched the shifts, but I also let them go because I wasn't living there anymore.

I've written that in the four years between the ego (personal thought system) falling away and my acknowledging it, I experienced the Awareness of Truth (Holy Spirit) and therefore peace, but also a barren place in my mind. There was also a thread of pain that accompanied the barren feeling which grew as time went on. I now understand that the barren experience was the missing ego. It was what told me to identify with the self. Without it, I was simply experiencing the self's shifts as distant and interesting, but nothing I spent much time thinking about. My attention was on Truth. And the pain I felt was a sense of loss. The barrenness and pain were things I expected to understand more in time. And, of course, I now do!

Without realizing it, more and more I was letting the self just be in the flow of the universe as I rested in Truth. Of course, even if I'd paid more attention I would not have understood what was coming. And I did, eventually, sense something big was coming. I just didn't know it would be HUGE.

The lesson here is that whatever you are conscious of, your part in the Undoing is always unfolding through you.

197. Ask: Do we receive abstract answers to linear problems from the Holy Spirit? (October 19, 2018)

"I have been staying Present a lot more, but recently saw myself bringing a problem in the illusion to the Truth to resolve rather than the Truth to illusion.

Do the answers we receive from HS come in the world abstract for a linear problem? Is that how we can recognize it? Or how can we recognize HS's answer for an action we need solved?" – MR

In fact, you *want* to bring illusions to Truth rather than Truth to the illusion! To bring illusions to Truth is to correct the illusion. To attempt to bring Truth to the illusion is an attempt to "spiritualize" illusion—to make illusion Truth-like.

"You have been told to ask the Holy Spirit for the answer to any specific problem, and that you will receive a specific answer if such is your need. You have also been told that there is only one problem and one answer. In prayer this is not contradictory. There are decisions to make here, and they must be made whether they be illusions or not. You cannot be asked to accept answers which are beyond the level of need that you can recognize. Therefore, it is not the form of the question that matters, nor how it is asked. The form of the answer, if given by God, will suit your need as you see it. This is merely an echo of the reply of His Voice. The real sound is always a song of thanksgiving and of Love." (S-1.I.2)

While the Holy Spirit (the Awareness of Truth in your mind) is Abstract, Its answers take a form that have meaning for you where you are. That's why all you need to do is touch the Holy Spirit and the answer will come. There's a metaphor for this in the Bible, where all one needed to do was touch Jesus's robe and be healed.

You can recognize an answer from the Holy Spirit by how you feel. You will feel guilt and fear lift. You will experience clarity. When the answer is from the ego (personal thought system in your mind), guilt and fear continue or grow.

198. Ask: Can you interpret "all things work together for good"? (October 26, 2018)

"Please interpret this phrase from the text 4:V:1: 'All things work together for good. There are no exceptions except in the ego's judgment.' In the ego-world/battlefield it hardly seems possible that 'all things works together for good'. I can understand that on a metaphysical level it is possible; however, the world we see with the body's eyes is a battlefield." – KA

The world you see is always an interpretation. You see forms moving about and decide what they mean. In fact, a practice I learned was to sort out fact from my projection of meaning. For example, let's say you see John shoot George. The facts is one body shot the other body. But, depending on the context, you may interpret that as good or bad. If it is during war and John is on your side and George is the enemy, you will probably see it as good. Or, if George is someone you judge as a "bad guy" you may also see it as good. Maybe John shot George in self-defense and you think it's regrettable, but justified. Or you could see things in black and white and think that anybody shooting anybody else for any reason is wrong, so it is bad.

However, you could say, "John shot George" and decide you don't know, in the big picture, what this means. You may pity one or the other or both. But you could make no judgment on it in the recognition that you don't know why things unfolded that way.

Now to your quote: The unfolding story of the universe of form is the moment of the idea of not-Truth/the-undoing-of-the-idea-of-not-Truth in the Mind of Truth (God) played out in time. So we are always living in the undoing (Atonement) of the idea-of-not-Truth, even if, in the moment, we cannot see that larger story. So all things, no matter how they appear, do work for good if you judge the Undoing as "good"!

"In order to judge anything rightly, one would have to be fully aware of an inconceivably wide range of things; past, present and to come. One would have to recognize in advance all the effects of his judgments on everyone and everything involved in them in any way. And one would have to be certain there is no distortion in his perception, so that his judgment would be wholly fair to everyone on whom it rests now and in the future." (M-10.3)

When you watch a movie and you don't know the outcome, you may fret over the protagonist's every challenge. But if you know there will be a happy ending, you relax and understand that everything that happens leads to that ending. You can look at the world the same way, knowing that, no matter how things appear right now, it is happening as part of the Undoing, the happy ending.

199. The Fact of Spirit (November 2, 2018)

It is not appropriate to exalt or to worship Spirit or anyone who has attained the awareness of Spirit. Of course, when you identify with the self and ego (personal thought system), Spirit seems "other". It can seem remote, mysterious, and/or magical. It is none of these things. It is What is Real in you, It is always right here and available, and It is miraculous, meaning It is simply Truth. It is the ego that tells you to exalt and worship Spirit to make Spirit seem foreign, exotic, and unobtainable. And to diminish you.

A few of months ago I experienced myself as Spirit for the first time. I was actually crouched down cleaning the shower door in my former house when it occurred. I don't remember what I was thinking before the experience. But suddenly I knew I have no beginning and no end. I am Invulnerable; I am Immortal. I am Spirit.

Even when I act as a person, I am Spirit.

I have had many higher miracles that have shown me the Truth is true or that illusion is illusion or both. Those are usually pretty dramatic because of their contrast to my usual experience. But when I experienced the awareness that I am Spirit it was simple and subtle and not at all dramatic. Yet the experience left me gobsmacked. I actually froze in place, my mouth gaping open, sponge in hand, for probably a good minute. More than once.

But then I experienced it again a few weeks ago and I was not gobsmacked. It was simply a lovely fact that has remained in my awareness ever since.

Four years ago when the ego fell away I began to rise in consciousness. It was as though the ego had been an anchor holding me down. I didn't realize it at the time, but the feeling I had in the following three years that I was a "ghost in the world" was the outer edges of the realization that I am Spirit. But for those years I was more focused on the emptiness left in the ego's absence than on the Life growing in my awareness.

So I can tell you from experience that Spirit, and anyone who is aware of Spirit as their Being, is not to be exalted or worshipped. We simply demonstrate that anyone can rise to this awareness.

200. Life As Spirit (so far) (November 9, 2018)

Whenever I express to others a dramatic shift in my experience I am asked to describe how life is different from the way it was before the shift. Of course I have been asked this since I have shared with others that this mind has attained the ongoing awareness that I am Spirit.

Life goes on as usual for the self (body/personality) on the outside. Well, *as usual* for living in the countryside in south Western Australia, which is wholly unlike the life I lived in a desert city in the southwestern US just a few weeks ago! But I mean the self appears as usual like a person, doing what people normally do every day, and I am experienced as a person by others.

The dramatic difference is within. I live so wholly in the moment. I call this experience *Hereness*. (It could also be called the "Spaciousness" I have referred to before. Or just being wholly present, centered, or in Presence). I am like an island in the stream of time, around which time flows. I am often staring out windows or sitting outside looking at the garden. Well hell, there isn't a single bad view here, who wouldn't? But often I'm not thinking about anything. I am simply being. What else is there to do, really? Until I am moved to think about something or do something with the self. And then I do all the usual thinking and doing, as needed.

I don't ask for the right action or the right time to take action. I just know what and when. I don't concern myself with the thoughts being "good" or "right" or whatever. Judgment isn't needed, not even on judgments.

Sometimes the very recent past, when I dismantled an entire life to make room for this new one, will surface with all the feelings of bafflement and grief and resistance one would expect. But each time the feelings are milder and I have learned to let them come up and go by without doing anything with them. They come up because they are still here in this mind, that's all. They pass.

Attachments fall away as they need to. Most of the time I didn't even know they were there until I watch them fall.

It used to be I saw dark thoughts as blocking my awareness of Truth, like clouds before the sun. Truth was still there, but I was not aware of It. But now I see it from the other side. When dark thoughts roll around, they do no block my awareness of Truth, but rather the extension of Truth (Love) through me. So they *limit* my awareness of Truth for a short time, but that is all. No biggie.

I experience others as passing, too. I am with them for the time I am with them, but do not give them any further thought, unless there is some reason to do so. Then that happens naturally and spontaneously, too.

I find it easy to just be quiet with others. Many thoughts of things to say will cross my mind, but most go unspoken. Then I find the self speaking and I just watch and listen. That moment in time will pass, too, after all.

In other words, this mind is a *lot* quieter.

I feel ethereal instead of concrete. I am everywhere, always, and yet nowhere specific. I am the grass, the trees, that person, this person, that house, that road, etc. But I am all of them at once.

I am you and you are me. But I do not go around thinking "I am you and you are me." I just know this.

I also do not go around thinking "I am Spirit." I just know that, too. I act as a person, but I know I am not that. I wear the person lightly.

I often feel "disappeared", which is really another way I experience the expansion of my awareness to Limitless Being. I feel "disappeared" because boundaries are gone.

I feel I cannot have a presence for others; I must be like empty space. But Hannah tells me I do, because the self still expresses thoughts and opinions and stories. These are insignificant and passing to me. However, I understand that to others they are real and meaningful. They still see a body, a personality, a *person*, and she is concrete to them because they project their own seemingly-concrete "reality" onto her.

Spacetime collapsed for me at that moment I called The Break, when in May I felt hurled upward in consciousness and outward toward Australia. The future seemed present and more real to me than what was actually manifestly present. I am in that future now. What was future then continues to unfold in the present. What I still see in the future unfolds from the present.

I feel the personality called "Liz" being reworked and remolded. She used to be, for this mind, an expression of ego (personal thought system). But that version of her passed away when the ego fell away. Now she is an expression of Spirit, and that is transforming her. She is in a process I watch.

201. Ask: Why doesn't Truth hold our attention? (November 16, 2018)

"Aldous Huxley wrote 'Distraction is the original sin of the mind'. Distraction appears to be the ego's most valued weapon in the world with a vast arsenal and growing steadily. So then it seems that it's what you give your attention to that will determine the level of inner peace or chaos in your experience in the world. This Distraction/Attention dynamic seems to me to be at the core of Truth/not Truth discovery within. While in this dualistic drama not-Truth claims easy victories distracting personal selves through attention and distraction, Truth on the other hand stands silently and waits for our mighty power of attention to turn towards it. It's as if Truth knows you will ultimately come back to it. The sound and fury of the ego has no effect on it but it does on you. Why doesn't Truth pull our attention?" – E St. A

Make no mistake: Not-Truth (including the ego/personal thought system) has no power over you. You empower it by valuing it. Truth doesn't hold your attention because you also value not-Truth. Sometimes you value not-Truth for what you think it will give you over what Truth will give you. Sometimes you value not-Truth because you are afraid of Truth.

This is why *A Course in Miracles* lays out the path to peace as "the development of trust". You do not trust that only Truth will give you what you want or that Truth will give you more than you give up. It takes a long while for you to let It in via the Awareness of Truth (Holy Spirit) in your mind. And then your trust builds slowly—often three steps forward and two steps back. You are very skittish in your distrust.

However, slowly but surely, you will trust It and let It in more and more and your peace will grow.

202. Ask: What does the Course mean when it says "ideas leave not their source"? (November 23, 2018)

"...What does the Course *mean when it says: ideas leave not their source? I just can't seem to get a true understanding of that."* - LDP

"Ideas leave not their source, and their effects but seem to be apart from them. Ideas are of the mind. What is projected out, and seems to be external to the mind, is not outside at all, but an effect of what is in, and has not left its source." (T-26.VII.4)

"There is no world apart from your ideas because ideas leave not their source, and you maintain the world within your mind in thought." (W-132.10)

Your experience of peace or conflict is the effect of thoughts (beliefs) in your mind. You may project the source of your experience outward and feel that someone or something else has caused your experience, but that does not make it so. Your "world" (experience) has its source in your thoughts (beliefs, perceptions), which never actually leave you when you deny them by projecting them away.

For example, let's say a friend has treated you in a way that you see as unfair. Because you believe this, you are angry with them. Your view of their actions determines how you experience their actions. After your initial emotional response (defensive anger), you can think it through. Did they really treat you unfairly? Was that their intention or an unintended consequence of actions they took? The answer you come to will determine whether you continue to be angry and whether you continue to have this person in your life. You also want to look at your own determination of their actions as "good" or "bad" or "right" or "wrong" and at the story you tell yourself with these judgements.

You see how you build your world with your thoughts? The source of your thoughts is you, not someone or something else. And your thoughts never leave you.

This is important to know so you can change your experience by changing your mind.

"A thought is in the mind. It can be then applied as mind directs it. But its origin is where it must be changed, if change occurs. Ideas leave not their source. The emphasis this course has placed on that idea is due to its centrality in our attempts to change your mind about yourself. It is the reason you can heal. It is the cause of healing." (W-167.3)

Another corollary to this idea is that, as a thought, or part of, God's Mind, you have never left God, your Source. Therefore, the ego's (personal thought system's) premise for guilt is erroneous.

"I walk with God in perfect holiness.
Today's idea but states the simple truth that makes the thought of sin impossible. It promises there is no cause for guilt, and being causeless it does not exist. It follows surely from the basic thought so often mentioned in the text; ideas leave not their source. If this be true, how can you be apart from God? How could you walk the world alone and separate from your Source?" (W-156.1)

"God wills you learn what always has been true: that He created you as part of Him, and this must still be true because ideas leave not their source." (T-26.VII.13)

203. Truth, the Awareness of Truth, and Its Effects (November 30, 2018)

Lately, I have been pulled back inward to the Awareness of Truth (Holy Spirit). I've certainly been experiencing It a great deal spontaneously, but this pull inward is something different. It seems to be coming from a conscious recognition of the difference between Truth, the Awareness of Truth, and Its effects.

It began with experiencing again Truth's complete indifference to the experience of not-Truth. Contemplating this I became aware how caught up I've been in what are merely the effects of the awareness of Truth. Frankly, my life has transformed so greatly I had to be. The transformation began with the experience I call The Golden, when the Golden Light of Love came into my mind and brought a romance novel with It. During that time, I also reached a point where I recognized that the Light Itself and the love and joy that accompanied It, were really only effects of being aware of Truth. They were not Truth, nor were they the Awareness of Truth, and I didn't want to lose sight of Truth. For a brief spell I was pulled back, like now, to turning inward to Truth. But not long afterward my seemingly-outer life went through a huge transformation and required my attention.

(When I write "awareness" with a lowercase "a" I am writing about the *action* of being aware of Truth. When I write "awareness" with an uppercase "A" I am writing about the *state* of being aware of Truth, also called the Holy Spirit.)

During the time I call The Dismantling, when I was undoing my entire outer life, I'd sometimes think about how I was experiencing the Awareness of Truth as the underlying Wave I was riding, but I was not consciously aware of Truth. When I tried to be, I felt it was not time. I would have to force the effort. My conscious efforts were needed in the dismantling of the life that had passed so I could move on to the new life I was given. The most I could do was rest in the Awareness of Truth; the Wave I was riding.

And here, in this new life, I've experienced what I call the Hereness. While the outward shifts in my life were effects of being aware of Truth, the Hereness is the Awareness of Truth Itself. It is the same as my experience that I am Spirit.

This has helped me clarify:

Truth is That-Which-is. It is wholly apart from not-Truth; It is wholly apart from the limited experience of form (including non-material forms like thoughts and energy), so wholly untouched by it. To understand this is to experience what *A Course in Miracles* means by "forgiveness".

The *Awareness of Truth* (also called Spirit or Holy Spirit or Christ Consciousness) is the state of being aware of Truth *as* truth while also being aware of not-Truth.

The *effects of the Awareness of Truth* are the experiences that follow from being aware of Truth: Love, Peace, Joy; detachment from not-Truth; a transformed perception of not-Truth, which ACIM calls "the Real World", "Vision", or "Real Perception"; and, sometimes, to a transformed life in the world.

Truth does not exist so that it can cause effects in your not-Truth darkened mind any more than the sun shines to make plants grow. The sun shines <u>and</u> plants grow. Truth exists and comes into your awareness <u>and</u> this has the effect of not-Truth being undone in your mind. These effects in turn "prove" the existence of Truth and reveal the Awareness of Truth in your mind.

204. Truth Rising to Conscious Awareness (December 7, 2018)

I recently read Jan Frazier's, "When Fear Falls Away". She asked for fear to be removed and woke up the next morning to find the ego (personal thought system) gone. Then she went on to write about the effects of this and all that it taught her about her mind before and after. Reading her experience validated mine, and though my experience is unfolding in a very different way, her story has helped me to understand mine better.

I didn't have a sudden awakening where I *consciously* recognized what had happened. In fact, some of what she realized after her sudden shift in awareness I have realized slowly over the past few years. For me, the experience of the ego (personal thought system) falling away has been a slow dawning on my conscious mind that this has occurred. It is as if, when it comes to my *conscious* awareness, what she realized suddenly has been dawning in slow motion.

I've only realized in the past few months how new things are in this mind and for how long they have been so. It was over four years ago that the ego fell away and for a long time I was only dimly aware of new experiences and a new way of seeing. Much of this was chronicled in these articles at the time. I simply did not realize how significant the shift was because I didn't have a *conscious* moment of stark contrast where I could say "yesterday I saw that way; today I see this way".

In August of 2017 things did shift consciously for me when the Golden Light came into my conscious awareness. At the time I thought It was signaling something new coming, not the dawning in my conscious awareness of what had already occurred unconsciously. I've written a lot in the past couple of years about how, as spiritual students, we put too much emphasis on what happens at the conscious level. We shift unconsciously toward Peace and we don't know how much until we face something that makes us aware. I thought I was writing from my past experiences of discovering this. I didn't realize I was writing about what was going on with me at the time!

I finally caught on earlier this year that the ego had fallen when I was moved to make a radical transformation in my outer life. As I dismantled my outer life I was aware of old habits of thinking that still hung around in my conscious awareness. An echo of the ego is still showing up as shallow, knee-jerk responses that are quickly resolved, but that are clearly still here in my conscious mind. I simply have not let go of turning into the void where the ego was to ask it who I am, what things means, how I should respond, etc. And this is how I make its echo. When I look deeper, however, the bottom drops out, and I cannot find the *actual* ego.

I have rolling insights throughout every day that signal to me how close I am to the Awareness of Truth. Insights and shifts (miracles) are not stepping stones to Truth, but are the evidence that Truth is in my mind. They are the effects of Light dispelling darkness in my mind. However, their result is only to spiritualize the personal experience. They shift my personal experience, but they do not transcend it.

I have moments, hours, days, of transcending self-identification in conscious awareness, but I do not stay there, so I have not yet transcended it completely. It is like the thinnest thread is still tied to self-identification. I feel so close that I cannot imagine it won't fall away, too. However, I also accept that perhaps that's not my role to play. I am aware now that I am a part of something larger that lives through me. I am not independent of it. It may well be that, for this mind, at the conscious level, for whatever reason, it never will totally drop self-identification.

205. The Difference Between Psychological and Spiritual Wholeness (December 14, 2018)

Psychological wholeness is not the same as the awareness of inherent Wholeness that is the Awareness of Truth (Holy Spirit/Christ Consciousness). Psychological wholeness results when, through life experience and/or spiritual awareness, you realize that you will be okay no matter what happens. You are aware of your inner strength, be it personal or your awareness of Truth, and you realize you can survive anything. On a worldly level, this is no small thing. It's a lovely awareness to have in that context. But it is not the Wholeness of the Awareness of Truth.

To be in an Awareness of Truth is to be in an entirely different state of mind. It is a state of Abundant Wholeness, or Love. There simply is no lack in the Awareness of Truth. It is an unshakable state. You know it to reflect Truth, so it remains the same no matter what is happening in your life, to those closest to you, and to the world around you. You see that others feel that they are in lack all the time, even when they don't acknowledge it. But you know for them that it isn't true, so you have no need to correct them.

It is important to understand that you cannot make the not-Truth state of mind like the Awareness of Truth. To be in the Awareness of Truth requires a wholesale shift of consciousness. It is not merely a different point of view at the same level you are in when you are not in an Awareness of Truth. So there is no need to struggle to see what you simply cannot see at that level. However, when you invite the Awareness of Truth into your awareness It will shift the view for you at your level. You will see a given situation differently if you are willing. But understand that is not the same as being in the Awareness of Truth, Which presents you with such a different experience it really is a different "world".

206. The Shift in "I" (December 21, 2018)

My experience of "I" has changed. I no longer experience my motivations and actions as coming from a limited, personal, autonomous place. I used to feel "I" was an independent thread in a tapestry of other independent threads. Now I experience "I" as the Tapestry expressing Itself through this thread.

A Course in Miracles says you cannot know What you are in yourself alone. This means you cannot understand yourself as only one thread in the Tapestry. You are the Tapestry as a whole expressing as a single thread.

ACIM speaks in terms of your relationships with others, but, for me, even the way I read that for a long time was limiting. Not yet able to allow the Tapestry to express through me, I tried to understand the Tapestry one thread (relationship) at a time, and it didn't work. I was relating at the level of the thread rather than at the level of the Tapestry.

The mystical Holy Relationship with another has been my way into understanding this. A mystical Holy Relationship is experienced with Spiritual Vision. On the surface, it appears as though one thread is relating to another thread. But in relating with Spiritual Vision to another, each thread becomes aware it is not isolated or autonomous. It is not even *part of* the Tapestry; it is the Tapestry Itself. The entire Tapestry is contained in a Holy Relationship. In what seems to be a singular relationship in a plurality of relationships I experience the One Relationship. In other words, a Holy Relationship is never just two threads in the Tapestry. It is the Tapestry expressing Itself as those two threads. It is the whole Tapestry.

I can no longer distinguish "I" from anyone or anything else. When I am centered, I feel I am with everyone. Not just my loved ones and not just those near me or whom I can see. But everyone, everywhere. The whole Tapestry. And I feel available to everyone, everywhere if I am moved to be there for them. But I have no personal motivation to be there for anyone because everything is unfolding perfectly. Any action I am moved to make is part of the perfect unfolding. And this is not something I discern from the personal level.

In this state, I am detached from the personal level with others because I am with everyone on the other level. I am actually detached from the personal level in me. This is why some refer to spiritual awareness as "lonely" at the personal level. You do not relate person-to-person. You do not even relate Spirit to Spirit as there is only one Spirit. You are simply Spirit.

207. Seek Truth, Not Its Effects (December 28, 2018)

A few weeks ago I wrote about Truth and Its effects and not confusing them. What inspired that article was my reading of Jan Frazier's book, *When Fear Falls Away*. While the book was directly useful to me by validating my experience and helping me to delineate the distinction between psychological wholeness and spiritual Wholeness, I felt something was missing from her story. And that was Truth Itself. This is what reminded me to turn inward to Truth. And, as it always does, this caused important shifts for me.

I first wrote about this in March, 2017, after I'd realized, with great relief, that love and peace, and joy were only effects. Like everyone I chased these, but chasing them misses the point. Truth is the point, not Its effects. They are important because they indicate Truth is here, but to seek them for themselves is to lose sight of Truth.

When the Golden Light of Love burst into my mind in August of '17 I was so caught up in It that I almost forgot about Truth Itself. When I remembered, I felt relief. All tension left me.

I had this experience again when I was going through the dismantling of my former life. I was so consumed with it I'd forget the shifts were caused by my awareness of Truth. Truth, not the shifts in my consciousness or in my outer life, is What matters. Because Truth is the truth!

And it happened again the other day. I was comparing the ego's (personal thought system's) limited world and the Vision of Spirit, Which reflects the Love I am back to me. At the time I was putting together my next collection of articles for publication and came across an article in which I discussed the difference between a Revelation (a direct experience of Truth) and a higher miracle (reflection of Truth). I finished that article with "But I can tell you, as joyous as the reflection is, it is as different from Heaven as a photon is from the sun." And woooosh! All the tension left my body.

Only the Truth is true. Anything else, even Its reflections (miracles), are illusions. To chase Truth's reflections is to chase illusions. The reason I feel relief each time I remember Truth is, well, *truth*, is because I experience the true forgiveness that *A Course in Miracles* teaches. The higher state of consciousness that results, where the Love I am is reflected back at me everywhere, always, is not forgiveness, but *the state of forgiveness*. It is an effect, not a cause.

It doesn't make sense to seek a higher state of consciousness. Instead, grow your awareness of Truth and the higher state of consciousness will result.

About the Author

Liz Cronkhite is a spiritual teacher, life coach, and author. She became a student of *A Course in Miracles* in 1984 and a life coach in 2000. In 2006 she combined these into ACIM Mentor, where she works one-on-one with students of ACIM and *4 Habits for Inner Peace,* as well as other non-dualistic spiritual paths, to help them remove their obstacles to peace.

Liz is the translator of *The Plain Language A Course in Miracles*, which is a translation of ACIM into plain, everyday language through her own spiritual experiences. She published *4 Habits for Inner Peace*, an encapsulation of the practice she learned from ACIM, in 2011, and *Releasing Guilt for Inner Peace*, a companion to 4HIP, in 2013.

You can learn more about her and what she has to offer at www.lizcronkhite.com.

Printed in Great Britain
by Amazon

40626277R00118